A Freneau Sampler

Edited by

Philip M. Marsh

The Scarecrow Press, Inc.
New York   1963

PS 755
.A5 M28

CONTENTS

Page

Introduction

iii

INTRODUCTION

Life

Philip Morin Freneau, the first child of Pierre Fresneau (old spelling), an American-born French Huguenot, and of a Scotch-American mother, Agnes Watson Fresneau, was born on January 2, 1752 (old-style), in an unknown house on Frankfort Street, New York City. His father, a wine merchant, soon settled on an estate in Monmouth (now Matawan, Monmouth County), New Jersey. For some years the family prospered; and Philip attended good schools in New York and New Jersey, preparing for college and the ministry, by his father's wish. In 1767, however, Pierre Fresneau died, in financial difficulties. Yet there was enough money to educate the oldest child; and a year later Philip entered Princeton (then the College of New Jersey), well schooled in the classics, as a sophomore.

At college, under a vigorous new president, John Witherspoon, he roomed with James Madison and became a friend of Hugh Brackenridge. He, with them, wrote satires on the Tories in verse, and some serious poems, and in general led a rather gay life. At graduation in 1771, Brackenridge read their joint poem, "The Rising Glory of America," which predicted a great future for the English colonies:[1]

A new Jerusalem, sent down from heaven,
Shall grace our happy earth--perhaps this land,
Whose ample breast shall then receive, tho' late,
Myriads of saints, with their immortal king,
To live and reign on earth a thousand years.

After graduating, Freneau tried teaching, and disliked

9

it; later he taught under Principal Brackenridge in a Maryland academy; but he turned to theology, the hope of his father. After two years, however, he discarded the ministry as too confining to the mind. He had been educated too broadly to accept a narrow sectarianism, and was already becoming a deist, like Franklin and Jefferson. Moreover, exciting political events were urging him to write more poetry--praises of freedom and attacks on English tyranny.

In 1775, after the Battles of Lexington, Concord, and Bunker Hill, and the mobilization for war, he composed several satires on the British, like "General Gage's Soliloquy" and "Libera nos, Domine," which concludes thus:[2]

> From an island that bullies, and hectors, and swears,
> I send up to heaven my wishes and prayers
> That we, disunited, may freemen be still,
> And Britain go on--to be damn'd, if she will.

Such poems gave him the name, "poet of the Revolution"-- yet he was no fire-eater, but a lover of peace. And so, shortly after the first of the next year, fearing an oncoming war, he sailed to the West Indies and lingered there over two years. Returning to New Jersey in July, 1778, he joined the militia as a private, but saw no real action. Three months later he sailed again for the West Indies, now master of a small ship, and went there twice more in 1779. Meanwhile he was contributing poems and essays to Brackenridge's United States Magazine (Philadelphia), notably his tale of the death of Death, "The House of Night:"[3]

> Turning to view from whence the murmur came,
> My frightened eyes a horrid form survey'd!
> Death, dreary death, upon the gloomy couch,
> With flesh-less limbs in rueful form was laid.

In May, 1780, Freneau shipped out of Philadelphia on the Aurora, a privateer, for the West Indies, as a passenger, though mistakenly enrolled as third mate. Near the sea in

Delaware Bay, the ship, after a battle, was captured by a
British frigate; and Freneau was imprisoned aboard a prison
ship, then a hospital ship, in New York Harbor, for six
weeks. From then on he hated the British bitterly; and his
poem, "The British Prison Ship," was a result:[4]

> The various horrors of these hulks to tell,
> These Prison Ships where pain and horror dwell,
> Where death in tenfold vengeance holds his reign,
> And injur'd ghosts, yet unaveng'd, complain;
> This be my task--ungenerous Britons, you
> Conspire to murder those you can't subdue.

After his release, ill and weak, Freneau rested at
home. Then he went to Philadelphia, where he worked as
printer, postal clerk, and assistant editor on Francis
Bailey's Freeman's Journal, to which he was also a voluminous contributor in prose and verse. Notable essays appeared in The Pilgrim, a primitivistic series, later the basis
for the series, The Philosopher of the Forest.

In 1784 the sailor poet returned to the sea, cruising
the Atlantic coast and the West Indies, writing and publishing
poems and essays. In 1786 Bailey published Freneau's first
collection in book form, The Poems of Philip Freneau. One
of its memorable poems is "Eutaw Springs," which commem-
orated the soldiers who died at the 1781 battle of that name,
in South Carolina:[5]

> At Eutaw Springs the valiant died:
>   Their limbs with dust are cover'd o'er--
> Weep on, ye springs, your tearful tide;
>   How many heroes are no more!

And in 1788 Bailey published The Miscellaneous Works of Mr.
Philip Freneau, half poetry, half prose, with essays by an
eccentric weaver bachelor, "Robert Slender," and the Philosopher of the Forest series. Both volumes were fairly well
received, and now Freneau was a writer with an established
repute. Particularly fine in the 1788 volume is the lyric,

11

"The Wild Honey Suckle:"

> Fair flower, that dost so comely grow,
> Hid in this silent dull retreat,
> Untouch'd thy honey'd blossoms blow,
> Unseen thy little branches greet:
>> No roving foot shall find thee here,
>> No busy hand provoke a tear.

In 1790 Captain Freneau, having decided to settle down, married Eleanor Forman, pretty and poetic daughter of a neighboring family. He moved to New York City and resumed his journalistic career, as assistant editor to Francis Childs and John Swaine, publishers of the popular Daily Advertiser. But Childs, apparently the real editor, was a Federalist; and though Freneau was allowed to contribute liberally, he wrote no political editorials (which would have been Whig). So he chafed at the restriction and planned to be an independent publisher.

This he was about to do in 1791, with a New Jersey newspaper, when Jefferson, Secretary of State, urged by Madison, now a Virginia congressman, offered Freneau a part-time translatorship. The intent was to induce the poet to establish his newspaper in Philadelphia. There, John Fenno's Gazette of the United States was giving strong support to Secretary of the Treasury Hamilton's financial measures--and this influence, Republicans felt, needed an antidote.

At first Freneau declined, feeling a duty to subscribers of his project, and having no confidence in his ability as a translator. Finally he made arrangements with Childs and Swaine, whereby he was to edit, and they to publish, the National Gazette, which was begun in Philadelphia on October 31, 1791. Much has been written about the supposed collusion between Jefferson and Freneau, editor of a newspaper attacking the administration that paid his salary.

12

Critics have chosen to believe Hamilton, who, annoyed at Freneau's attacks and believing Jefferson to be their inspiration (if not an author), struck back anonymously in 1792. He charged that Jefferson was the real editor and Freneau his bribed tool. Jefferson denied the charges privately to Washington and to Edmund Randolph (Attorney General). But Hamilton--despite Freneau's published affidavit of denial-- went on brilliantly and convincingly, till silenced by James Monroe and his own lack of proof.

The National Gazette did prove to be an antidote to Fenno's Hamilton-worshipping, aristocratic Gazette of the United States. Freneau and his contributors--Madison, George Logan, John Taylor, John Beckley, probably Monroe, and others--attacked the Treasury funding system and excise taxes, the national bank and the resultant stock speculation, and the federal assumption of state war debts. It also criticized President Washington's proclamation of neutrality in 1793, and argued for France and against Britain in the European war of that year. Editor Freneau staunchly supported the impetuous French ambassador, Genet, who was finally recalled. In the summer of 1793, yellow fever struck the capital city and slowed business to a standstill. Now Childs withdrew his support from the National Gazette, which had never made money. So Freneau reluctantly gave up, leaving a record of liberal-radical ideas, and of halting the Federalists in their march toward an aristocratic oligarchy, if not monarchy. Jefferson retired soon after Freneau, to return to Philadelphia as Vice President under Adams in 1797. Actually Hamilton, Madison, Monroe, and the National Gazette had combined to make him, in the eyes of the public, the symbol of democracy.

Meanwhile Washington, watching jealously over the new

government, had become annoyed at Freneau--who admired the President, but felt he was used as a figurehead for Hamilton's program, and that he was a symbol of the monarchial formality surrounding the presidency. At one time Washington evidently wanted Jefferson to discharge his translator; but Jefferson would not, writing in his <u>Anas</u> (May 23, 1793), "His paper has saved our Constitution, which was galloping fast into monarchy, and has been checked by no one means so powerfully." On another occasion, in a Cabinet meeting, the President angrily referred to the democratic editor as "that <u>rascal Freneau</u>."[6]

But despite Hamilton's brilliant arguments, his case against Freneau and Jefferson was almost wholly circumstantial. No real evidence has been uncovered to support it; and it is best explained as a petulant exhibition of an immature politician used to having his way. One important result, however, was the beginning of the American two-party system, as the conservatives joined Hamilton and the liberals lined up with Jefferson.

Freneau returned to his New Jersey home--he was always going back there--and tried to pick up the threads of a tangled literary career. In the political conflict he had written almost no verse or prose in a literary vein. He took with him new types, set up a country press, and published <u>The Monmouth Almanac</u> (for 1795); another volume of <u>Poems</u> (1795); and the <u>Jersey Chronicle</u>, a weekly newspaper with echoes of the <u>National Gazette</u>. This little periodical lived only a year (1795-1796), and is chiefly notable for the essays by "Tomo Cheeki," a supposed Indian chief in Philadelphia, who criticizes whites' ways and champions the primitive life of the red men. These essays are Freneau's best prose.

In 1797, Freneau again tried editing-publishing. With
Alexander Menut, and later Matthew Davis, in New York, he
published The Time Piece, a semi-literary, thrice-weekly
newspaper. At first non-political, it soon became a radical
pro-France, anti-Britain, anti-Federalist political sheet--and
like the National Gazette, it failed to make money. So the
editor, beset by debts, retired at the end of the year. The
Time Piece was his last publishing or editing venture.

In 1799, however, he began a long series of political
essays in the Philadelphia Aurora--at first edited by Benjamin Franklin Bache, but now by William Duane. (Both Bache
and Fenno had died of yellow fever in 1798.) Freneau now
resumed the pen name of "Robert Slender"--but this Slender
was a much-married cobbler who pretended humility and ignorance, while slashing at Federalism, Britain, monarchy,
and President Adams. He defended Republican (Democratic)
policies, France, Jefferson, Thomas McKean (local politician), and the common man. These essays, numbering
nearly forty, ran till February, 1801, when Jefferson was
elected President by the House of Representatives. A collection of them, Letters on Various interesting and important Subjects, was published in December, 1799.

After living on the farm a few years, Freneau again
went to sea. Then, in 1804, he evidently returned to the
Philadelphia political wars in a series of twenty essays in
the Aurora, by members of the "Bunker" family. These
closely resemble the Slender letters of 1799-1801; they were
climaxed by three essays signed "Tomo Cheeki," good evidence that Freneau was in the city, and writing.

Jefferson's Embargo Act (1807) forced Freneau from
the sea, and he settled again at Mount Pleasant, his farm.
In 1809 he supervised a two-volume edition of his Poems in

Philadelphia, and published another after the War of 1812, in New York in 1815. The latter was a collection of new poems, among which was "Lines Addressed to Mr. Jefferson," with a reference to Hamilton's attacks:

> You, when an angry faction vex'd the age,
> Rose to your place at once, and check'd their rage;
> The envenom'd shafts of malice you defied,
> And turn'd all projects of revolt aside:--
> We saw you libell'd by the worst of men,
> While hell's red lamp hung quivering o'er his pen,
> And fiends congenial every effort try
> To blast a merit which shall never die.

There were also some deistic poems, for example "On the Religion of Nature:"

> Religion, such as nature taught,
>   With all divine perfection suits;
> Had all mankind this system sought
>   Sophists would cease their vain disputes,
>   And from this source would nations know
>   All that can make their heaven below.

Though previous editions had sold well, chiefly because of their patriotic poems, the 1815 edition was a failure, perhaps because it was less enthusiastic and more philosophical. In his old age Freneau became more and more reflective, more inclined to a calm, philosophical view of life and its struggles.

From 1808 on, evidently he often drifted into Philadelphia to meet old friends and learn the latest news, and probably to help Duane print or edit the Aurora. Here his essays continued to appear, by all apparent signs, dealing with current political problems mostly, though also with national issues.

These Aurora essays are signed by pseudonyms already familiar to the columns of the Freeman's Journal and the National Gazette--"Hawser Trunnion," "L.," "An American," "Juba," "An Old Soldier," and others whose style al-

16

so stamps them as Freneau's. Generally they advocated ideas similar to those of the National Gazette--opposition to Britain, the Federalists, and monarchy, and enthusiastic support of France, republicanism, and the Democrats. They supported Jefferson's Embargo Act, argued for war with England long before it occurred, and appealed for cooperation with President Madison. For some reason, they showed no enthusiasm for the Monroe administration. The "Old Soldier" essays number more than four score, and were largely concerned with the problem of the American Indian. Now Freneau seems to have lost his early "noble savage," romantic concept of the red man--as appears in some poems and the "Tomo Cheeki" essays--which is replaced by a more realistic attitude. He had evidently adopted the Brackenridge view, that Indians were dangerous savages, that they had no legal right to their lands, and that they must be treated firmly.[7]

The Mount Pleasant home was burned in 1818, and with it many manuscripts; and after a few years the Freneaus settled on a farm near Freehold, New Jersey. To pay debts, the old poet occasionally sold a part of his land, but seems to have done little or no real work from 1818 on. Yet he continued to write. From 1821 to 1824, The True American of Trenton published many of his poems and some essays. For Freneau it was a time for recollections, memories of the Revolution, and of other experiences. This was his last extended literary effort.

Stringent finances in 1832 forced him to apply for a federal pension of $35 a year, which was granted. In applying, as might be expected of a nearly destitute old man, he made some statements whose exact truth may be questioned. But he was not to enjoy the little pension. In the evening of December 18, 1832, he left the Freehold country store where he was accustomed to talk of old times. Probably a bit tipsy from wine, he started across the swamp towards his home. It was snowing, and he evidently lost his way, fell, and was unable to go on; his body was found next morning. He was buried on the old estate, Mount Pleasant, where a tiny village is now called Freneau, under a monument marked "Poet's Grave."

Freneau left a widow and four daughters--Helena, Agnes, Catherine, and Margaret--but no son. His grandson, Philip Freneau Leadbeater, changed his name to Philip Leadbeater Freneau, but died without a son. A great-grandson is Edmond Sweeny Freneau, whose daughter, I. D. Freneau, has published a volume of poems, July and Winter (1950), first collection by a Freneau since 1815. All were presumably descendants of Freneau's second daughter Agnes.

Evaluations

Philip Freneau was a deist, like Franklin, Paine, Washington, and Jefferson; a Democrat (or early Republican) and follower of, but more radical than, Jefferson; and an independent voice for freedom and liberalism, a fanatical enemy of brutality and tyranny. Steeped in the classics and devoted to the English authors, particularly Shakespeare, Pope, Dryden, and Gray, yet he was an instinctive romanticist. He was drawn irresistibly to the revolutionary ideas of Rousseau and Paine. But he was not a violent person; he usually shrank from the idea of war. His warlike poems and prose are mostly exhortations to resist tyranny and help the weak. Even his hatred of English force in "The British Prison Ship" is confined chiefly to protest and denunciation; there is little advocacy of battle, and that is an appeal to defend America and strike back at cruelty:[8]

18

Rouse from your sleep, and crush the thievish band,
Defeat, destroy, and sweep them from the land.

Far more typical is this resigned rebuke:

Ah! traitors, lost to every sense of shame,
Unjust supporters of a tyrant's claim;
Foes to the rights of freedom and of men,
Flush'd with the blood of thousands you have slain,
To the just doom the righteous skies decree
We leave you, toiling still in cruelty.

The Poems

Critics and historians generally rate Freneau as the first important American poet, basing the judgment on his better lyrics like "The Wild Honey Suckle," "The Indian Burying Ground," "Eutaw Springs," etc. Lewis Leary's subtitle to That Rascal Freneau, "A Study in Literary Failure," is a judgment many would protest. Freneau failed financially, failed to establish himself as a lasting popular favorite; but his work as a whole hardly suggests failure. It is a sort of combined literary and journalistic success of a minor order. Pattee calls him "the father of American poetry" and the "first true poet born upon our continent." Clark joins Pattee in the fatherhood idea, adding that Freneau was an "Apostle of the Religion of Nature and Humanity," devoted to faith in natural goodness, despite his bitter satires. Murdock calls him "the best American poet after Taylor and before Bryant."[9] Such opinions are founded on ten or fifteen of his best poems; but the great bulk of his verse is mediocre, much of it written in haste, in angry retort to political enemies. Even so, this verse is better than most of his rivals' in that field, and has some historical value.

The Prose

Few historians are familiar with Freneau's prose,

19

which has been almost entirely ignored, because buried in old newspaper and magazine files or rare books. The Duyckincks say the Miscellaneous Works essays are "pleasant papers...simple and elegant in style, independent in thought, playful and humorous."[10] Tyler called Freneau a "master of a delightful prose style, easy, sinewy, touched with delicate humor, crisp, and keen-edged."[11] Pattee offers no sweeping judgment on the prose, yet characterizes the Pilgrim essays "graceful" and the "Robert Slender" Letters' style easy and the characterization natural.[12] Clark names Freneau the "father of American prose,"[13] though Franklin probably is a wiser choice for this honor. Leary avoids a general evaluation, but in the Literary History of the United States says, "Freneau's prose became progressively more indigenous."[14] Murdock says the prose is "often very good," that Freneau did "some excellent essays."[15]

Critics generally have been timid about such judgments, being strangers to most of the prose, whose only large body was available in the Miscellaneous Works and the Slender Letters. But it has historical and political values. At one time Freneau was the leading democratic editor in the country (1792-1793); at other times he was a critical force for liberal ideas. Most of his political essays, from a literary view, are worthless; but they were once important as propaganda for the rise of the Democratic Party and the demolition of Federalism, as well as the fall of John Adams and Hamilton from power and influence. And it is quite possible that Jefferson was right--that there did exist, in the early 1790's, a real threat to the republic, a real possibility of a limited American monarchy. If we accept this, the Jefferson estimate of Freneau's service--saving the Constitution from monarchy--must also be accepted.

Among the non-political essays, the Tomo Cheeki series is the best; next in value from a literary standpoint are the Philosopher of the Forest numbers; and there are many scattered pieces of good quality, in the Miscellaneous Works, the Time Piece, and elsewhere. Freneau also wrote a few short stories, like "The City Poet" (MW), though most have an essay intent. One, "Light, Summer Reading" (MW), satirizes romantic fiction. Many of Freneau's writings, prose and verse, are in dramatic form; and he wrote three acts of a play, The Spy,[16] about Arnold and André, a third of it in prose. The prose of Freneau may be divided into literary, expository, and political items.[17]

Comparisons

As a poet, excepting Edward Taylor--a Puritan metaphysical poet who wrote nothing of the American scene or issues--we have in Freneau the first important American poet, the best of his time. As a prose writer, he compares favorably with any other American up to 1800, and, with the exception of Hopkinson, is more versatile than his rivals. None of them did anything so original as The Pilgrim or the Tomo Cheeki essays. And he is one of the most voluminous of all, having done over 500 known poems and many others not positively ascribable, but evidently his--to say nothing of some 1100 prose pieces (positive ascriptions and probable). Thus he and his work have served as a rich background for writers of the nineteenth century--Irving, Bryant, Cooper, Emerson, and Poe.

Notes

1.   From the 1786 Poems.
2.   From the 1786 Poems.
3.   United States Magazine, Aug., 1779.   Poem enlarged,

in 1786 Poems.

4. From the 1786 Poems.

5. Ibid. Original title, "To the Memory of the Brave Americans, under General Greene, who fell in the action of September 8, 1781."

6. Anas, Aug. 2, 1793.

7. See Freeman's Journal, April 30, 1783, ff.--also Indian Atrocities, Nashville, 1843, Brackenridge's introduction.

8. From the 1786 Poems.

9. The Literature of the American People, Arthur H. Quinn, editor, New York, 1951, page 169. Kenneth B. Murdock wrote Part I, "The Colonial and Revolutionary Period."

10. Evert A. and George L. Duyckinck, Cyclopaedia of American Literature, New York, 1855, I, 328.

11. Moses C. Tyler, The Literary History of the American Revolution, New York, 1900, II, 275, note.

12. Pattee, I, xxxvi, lxxvii.

13. Harry H. Clark, "What Made Freneau the Father of American Prose?" Transactions of the Wisconsin Academy of Sciences, Arts, and Letters, May, 1930.

14. Literary History of the United States, Robert E. Spiller, editor, New York, 1953, page 173.

15. Op. cit., page 167.

16. Included in Pattee's Poems of Philip Freneau.

17. The Prose of Philip Freneau, Philip M. Marsh, editor, New Brunswick, N.J., 1955, includes about 170 selections of all types.

SELECTED BIBLIOGRAPHY
Collections

New Travels Through North-America, by Abbé Claude Robin, translated by Philip Freneau. 13 essays. Philadelphia, 1783; Boston, 1784.

The Poems of Philip Freneau, Philadelphia, 1786.

The Miscellaneous Works of Mr. Philip Freneau, Philadelphia, 1788. MW.

The Monmouth Almanac, Middletown-Point, N.J., for 1795.

Poems Written between the Years 1768 & 1794, Monmouth, N.J., 1795.

Letters...By Robert Slender, Philadelphia, 1799.

Poems Written and Published during the American Revolutionary War...with Translations from the Ancients, and Other Pieces Not Heretofore in Print, Philadelphia, 1809. 2 volumes.

A Collection of Poems...Written between the Year 1797 and the Present Time, New York, 1815. 2 volumes.

The Poems of Philip Freneau, Fred L. Pattee, editor, Princeton, 1902-1907. 3 volumes. Here known as "Pattee."

Poems of Freneau, Harry H. Clark, editor, New York, 1929.

The Last Poems of Philip Freneau, Lewis Leary, editor, New Brunswick, N.J., 1945.

The Prose of Philip Freneau, Philip M. Marsh, editor, New Brunswick, N.J., 1955.

23

Bibliographies

Fred L. Pattee, "Bibliography of Philip Freneau," The Bibliographer, March, 1902.

---- ----, "Bibliography of the Poetry of Philip Freneau," Poems of Philip Freneau, Princeton, 1907. Vol. III.

Victor H. Paltsits, A Bibliography of the Separate and Collected Works of Philip Freneau, New York, 1903.

Lewis Leary, "Bibliography," That Rascal Freneau, New Brunswick, N. J., 1941.

Philip M. Marsh, "Selected Bibliography," The Prose of Philip Freneau, New Brunswick, N. J., 1955.

---- ----, Freneau's Published Prose: a Bibliography-- to be published.

Owen P. Thomas, "Philip Freneau: A Bibliography," N. J. H. S. Proceedings, July, 1957. List of items about Freneau.

Biographies

Evert A. and George L. Duyckinck, Cyclopaedia of American Literature, New York, 1855. 2 vols. I, 327-348.

Evert A. Duyckinck, "Introductory Memoir," Poems relating to the American Revolution by Philip Freneau, New York, 1865.

Mary Austin, Philip Freneau, The Poet of the Revolution, New York, 1901.

Samuel E. Forman, The Political Activities of Philip Freneau, Baltimore, 1902.

Fred L. Pattee, "Life of Philip Freneau," Poems of Philip Freneau, Princeton, 1902-1907. 3 vols. I, xiii-cxii.

Lewis Leary, That Rascal Freneau, New Brunswick, N. J., 1941.

Philip M. Marsh, "Introduction," The Prose of Philip Fren-

24

eau, New Brunswick, N.J., 1955.

Critical Essays

Harry H. Clark, "The Literary Influences of Philip Freneau," Studies in Philology, Jan., 1925.

---- ----, "Introduction," Poems of Freneau, New York, 1929.

Frank Smith, "Philip Freneau and The Time-Piece and Literary Companion," American Literature, Nov., 1932.

Philip M. Marsh, "Freneau and Jefferson," American Literature, May, 1936.

---- ----, " 'The Vindication of Mr. Jefferson, '" South Atlantic Quarterly, Jan., 1946.

---- ----, Monroe's Defense of Jefferson and Freneau against Hamilton, Oxford, Ohio, 1948.

Lewis Leary, "Philip Freneau in Charleston," The South Carolina Historical and Genealogical Magazine, July, 1941.

---- ----, "Introduction," The Last Poems of Philip Freneau, New Brunswick, N.J., 1945.

Newspapers and Magazines

United States Magazine, Hugh Brackenridge, editor, Philadelphia, 1779. USM.

The Freeman's Journal, Francis Bailey, editor-publisher, Philadelphia, 1781-1789. FJ.

The Daily Advertiser, Francis Childs and John Swaine, publishers, New York, 1790-1791. DA.

Gazette of the United States, John Fenno, editor, New York and Philadelphia, 1789-1798. GUS.

National Gazette, Philip Freneau, editor, Philadelphia, 1791-1793. NG.

The Aurora, Benjamin F. Bache, editor-publisher till 1798; William Duane, editor most of the time, 1798 on, Philadelphia, 1793-1824.

Jersey Chronicle, Philip Freneau, editor-publisher, Monmouth, N.J., 1795-1796. JC.

The Time-Piece, Philip Freneau, editor and co-publisher with Alexander Menut, later Matthew Davis, New York, 1797-1798. TP.

The New York Weekly Museum, James Oram, editor-publisher, New York, 1814-1817. WM.

The True American, James Wilson, editor-publisher, Trenton, 1821-1824. TA.

CHRONOLOGY

1752:   Jan. 2 (old style), born on Frankfort Street, New York City, first child of Pierre Fresneau and Agnes Watson Fresneau.

1767:   Oct. 17, Pierre Fresneau died.

1768:   Nov. 7, entered Princeton (then College of New Jersey).

1771:   Sept. 25, graduated from college.

1772:   April, after teaching 13 days at Flatbush, Long Island, left. In New York, published The American Village, with several short poems.
         In Philadelphia, published A Poem, on the Rising Glory of America, the version in which Brackenridge collaborated.

1773-74: Studying theology.

1775:   Writing patriotic and satiric poems, also "The House of Night."
         In New York, published American Liberty, in Philadelphia as "The Present Situation of Affairs in North-America."
         In Philadelphia, published A Voyage to Boston.

1776:   From New York, in February (?) sailed to Santa Cruz, Virgin Islands.

1776-78: As supercargo of the Liberty, visited Bermuda and various points in the Caribbean.

1778:   April, visited Bermuda, probably courting Frances Bruere, daughter of the governor.
         July, en route to the United States, captured by a

British ship and released.

July, enlisted as private in New Jersey militia.

In Philadelphia, published American Independence.

October, sailed as master of the Indian Delaware.

1779:   Contributed prose and poetry to Brackenridge's United States Magazine, Philadelphia.

July, sailed as master of the John Courter.

September, sailed as supercargo of the Rebecca.

December, helped take a shipwreck, off New Jersey coast.

1780:   May 1, quit the N. J. Militia.

May 20, left Philadelphia, passenger on the Aurora, mistakenly enrolled as third mate, captured by British frigate Iris on May 26.

May 26-July 13, prisoner, mostly in New York Harbor, on the Scorpion and the Hunter.

Summer-fall, wrote "The British Prison Ship" and play, The Spy.

1781:   Published The British Prison Ship, broadside, Philadelphia.

Summer, began to help edit The Freeman's Journal, Philadelphia--Francis Bailey, publisher--contributing prose and verse.

1782:   Resigned assistant editorship of The Freeman's Journal, probably in August or September.

Autumn, began work as postoffice clerk in Philadelphia.

1783:   Translated New Travels Through North-America, by Abbe Claude Robin, French Army chaplain, Philadelphia.

1784:   In June, as supercargo, sailed for Jamaica.

In July, near Jamaica, nearly wrecked in hurricane.

November, returned to Philadelphia.

1785:   January, was printing for Patrick Rice, Philadelphia.

Ill in spring, left for Pacolet Springs, South Carolina.

November, sailed as captain of the Monmouth.

1785-89: Sailing along Atlantic Coast and in West Indies, captain of the Monmouth, the Industry, and the Columbia.

1789:   November, in Georgia, retired from sailing.

1790:   February, arrived in New York.

March (?), began to help edit The Daily Advertiser --Francis Childs and John Swaine, publishers--in New York.

April 15, married Eleanor Forman at her home in Middletown-Point (now Matawan) in New Jersey.

April, settled in New York City.

1791:   January, planning a New Jersey newspaper.

February, Jefferson offered Freneau part-time translatorship in State Department in Philadelphia.

March, Freneau declined Jefferson's offer.

July, agreed, with Childs and Swaine, to edit newspaper in Philadelphia.

August, accepted Jefferson's offer and became translator in Department of State, at $250 a year.

October 31, published first issue of the National Gazette.

1792:   July 25, Hamilton (in Gazette of the United States) began anonymous attacks on Freneau and Jefferson.

August 8, Freneau (in GUS) denied charges, by affidavit.

September 9, Jefferson, in letter to Washington, de-

29

nied charges.

September 22, Monroe, helped by Madison (in American Daily Advertiser) began refutation of Hamilton's charges, till Hamilton desisted in December.

1793:   May 23, Washington, talking with Jefferson, seemed
to wish Freneau discharged; but Jefferson com-
mented in his Anas, "His paper has saved our
Constitution, which was galloping fast into monarchy."

August 2, Washington, in a Cabinet meeting, burst
out against "that rascal Freneau"--from Jefferson's Anas.

October 11, resigned as translator, effective Oct. 1.

October 26, published last issue of the National
Gazette.

November (?), returned to home in New Jersey.

1794:   In Philadelphia, published The Village Merchant,
with "The Country Printer."

At Middletown-Point, published The Monmouth Almanac for 1795.

1795:   At Middletown-Point, published volume of Poems,
printed by himself, advertised for sale in April.

May 2, began the Jersey Chronicle, weekly rural
newspaper.

1796:   April 30, printed last issue of the Jersey Chronicle.

1797:   March 13, with Alexander Menut, began The Time
Piece, in New York.

September 13, Menut replaced by Matthew Davis.

1798:   January, retired from active editorship of TP.

January 3, sailed for Charleston, S. C.

March 14, returned to New York.

March 21, officially retired from TP publishing.

1799:   March 25, began new "Robert Slender" series of
        essays in the Aurora, Philadelphia, now edited by
        William Duane.

        Dec. 30, Letters by "Robert Slender," published in
        Philadelphia.

1800:   Continued occasional contributions, under "Robert
        Slender" and other pseudonyms, in the Aurora.

        April (?), was sued for debts in New York.

1801:   February 19, contributed last essay of the "Slender"
        series to the Aurora.

        Autumn (?), resumed sailing as master of the John,
        owned by his brother, Peter Freneau.

1802:   January, returned to New York from Guadeloupe, as
        master of the Fanny.

1803-07: Sailing as captain of the Washington and other ships,
        owned by Peter Freneau.

1804:   August-October, evidently in Philadelphia, wrote po-
        litical essays for the Aurora, mostly by members
        of the "Bunker" family and by "Tomo Cheeki."

1807:   Retired from the sea because of the Embargo Act.

1809:   In Philadelphia, contributed essays to the Aurora
        and supervised the edition of the 1809 Poems,
        published by Lydia Bailey.

1815:   In New York, a new edition of Poems was published
        by David Longworth.

1818:   October 18, his home was burned, with many books
        and manuscripts.

1821-24: Published many poems and a few essays in The
        True American of Trenton.

1824:   Moved to farm near Freehold, New Jersey.

1827:   Last known published poem in True American, June
        30.

1832:   August 7, applied for $35 annual federal pension
(granted).

December 18, died in snowstorm, near his home in
Freehold, New Jersey.

SELECTIONS FROM THE POEMS

The American Village[1]

Where yonder stream divides the fertile plain,
Made fertile by the labours of the swain;
And hills and woods high tow'ring o'er the rest,
Behold a village with fair plenty blest...

Though <u>Goldsmith</u> weeps in melancholy strains,
Deserted Auburn and forsaken plains,
And mourns his village with a patriot sigh,
And in that village sees Britannia die:
Yet shall this land with rising pomp divine,
In its own splendor and Britannia's shine.
O muse, forget to paint her ancient woes,
Her Indian battles, or her Gallic foes;
Resume the pleasures of the rural scene,
Describe the village rising on the green,
Its harmless people, born to small command,
Lost in the bosom of this western land:
So shall my verse run gentle as the floods,
So answer all ye hills, and echo all ye woods;
So glide ye streams in hollow channels pent,
Forever wasting, yet not ever spent...

Now fairest village of the fertile plain,
Made fertile by the labours of the swain...
Wou'd fate but raise me o'er the smaller cares,
Of life unwelcome and distressful years,
Pedantic labours and a hateful ease,
Which scarce the hoary wrinkled rage cou'd please.
Hence springs each grief, each long reflective sigh,
And not one comfort left but poetry.
Long, long ago with her I could have stray'd,
To woods, to thickets or the mountain shade;
Unfit for cities and the noisy throng,
The drunken revel and the midnight song;
The gilded beau and scenes of empty joy,
Which please a moment and forever die.
Here then shall center ev'ry wish, and all

33

The tempting beauties of this spacious ball:
No thought ambitious, and no bold design,
But heaven born contemplation shall be mine.
In yonder village shall my fancy stray,
Nor rove beyond the confines of to-day...
The summer morns and vernal eves should see,
MILTON, immortal bard, my company;
Or SHAKESPEARE, DRYDEN, each high sounding name,
The pride of BRITAIN, and one half her fame:
Or him who wak'd the fairy muse of old
And pleasing tales of lands inchanted told.
Still in my hand, he his soft verse shou'd find,
His verse, the picture of the poet's mind:
Or heav'nly POPE, who now harmonious mourns,
"Like the rapt seraph that adores and burns,"
Then in sharp satire, with a giant's might,
Forbids the blockhead and the fool to write:
And in the centre of the bards be shown
The deathless lines of godlike ADDISON;
Who, bard thrice glorious, all delightful flows,
And wrapt the soul of poetry in prose.

The Power of Fancy[2]

Wakeful, vagrant, restless thing,
Ever wandering on the wing,
Who thy wondrous source can find,
FANCY, regent of the mind;
A spark from Jove's resplendent throne,
But thy nature all unknown.

This spark of bright, celestial flame,
From Jove's seraphic altar came,
And hence alone in man we trace,
Resemblance to the immortal race.

Ah! what is all this mighty WHOLE,
These suns and stars that round us roll!
What are they all, where'er they shine,
But Fancies of the Power Divine!
What is this globe, these lands, and seas,
And heat, and cold, and flowers, and trees,
And life, and death, and beast, and man,
And time--that with the sun began--
But thoughts on reason's scale combin'd,
Ideas of the Almighty mind?

On the surface of the brain
Night after night she walks unseen;
Noble fabrics doth she raise
In the woods or on the seas,
On some high, steep, pointed rock,
Where the billows loudly knock
And the dreary tempests sweep
Clouds along the uncivil deep.
Lo! she walks upon the moon,
Listens to the chimy tune
Of the bright, harmonious spheres,
And the song of angels hears;
Sees this earth a distant star, [3]
Pendant, floating in the air;
Leads me to some lonely dome,
Where Religion loves to come,
Where the bride of Jesus dwells,
And the deep ton'd organ swells
In notes with lofty anthems join'd,
Notes that half distract the mind.

Now like lightning she descends
To the prison of the fiends,
Hears the rattling of their chains,
Feels their never ceasing pains--
But, O never may she tell
Half the frightfulness of hell.

Now she views Arcadian rocks,
Where the shepherds guard their flocks,
And, while yet her wings she spreads,
Sees chrystal streams and coral beds,
Wanders to some desert deep,
Or some dark, enchanted steep;
By the full moon light doth shew
Forests of a dusky blue,
Where, upon some mossy bed,
Innocence reclines her head.

Swift, she stretches o'er the seas
To the far off Hebrides;
Canvas on the lofty mast
Could not travel half so fast--
Swifter than the eagle's flight
Or instantaneous rays of light!
Lo! contemplative she stands
On Norwegia's rocky lands--

Fickle Goddess, set me down
Where the rugged winters frown
Upon Orca's howling steep,
Nodding o'er the northern deep,
Where the winds tumultuous roar,
Vext that Ossian sings no more.
Fancy, to that land repair;
Sweetest Ossian slumbers there;
Waft me far to southern isles
Where the soften'd winter smiles,
To Bermuda's orange shades,
Or Demerara's lovely glades;
Bear me o'er the sounding cape,
Painting death in every shape,
Where daring Anson spread the sail
Shatter'd by the stormy gale--
Lo! she leads me wide and far;
Sense can never follow her--
Shape thy course o'er land and sea;
Help me to keep pace with thee;
Lead me to yon' chalky cliff,
Over rock and over reef,
Into Britain's fertile land,
Stretching far her proud command.
Look back and view, thro' many a year,
Caesar, Julius Caesar, there.

Now to Tempe's verdant wood,
Over the mid-ocean flood;
Lo! the islands of the sea
--Sappho, Lesbos mourns for thee:
Greece, arouse thy humbled head,
Where are all thy mighty dead,
Who states to endless ruin hurl'd
And carried vengeance through the world?--
Troy, thy vanish'd pomp resume,
Or, weeping at thy Hector's tomb,
Yet those faded scenes renew,
Whose memory is to Homer due.
Fancy, lead me wandering still
Up to Ida's cloud-topt hill;
Not a laurel there doth grow
But in vision thou shalt show, --
Every sprig on Virgil's tomb
Shall in livelier colours bloom,
And every triumph Rome has seen
Flourish on the years between.

36

Now she bears me far away
In the east to meet the day,
Leads me over Ganges' streams,
Mother of the morning beams--
O'er the ocean hath she ran,
Places me on Tinian;
Farther, farther in the east,
Till it almost meets the west,
Let us wandering both be lost
On Taitis sea-beat coast;
Bear me from that distant strand,
Over ocean, over land,
To California's golden shore--
Fancy, stop, and rove no more.

Now, tho' late, returning home,
Lead me to Belinda's tomb;
Let me glide as well as you
Through the shroud and coffin too,
And behold, a moment, there,
All that once was good and fair--
Who doth here so soundly sleep?
Shall we break this prison deep?--
Thunders cannot wake the maid,
Lightnings cannot pierce the shade,
And tho' wintry tempests roar,
Tempests shall disturb no more.

Yet must those eyes in darkness stay,
That once were rivals to the day--?
Like heaven's bright lamp beneath the main
They are but set to rise again.

Fancy, thou the muses pride,
In thy painted realms reside
Endless images of things,
Fluttering each on golden wings;
Ideal objects, such a store,
The universe could hold no more:
Fancy, to thy power I owe
Half my happiness below;
By thee Elysian groves were made;
Thine were the notes that Orpheus play'd;
By thee was Pluto charm'd so well
While rapture seiz'd the sons of hell--
Come, O come--perceiv'd by none,
You and I will walk alone.

The Rising Glory of America[4]
Written 1771.

----Venient annis
Saecula seris, quibus oceanus
Vincula rerum laxet, et ingens
Pateat tellus, Typhisque novos
Detegat orbes; nec sit terris
Ultima Thule. ----

Seneca. Med. Act III. V. 375.

ARGUMENT.

The subject proposed--The discovery of America by Colum-
bus--A philosophical enquiry into the origin of the savages
of America--The first planters from Europe--Causes of
their migration to America--The difficulties they encountered from the jealousy of the natives--Agriculture
descanted on--Commerce and navigation--Science--Future
prospects of British usurpation, tyranny, and devastation
on this side the Atlantic--The more comfortable one of
Independence, liberty, and peace--Conclusion.

Acasto.

Now shall the adventurous muse attempt a strain
More new, more noble, and more flush of fame
Than all that went before--
Now through the veil of ancient days renew
The period fam'd when first Columbus touch'd
These shores so long unknown--through various toils,
Famine, and death, the hero forc'd his way,
Thro' oceans pregnant with perpetual storms,
And climates hostile to advent'rous man.
But why, to prompt your tears, should we resume
The tale of Cortez, furious chief, ordain'd
With Indian blood to dye the sands, and choak,
Fam'd Mexico, thy streams with dead? or why
Once more revive the tale so oft rehears'd
Of Atabilipa, by thirst of gold,
(All conquering motive in the human breast)
Depriv'd of life, which not Peru's rich ore
Nor Mexico's vast mines could then redeem?
Better these northern realms demand our song
Design'd by nature for that rural reign,
For agriculture's toil. --No blood we shed
For metals buried in a rocky waste.

Curs'd be that ore, which brutal makes mankind,
And prompts mankind to shed a brother's blood.

Eugenio.

                    But whence arose
That vagrant race who love the shady vale,
And choose the forest for their dark abode?--
For long has this perplext the sages' skill
To investigate.--Tradition seems to hide
The mighty secret from each mortal eye,
How first these various nations, north and south,
Possest these shores, or from what countries came.--
Whether they sprang from some primaeval head
In their own lands, like Adam in the east,--
Yet this the sacred oracles deny,
And reason, too, reclaims against the thought:
For when the general deluge drown'd the world
Where could their tribes have found security,
Where find their fate, but in the ghastly deep?--
Unless, as others dream, some chosen few
High on the Andes, wrapt in endless snow,
Where winter in his wildest fury reigns,
And subtle ether scarce our life maintains.--
But here Philosophers oppose the scheme;
This earth, say they, nor hills nor mountains knew
Ere yet the universal flood prevail'd;
But when the mighty waters rose aloft,
Rous'd by the winds they shook their solid base,
And, in convulsions, tore the delug'd world,
Till by the winds assuag'd, again they fell,
And all their ragged bed expos'd to view.

    Perhaps far wandering toward the northern pole
The streights of Zembla, and the frozen zone,
And where the eastern Greenland almost joins
America's north point, the hardy tribes
Of banish'd Jews, Siberians, Tartars wild
Come over icy mountains, or on floats
First reach'd these coasts, hid from the world beside.--
And yet another argument more strange,
Reserv'd for men of deeper thought, and late,
Presents itself to view:--In Peleg's days[5]
(So says the Hebrew seer's unerring pen)
This mighty mass of earth, this solid globe
Was cleft in twain,--divided east and west,

39

While straight between, the deep Atlantic roll'd.--
And traces indisputable remain
Of this primaeval land, now sunk and lost.--
The islands rising in our eastern main
Are but small fragments of this continent,
Whose two extremities were Newfoundland
And St. Helena.--One far in the north,
Where shivering seamen view with strange surprize
The guiding pole-star glittering o'er their heads;
The other near the southern tropic rears
Its head above the waves--Bermudas' isles,
Cape Verd, Canary, Britain, and the Azores,
With fam'd Hibernia, are but broken parts
Of some prodigious waste, which once sustain'd
Nations and tribes of vanish'd memory,
Forests, and towns, and beasts of every class,
Where navies now explore their briny way.

Leander.

Your sophistry, Eugenio, makes me smile:
The roving mind of man delights to dwell
On hidden things merely because they're hid:
He thinks his knowledge far beyond all limit,
And boldly fathoms nature's darkest haunts--
But for uncertainties, your broken isles,
Your northern Tartars, and your wandering Jews,
(The flimsy cobwebs of a sophist's brain)
Hear what the voice of history proclaims--
The Carthaginians, ere the Roman yoke
Broke their proud spirits, and enslav'd them too,
For navigation were renown'd as much
As haughty Tyre with all her hundred fleets;
Full many a league their vent'rous seamen sail'd
Thro' streight Gibraltar, down the western shore
Of Africa, to the Canary isles,
By them call'd Fortunate; so Flaccus[6] sings,
Because eternal spring there clothes the fields
And fruits delicious bloom throughout the year.--
From voyaging here, this inference I draw;
Perhaps some barque with all her numerous crew
Falling to leeward of her destin'd port,
Caught by the eastern <u>trade</u>, was hurried on
Before the unceasing blast to Indian isles,
Brazil, La Plata, or the coasts more south--
There stranded, and unable to return,

40

Forever from their native skies estrang'd,
Doubtless they made these virgin climes their own,
And in the course of long revolving years
A numerous progeny from these arose,
And spread throughout the coasts--those whom we call
Brazilians, Mexicans, Peruvians rich,
The tribes of Chili, Patagon, and those
Who till the shores of Amazonia's stream.
When first the powers of Europe here attain'd
Vast empires, kingdoms, cities, palaces
And polish'd nations stock'd the fertile land.
Who has not heard of Cusco, Lima, and
The town of Mexico--huge cities form'd
From Europe's architecture; ere the arms
Of haughty Spain disturb'd the peaceful soil. --
But here, amid this northern dark domain,
No towns were seen to rise.--No arts were here;
The tribes unskill'd to raise the lofty mast,
Or force the daring prow thro' adverse waves,
Gaz'd on the pregnant soil, and crav'd alone
Life from the unaided genius of the ground, --
This indicates they were a different race;
From whom descended 'tis not ours to say--
That power, no doubt, who furnish'd trees, and plants,
And animals, to this vast continent,
Spoke into being man among the rest,
But what a change is here!--what arts arise!
What towns and capitals! how commerce waves
Her gaudy flags, where silence reign'd before!

Acasto.

Speak, my Eugenio, for I've heard you tell
The dismal history, and the cause that brought
The first adventurers to these western shores;
The glorious cause that urg'd our fathers first
To visit climes unknown, and wilder woods
Than e'er Tartarian or Norwegian saw,
And with fair culture to adorn that soil
Which never felt the industrious swain before.

Eugenio.

All this long story to rehearse, would tire;
Besides, the sun toward the west retreats,
Nor can the noblest theme retard his speed,

Nor loftiest verse--not that which sang the fall
Of Troy divine, and fierce Achilles' ire.
Yet hear a part:--By persecution wrong'd,
And sacerdotal rage, our fathers came
From Europe's hostile shores to these abodes,
Here to enjoy a liberty in <u>faith,</u>
Secure from tyranny and base controul.
For this they left their country and their friends,
And dar'd the Atlantic wave in quest of peace,
And found new shores, and sylvan settlements,
And men, alike unknowing and unknown.
Hence, by the care of each advent'rous <u>chief</u>
New governments (their wealth unenvied yet)
Were form'd on liberty and virtue's plan.
<u>These</u> searching out uncultivated tracts
Conceiv'd new plans of towns, and capitals,
And spacious provinces--Why should I name
Thee, Penn, the Solon of our western lands;
Sagacious legislator, whom the world
Admires, and mourns: an infant colony,
Nurs'd by thy care, now rises o'er the rest
Like that tall Pyramid in Egypt's waste
O'er all thy neighbouring piles, they also great.
Why should I name these heroes so well known,
Who peopled all the rest from Canada
To Georgia's farthest coasts, West Florida,
Or Apalachian mountains?--Yet what streams
Of blood were shed! what Indian hosts were slain,
Before these days of peace were quite restor'd!

Leander.

Yes, while they overturn'd the rugged soil
And swept the forests from the shaded plain
'Midst dangers, foes, and death, fierce Indian tribes
With vengeful malice arm'd, and black design,
Oft murder'd or dispers'd these colonies--
Encourag'd, too, by Gallia's hostile sons,
A warlike race, who late their arms display'd
At <u>Quebec</u>, <u>Montreal</u>, and farthest coasts
Of <u>Labrador</u>, or <u>Cape Breton</u>, where now
The British standard awes the subject host.
Here, those brave chiefs, who, lavish of their blood,
Fought in Britannia's cause, in battle fell!--
What heart but mourns the untimely fate of <u>Wolfe</u>,
Who, dying, conquer'd!--or what breast but beats
To share a fate like his, and die like him!

42

Acasto.

But why alone commemorate the dead,
And pass these glorious heroes by, who yet
Breathe the same air, and see the light with us?--
The dead, Leander, are but empty names,
And they who fall to-day the same to us
As they who fell ten centuries ago--!
Lost are they all that shin'd on earth before;
Rome's boldest champions in the dust are laid,
Ajax and great Achilles are no more,
And Philip's warlike son, an empty shade!--
A WASHINGTON among our sons of fame
We boast--conspicuous as the morning star
Among the inferior lights--
To distant wilds Virginia sent him forth--
With her brave sons he gallantly oppos'd
The bold invaders of his country's rights,
Where wild Ohio pours the mazy flood,
And mighty meadows skirt these subject streams.--
But now, delighting in his elm tree's shade,
Where deep Potowmac laves the enchanting shore,
He prunes the tender vine, or bids the soil
Luxuriant harvests to the sun display.--

Behold a different scene--not thus employ'd
Were Cortez and Pizarro, pride of Spain,
Whom blood and murder only satisfy'd,
And all to glut ambition!--

Eugenio.

Such is the curse, Acasto, where the soul
Humane is wanting--but we boast no feats
Of cruelty like Europe's murdering breed--
Our milder epithet is merciful,
And each American, true hearted, learns
To conquer, and to spare; for coward souls
Alone seek vengeance on a vanquish'd foe.
Gold, fatal gold, was the alluring bait
To Spain's rapacious tribe--hence rose the wars
From Chili to the Caribbean sea,
And Montezuma's Mexican domains:
More blest are we, with whose unenvied soil
Nature decreed no mingling gold to shine,
No flaming diamond, precious emerald,

43

No blushing sapphire, ruby, chrysalite,
Or jasper red--more noble riches flow
From agriculture, and the industrious swain,
Who tills the fertile vale, or mountain's brow,
Content to lead a safe, a humble life
Among his native hills, romantic shades
Such as the Muse of Greece of old did feign,
Allur'd the Olympian gods from chrystal skies,
Envying such lovely scenes to mortal man.

Leander.

Long has the rural life been justly fam'd,
And bards of old their pleasing pictures drew
Of flowery meads, and groves, and gliding streams:
Hence, old Arcadia--wood-nymphs, satyrs, swains;
And hence Elysium, fancied heaven below!--
Fair agriculture, not unworthy kings,
Once exercis'd the royal hand, or those
Whose virtues rais'd them to the rank of gods.
See old Laertes[7] in his shepherd weeds
Far from his pompous throne and court august,
Digging the grateful soil, where round him rise
Sons of the earth, the tall aspiring oaks,
Or orchards boasting of more fertile boughs,
Laden with apples red, sweet scented peach,
Pear, cherry, apricot, or spungy plumb;
While through the glebe the industrious oxen draw
The earth-inverting plough. --Those Romans too,
Fabricius and Camillus, lov'd a life
Of neat simplicity and rustic bliss,
And from the noisy Forum hastening far,
From busy camps, and sycophants, and crowns,
'Midst woods and fields spent the remains of life,
Which full enjoyment only finds for fools.

How grateful, to behold the harvests rise,
And mighty crops adorn the extended plains!--
Fair plenty smiles throughout, while lowing herds
Stalk o'er the shrubby hill or grassy mead,
Or at some shallow river slake their thirst. --
The inclosure now succeeds the shepherd's care,
Yet milk-white flocks adorn the well stock'd farm,
And court the attention of the industrious swain--
Their fleece rewards him well; and when the winds
Blow with a keener blast, and from the north

44

Pour mingled tempests through a sunless sky
(Ice, sleet, and rattling hail) secure he sits
Warm in his cottage, fearless of the storm,
Enjoying now the toils of milder moons,
Yet hoping for the spring.--Such are the joys,
And such the toils of those whom heaven hath bless'd
With souls enamour'd of a country life.

Acasto.

Such are the visions of the rustic reign--
But this alone, the fountain of support,
Would scarce employ the varying mind of man;
Each seeks employ, and each a different way:
Strip Commerce of her sail, and men once more
Would be converted into savages--
No nation e'er grew social and refin'd
Till Commerce first had wing'd the adventurous prow,
Or sent the slow-pac'd caravan afar,
To waft their produce to some other clime,
And bring the wish'd exchange--thus came, of old,
Golconda's golden ore, and thus the wealth
Of Ophir to the wisest of mankind.

Eugenio.

Great is the praise of commerce, and the men
Deserve our praise, who spread the undaunted sail,
And traverse every sea--their dangers great,
Death still to combat in the unfeeling gale,
And every billow but a gaping grave:--
There, skies and waters, wearying on the eye,
For weeks and months, no other prospect yield
But barren wastes, unfathom'd depths, where not
The blissful haunt of human form is seen
To chear the unsocial horrors of the way--
Yet all these bold designs to Science owe
Their rise and glory--Hail, fair Science! thou,
Transplanted from the eastern skies, dost bloom
In these blest regions--Greece and Rome no more
Detain the Muses on Cithaeron's brow
Or old Olympus, crown'd with waving woods,
Or Haemus' top, where once was heard the harp,
Sweet Orpheus' harp, that gain'd his cause below,
And pierc'd the heart of Orcus and his bride;

That hush'd to silence by its voice divine
Thy melancholy waters, and the gales
O Hebrus! that o'er thy sad surface blow.--
No more the maids round Alpheus' waters stray,
Where he with Arethusa's wave doth mix,
Or where swift Tiber disembogues his waves
Into the Italian sea, so long unsung;
Hither they wing their way, the last the best
Of countries, where the arts shall rise and grow,
And arms shall have their day--Even now we boast
Of Franklin, prince of all philosophy,
A genius piercing as the electric fire,
Bright as the lightning's flash, explain'd so well
By him, the rival of Britannia's sage. [8]
This is the land of every joyous sound,
Of liberty and life, sweet liberty!
Without whose aid the noblest genius fails,
And Science irretrievably must die.

Leander.

But come, Eugenio, since we know the past--
What hinders to pervade with searching eye
The mystic scenes of dark Futurity!
Say, shall we ask what empires yet must rise,
What kingdoms, powers and STATES, where now are seen
Mere dreary wastes and awful solitude,
Where melancholy sits, with eye folorn,
And time anticipates, when we shall spread
Dominion from the north, and south, and west
Far from the Atlantic to Pacific shores,
And shackle half the convex of the main!--
A glorious theme!--but how shall mortals dare
To pierce the dark events of future years
And scenes unravel, only known to fate?

Acasto.

This we might do, if warm'd by that bright coal
Snatch'd from the altar of cherubic fire
Which touch'd Isaiah's lips--or of the spirit
Of Jeremy and Amos, prophets old,
Might swell the heaving breast--I see, I see
A thousand kingdoms rais'd, cities, and men,
Numerous as sand upon the ocean shore!--

The Ohio soon shall glide by many a town
Of note; and where the Mississippi stream,
By forests shaded, now runs weeping on,
Nations shall grow, and STATES not less in fame
Than Greece and Rome of old!--we too shall boast
Our Alexanders, Pompeys, heroes, kings,
That in the womb of time yet dormant lie,
Waiting the joyous hour of life and light--
O snatch me hence, ye muses, to those days
When through the veil of dark antiquity
Our sons shall hear of us as things remote,
That blossom'd in the morn of days--Alas!
How could I weep that we were born so soon,
Just in the dawning of these mighty times,
When scenes are pregnant with eternity!
Dissentions that shall swell the trump of fame,
And ruin brooding o'er one monarchy!

Eugenio.

Nor shall these angry tumults here subside
Nor murders[9] cease, through all these Provinces,
Till foreign crowns have vanish'd from our view
And dazzle here no more--no more presume
To awe the spirit of fair Liberty--
Vengeance shall cut the thread--and Britain, sure,
Will curse her fatal obstinacy for it!
Bent on the ruin of this injur'd country,
She will not listen to our humble prayers,
Though offer'd with submission.
Like vagabonds, and objects of destruction,
Like those whom all mankind are sworn to hate,
She casts us off from her protection,
And will invite the nations round about,
Russians and Germans, slaves and savages,
To come and have a share in our perdition--
O cruel race, O unrelenting Britain,
Who bloody beasts will hire to cut our throats,
Who war will wage with prattling innocence,
And basely murder unoffending women!--
Will stab their prisoners when they cry for quarter,
Will burn our towns, and from his lodging turn
The poor inhabitant to sleep in tempests !--
These will be wrong; indeed, and all sufficient
To kindle up our souls to deeds of horror,
And give to every arm the nerves of Sampson--

These are the men that fill the world with ruin,
And every region mourns their greedy sway,
Nor only for ambition!--
But what are this world's goods, that they for them
Should exercise eternal butchery?
What are these mighty riches we possess,
That they should send so far to finger them--?--
Already have we felt their potent arm--
And ever since that inauspicious day,
When first Sir Francis Bernard[10]
His canons planted at the council door,
And made the assembly room a home for strumpets,
And soldiers rank and file--e'er since that day
This wretched land, that drinks its children's gore,
Has been a scene of tumult and confusion--!
Are there not evils in the world enough?
Are we so happy that they envy us?
Have we not toil'd to satisfy their Harpies,
King's deputies, that are insatiable;
Whose practice is to incense the royal mind,
And make us despicable in his view?--
Have we not all the evils to contend with
That, in this life, mankind are subject to,
Pain, sickness, poverty, and natural death--
But into every wound that nature gave
They will a dagger plunge, and make them mortal!

Leander.

Enough, enough--such dismal scenes you paint,
I almost shudder at the recollection--
What, are they dogs that they would mangle us?--
To brighter skies I turn my ravish'd view,
And fairer prospects from the future draw--
Here independent power shall hold her sway,
And public virtue warm the patriot breast:
No traces shall remain of tyranny,
And laws, a pattern to the world beside
Be here enacted first.--

Acasto.

And when a train of rolling years are past,
(So sung the exil'd seer in Patmos isle)[11]
A new Jerusalem, sent down from heaven,

Shall grace our happy earth--perhaps this land,
Whose ample breast shall then receive, tho' late,
Myriads of saints, with their immortal king,
To live and reign on earth a thousand years,
Thence called <u>Millenium</u>. Paradise anew
Shall flourish, by no second Adam lost.
No dangerous tree with deadly fruit shall grow,
No tempting serpent to allure the soul
From native innocence.--A <u>Canaan</u> here,
Another <u>Canaan</u> shall excel the old,
And from a fairer <u>Pisgah's</u> top be seen.
No thistle here, nor thorn, nor briar shall spring,
Earth's cause before: The lion and the lamb
In mutual friendship link'd, shall browse the shrub,
And tim'rous deer with soften'd tygers stray
O'er mead, or lofty hill, or grassy plain:
Another Jordan's stream shall glide along,
And Siloah's brook in circling eddies flow:
Groves shall adorn their verdant banks, on which
The happy people, free from toils and death,
Shall find secure repose. No fierce disease,
No fevers, slow consumption, ghastly plague,
(Death's ancient ministers) again proclaim
Perpetual war with man: Fair fruits shall bloom
Fair to the eye and grateful to the taste;
Nature's loud streams be hush'd, and seas no more
Rage hostile to mankind--and, worse than all,
The fiercer passions of the human breast
Shall kindle up to deeds of death no more,
But all subside in universal peace.--

                    Such days the world,
And such, AMERICA, thou first shalt have,
When ages, yet to come, have run their round,
And future years of life alone remain.

On the Conqueror of America shut up in Boston[12]

<u>Rebels you are</u>--the British champion cries;
Truth, stand thou forth, and tell Tom. Gage he lies--
Rebels!--and see, this mock imperial Lord
Already threats those rebels with the <u>cord</u>--

    The hour draws nigh, the glass is almost run,
When truth must shine, and scoundrels be undone,
When this base miscreant shall forbear to sneer,
And curse his taunts and bitter insults here.

If to controul the cunning of a knave,
Freedom adore, and scorn the name of slave,
If to protest against a tyrant's laws,
And arm for vengeance in a righteous cause,
Be deem'd Rebellion--'tis a harmless thing;
This bug-bear name, like death, has lost its sting.

AMERICANS, at freedom's fane adore,
But trust to British clemency no more;
The generous genius of the isle has fled,
And left a mere impostor in his stead--
If conquer'd, rebels, their past records show,
Receive no mercy from this parent foe--
And even the grave, that sacred haunt of peace,
Where Nature gives the woes of man to cease,
Vengeance will search--and mangled corpses there
Be rais'd to feast the armies of the air. --
If Britain conquers, help us, heav'n, to fly;
Lend me your wings, ye ravens of the sky--
If Britain conquers--we exist no more:
These lands shall redden with their children's gore,
Who, turn'd to slaves, their fruitless toils shall moan,
Toils in these fields that once they call'd their own!

To arms! to arms!--and let the trusty sword
Decide who best deserves the hangman's cord,
Nor think the hills of Canada too bleak,
When desperate Freedom is the prize you seek;
For that the voice of honour bids you go
O'er frozen lakes and mountains wrapt in snow;
No toils can daunt the warlike and the bold;
They scorn all heat or wave-congealing cold;
Haste, to your tents in fetters bring
These slaves that serve their tyrant of a king,
So just, so virtuous is your cause, I say
Hell must prevail if Britain wins the day.

The House of Night: A Vision[13]

ADVERTISEMENT--This Poem is founded upon the authority of Scripture, inasmuch as these sacred books assert,
that the last enemy that shall be conquered is Death. For
the purposes of poetry he is here personified, and represented as on his dying bed. The scene is laid at a solitary
palace, (the time midnight) which, tho' before beautiful and
joyous, is now become sad and gloomy, as being the abode

and receptacle of Death. Its owner, an amiable majestic
youth, who had lately lost a beloved consort, nevertheless
with a noble philosophical fortitude and humanity entertains
him in a friendly manner, and by employing Physicians, endeavours to restore him to health, altho' an enemy; convinced of the excellence and propriety of that divine precept,
If thine enemy hunger, feed him; if he thirst, give him
drink. He nevertheless, as if by a spirit of prophecy, informs this (fictitiously) wicked being of the certainty of his
doom, and represents to him in a pathetic manner the vanity
of his expectations, either of a reception into the abodes of
the just, or continuing longer to make havock of mankind upon earth. The patient finding his end approaching, composes
his epitaph, and orders it to be engraved on his tombstone,
hinting to us thereby, that even Death and Distress have vanity; and would be remembered with honour after he is no
more, altho' his whole life has been spent in deeds of devastation and murder. He dies at last in the utmost agonies of
despair, after agreeing with an avaricious Undertaker to in-
tomb his bones. This reflects upon the inhumanity of those
men, who, not to mention an enemy, would scarcely cover a
departed friend with a little dust, without certainty of reward for so doing. The circumstances of his funeral are
then recited, and the visionary and fabulous part of the poem
disappears. It concludes with a few reflexions on the impro-
priety of a too great attachment to the present life, and in-
centives to such moral virtue as may assist in conducting us
to a better.

1.

Trembling I write my dream, and recollect[14]
A fearful vision at the midnight hour;
So late, Death o'er me spread his sable wings,
Painted with fancies of malignant power!

2.

Such was the dream the sage Chaldean saw
Disclos'd to him that felt heav'n's vengeful rod;
Such was the ghost, who through deep silence cry'd,
Shall mortal man--be juster than his God.

3.

Let others draw from smiling skies their theme,
And tell of climes that boast unfading light;
I draw a darker scene, replete with gloom;
I sing the horrors of the House of Night.

4.

Stranger, believe the truth experience tells;
Poetic dreams are of a finer cast
Than those which o'er the sober brain diffus'd,
Are but a repetition of some action past.

5.

Fancy, I own thy power--when sunk in sleep
Thou play'st thy wild delusive part so well
You lift me into immortality,
Depict new heavens, or draw the scenes of hell.

6.

By some sad means, when Reason holds no sway,
Lonely I rov'd at midnight o'er a plain
Where murmuring streams and mingling rivers flow,
Far to their springs, or seek the sea again.

7.

Sweet vernal May! tho' then thy woods in bloom
Flourish'd; yet nought of this could Fancy see;
No wild pinks bless'd the meads, no green the fields,
And naked seem'd to stand each lifeless tree:

8.

Dark was the sky, and not one friendly star
Shone from the zenith or horizon, clear,
Mist sate upon the woods, and darkness rode
In her black chariot, with a wild career.

9.

And from the woods the late resounding note
Issued of the loquacious Whip-poor-will, 15
Hoarse, howling dogs, and nightly roving wolves
Clamour'd from far off clifts invisible.

10.

Rude, from the wide extended Chesapeke
I heard the winds the dashing waves assail,
And saw from far, by picturing fancy form'd,
The black ship travelling through the noisy gale.

11.

At last, by chance and guardian fancy led,
I reach'd a noble dome, rais'd fair and high,
And saw the light from upper windows flame,
Presage of mirth and hospitality.

52

12.

And by that light around the dome appear'd
A mournful garden of autumnal hue,
Its lately pleasing flowers all drooping stood
Amidst high weeds that in rank plenty grew.

13.

The Primrose there, the violet darkly blue,
Daisies and fair Narcissus ceas'd to rise,
Gay spotted pinks their charming bloom withdrew,
And Polyanthus quench'd its thousand dyes.

14.

No pleasant fruit or blossom gaily smil'd.
Nought but unhappy plants and trees were seen,
The yew, the myrtle, and the church-yard elm,
The cypress, with its melancholy green.

15.

There cedars dark, the osier, and the pine,
Shorn tamarisks, and weeping willows grew;
The poplar tall, the lotos, and the lime,
And pyracantha did her leaves renew.

16.

The poppy there, companion to repose,
Display'd her blossoms that began to fall,
And here the purple amaranthus rose
With mint strong-scented, for the funeral.

17.

And here and there with laurel shrubs between
A tombstone lay, inscribed with strains of woe,
And stanzas sad, throughout the dismal green,
Lamented for the dead that slept below.

18.

Peace to this awful dome!--when strait I heard
The voice of men in a secluded room,
Much did they talk of death, and much of life,
Of coffins, shrouds, and horrors of a tomb.

19.

Pathetic were their words, and well they aim'd
To explain the mystic paths of providence;
Learn'd were they all, but there remain'd not I
To hear the upshot of their conference.

20.

Meanwhile from an adjoining chamber came
Confused murmurings, half distinguish'd sounds,
And as I nearer drew, disputes arose
Of surgery, and remedies for wounds.

21.

Dull were their feuds, for they went on to talk
Of Anchylosis, and the shoulder blade,
Os Femoris, Trochanters--and whate'er,
Has been discuss'd by Cheselden or Meade: 16

22.

And often each to prove his notion true
Brought proofs from Galen or Hippocrates--
But fancy led me hence--and left them so,
Firm at their points of hardy No and Yes.

23.

Then up three winding stairs my feet were brought
To a high chamber, hung with mourning sad,
The unsnuff'd candles glar'd with visage dim,
'Midst grief, in ecstasy of woe run mad.

24.

A wide leaf'd table stood on either side
Well fraught with phials, half their liquids spent,
And from a couch, behind the curtain's veil
I heard a hollow voice of loud lament.

25.

Turning to view the object whence it came,
My frighted eyes a horrid form survey'd;
Fancy, I own thy power--Death on the couch
With fleshless limbs, at rueful length, was laid.

26.

And o'er his head flew jealousies and cares,
Ghosts, imps, and half the black Tartarian crew,
Arch-angels damn'd, nor was their Prince remote,
Borne on the vaporous wings of Stygian dew.

27.

Around his bed by the dull flambeaux' glare,
I saw pale phantoms--Rage to madness vext,
Wan, wasting grief, and ever musing care,
Distressful pain, and poverty perplext.

28.

Sad was his countenance, if we can call
That <u>countenance</u>, where only bones were seen
And eyes sunk in their sockets, dark and low,
And teeth, that only show'd themselves to grin.

29.

Reft was his scull of hair, and no fresh bloom
Of chearful mirth sate on his visage hoar:
Sometimes he rais'd his head, while deep drawn groans
Were mixt with words that did his fate deplore.

30.

Oft did he wish to see the day light spring,
And often toward the window lean'd to hear,
Forerunner of the scarlet-mantled morn,
The early note of wakeful <u>Chanticleer</u>.

31.

Thus he--But at my hand a portly youth
Of comely countenance, began to tell,
"That this was Death upon his dying bed,
Sullen, morose, and peevish to be well;

32.

"Fixt is his doom--the miscreant reigns no more
The tyrant of the dying or the dead;
This night concludes his all-consuming reign;
Pour out, ye heav'ns, your vengeance on his head.

33.

"But since, my friends, (said he) chance leads you here,
With me this night upon the sick attend,
You on this bed of death must watch, and I
Will not be distant from the fretful fiend.

34.

"Before he made this lofty pile his home,
In undisturb'd repose I sweetly slept,
But when he came to this sequester'd dome
'Twas then my troubles came, and then I wept:

35.

"Twice three long nights, in this sad chamber, I
As though a brother languish'd in despair,
Have 'tended faithful round his gloomy bed,
Have been content to breathe this loathsome air.

36.

"A while relieve the languors that I feel,
Sleep's magic forces close my weary eyes;
Soft o'er my soul unwonted slumbers steal;
Aid the weak patient till you see me rise.

37.

"But let no slumbers on your eye-lids fall,
That if he ask for powder or for pill
You may be ready at the word to start,
And still seem anxious to perform his will.

38.

"The bleeding Saviour of a world undone
Bade thy compassion rise toward thy foe;
Then, stranger, for the sake of Mary's son,
Thy tears of pity on this wretch bestow.

39.

"'Twas he that stole from my adoring arms
Aspasia, she the loveliest of her land,
Lucretia's virtue, with a Helen's charms,
Charms of the face, and beauties of the mind.

40.

"The blushy cheek, the lively, beaming eye,
The ruby lip, the flowing jetty hair,
The stature tall, the aspect so divine,
All beauty, you would think, had center'd there.

41.

"Each future age her virtues shall extol,
Nor the just tribute to her worth refuse;
Fam'd, to the stars URANIA bids her rise,
Theme of the moral, and the tragic Muse.

42.

"Sweet as the fragrance of the vernal morn,
Nipt in its bloom this faded flower I see;
The inspiring angel from that breast is gone,
And life's warm tide forever chill'd in thee!

43.

"Such charms shall greet thy longing soul no more;
Her lively eyes are clos'd in endless shade;
Torpid, she rests on yonder marble floor;
Approach, and see what havock DEATH has made.

44.

"Yet, stranger, hold--her charms are so divine,
Such tints of life still on her visage glow,
That even in death this slumbering bride of mine
May seize thy heart, and make thee wretched too.

45.

"O shun the sight--forbid thy trembling hand
From her pale face to raise the enshrouding lawn, --
Death claims thy care; obey his stern command;
Trim the dull tapers, for I see no dawn!"

46.

So said, at Death's left side I sate me down;
The mourning youth toward his right reclin'd;
Death in the middle lay, with all his groans,
And much he toss'd and tumbled, sigh'd and pin'd.

47.

But now this man of hell toward me turn'd,
And strait, in hideous tone, began to speak;
Long held he sage discourse, but I forbore
To answer him, much less his news to seek.

48.

He talk'd of tomb-stones and of monuments,
Of Equinoxial climes and India shores;
He talk'd of stars that shed their influence,
Fevers and plagues, and all their noxious stores.

49.

He mention'd too the guileful <u>calenture</u>, [17]
Tempting the sailor on the deep sea main,
That paints gay groves upon the ocean floor,
Beckoning her victim to the faithless scene.

50.

Much spoke he of the myrtle and the yew,
Of ghosts that nightly walk the church-yard o'er,
Of storms that through the wint'ry ocean blow
And dash the well-mann'd galley on the shore,

51.

Of broad-mouth'd cannons, and the thunderbolt,
Of sieges and convulsions, dearth and fire,
Of poisonous weeds--but seem'd to sneer at these
Who by the laurel o'er him did aspire.

52.

Then with a hollow voice thus went he on,
"Get up, and search, and bring, when found, to me,
Some cordial, potion, or some pleasant draught,
Sweet, slumb'rous poppy, or the mild Bohea.

53.

"But hark, my pitying friend--!--and, if you can,
Deceive the grim physician at the door--
Bring half the mountain springs--ah! hither bring
The cold rock water from the shady bower.

54.

"For till this night such thirst did ne'er invade,
A thirst provok'd by heav'n's avenging hand;
Hence bear me, friends, to quaff, and quaff again
The cool wave bubbling from the yellow sand.

55.

"To these dark walls with stately step I came,
Prepar'd your drugs and doses to defy;
Smit with the love of never dying fame,
I came, alas! to conquer--not to die!"

56.

Glad, from his side I sprang, and fetch'd the draught,
Which down his greedy throat he quickly swills,
Then on a second errand sent me strait
To search in some dark corner for his pills.

57.

Quoth he, "These pills have long compounded been
Of dead men's bones and bitter roots, I trow;
But that I may to wonted health return,
Throughout my lank veins shall their substance go."

58.

So down they went--He rais'd his fainting head
And oft in feeble tone essay'd to talk;
Quoth he, "Since remedies have small avail,
Assist unhappy Death once more to walk."

59.

Then slowly rising from his loathsome bed,
On wasted legs the meagre monster stood,
Gap'd wide, and foam'd, and hungry seem'd to ask,
Tho' sick, an endless quantity of food.

60.

Said he, "The sweet melodious flute prepare,
The anthem, and the organ's solemn sound,
Such as may strike my soul with ecstacy,
Such as may from yon' lofty walls rebound.

61.

"Sweet music can the fiercest pains assuage,
She bids the soul to heav'n's blest mansions rise,
She calms despair, controuls infernal rage
And deepest anguish, when it hears her, dies.

62.

"And see, the mizzling, misty midnight reigns,
And no soft dews are on my eye-lids sent--!
Here, stranger, lend thy hand; assist me, pray,
To walk a circuit of so large extent. "--

63.

On my prest shoulders leaning, round he went,
And could have made the boldest spectre flee;
I led him up stairs, and I led him down,
But not one moment's rest from pain got he.

64.

Then with his dart, its cup unpointed now,
Thrice with main strength he smote the trembling floor,
The roof resounded to the fearful blow,
And Cleon started, domm'd to sleep no more.

65.

When thus spake Death, impatient of controul,
"Quick, move, and bring from yonder black bureau
The sacred book that may preserve my soul
From long damnation, and eternal woe.

66.

"And with it bring--for you may find them there,
The works of holy authors, dead and gone,
The sacred tome of moving Drelincourt,
Or what more solemn Sherlock mus'd upon:

67.

"And read, my Cleon, what these sages say,
And what the sacred Penman hath declar'd,
That when the wicked leaves his odious way,
His sins shall vanish, and his soul be spar'd. "

68.

But he, unmindful of the vain command,
Reason'd with Death, nor were his reasonings few:
Quoth he--"My Lord, what frenzy moves your brain,
Pray, what, my lord, can Sherlock be to you,

69.

"Or all the sage divines that ever wrote,
Grave Drelincourt, or heaven's unerring page;
These point their arrows at your hostile breast,
And raise new pains that time must ne'er assuage.

70.

"And why should thus thy woe disturb my rest?
Much of Theology I once did read,
And there 'tis fixt, sure as my God is so,
That Death shall perish, tho' a God should bleed.

71.

"The martyr, doom'd the pangs of fire to feel,
Lives but a moment in the sultry blast;
The victim groans, and dies beneath the steel,
But thy severer pains shall always last.

72.

"O miscreant vile, thy age has made thee doat--
If peace, if sacred peace were found for you,
Hell would cry out, and all the damn'd arise
And, more deserving, seek for pity, too.

73.

"Seek not for Paradise--'tis not for thee,
Where high in heaven its sweetest blossoms blow,
Nor even where gliding to the Persian main
Thy waves, Euphrates, through the garden flow!

74.

"Bloody has been thy reign, O man of hell,
Who sympathiz'd with no departing groan;
Cruel was thou, and hardly dost deserve
To have Hic Jacet stampt upon thy stone.

75.

"He that could build his mansion o'er the tombs,
Depending still on sickness and decay,
May dwell unmov'd amidst these drowsier glooms,
May laugh the dullest of these shades away.

76.

"Remember how with unrelenting ire
You tore the infant from the unwilling breast--
ASPASIA fell, and CLEON must expire,
Doom'd by the impartial God to endless rest:

77.

"In vain with stars he deck'd yon' spangled skies,
And bade the mind to heaven's bright regions soar,
And brought so far to my admiring eyes
A glimpse of glories that shall blaze no more!

78.

"Even now to glut thy devilish wrath, I see
From eastern realms a wasteful army rise:
Why else those lights that tremble in the north?
Why else yon' comet blazing through the skies?

79.

"Rejoice O fiend; Britannia's tyrant sends
From German plains his myriads to our shore.
The fierce Hibernian with the Briton join'd--
Bring them ye winds! but waft them back no more.

80.

"To you, alas! the fates in wrath deny
The comforts to our parting moments due,
And leave you here to languish and to die,
Your crimes too many, and your tears too few.

81.

"No cheering voice to thee shall cry, Repent!
As once it echoed through the wilderness--
No patron died for thee--damn'd, damn'd art thou
Like all the devils, nor one jot the less.

82.

"A gloomy land, with sullen skies is thine,
Where never rose or amaranthus grow,
No daffodils, nor comely columbine,
No hyacinths nor asphodels for you.

83.

"The barren trees that flourish on the shore
With leaves or fruit were never seen to bend,
O'er languid waves unblossom'd branches hang,
And every branch sustains some vagrant fiend.

84.

"And now no more remains, but to prepare
To take possession of thy punishment;
That's thy inheritance, that thy domain,
A land of bitter woe, and loud lament.

85.

"And oh that HE, who spread the universe,
Would cast one pitying glance on thee below;
Millions of years in torments thou might'st fry,
But thy eternity!--who can conceive its woe!"

86.

He heard, and round with his black eye-balls gaz'd,
Full of despair, and curs'd, and rav'd, and swore:
"And since this is my doom, said he, call up
Your wood-mechanics to my chamber door:

87.

"Blame not on me the ravage to be made;
Proclaim,--even Death abhors such woe to see;
I'll quit the world, while decently I can,
And leave the work to GEORGE my deputy."

88.

Up rush'd a band, with compasses and scales
To measure his slim carcase, long and lean--
"Be sure, said he, to frame my coffin strong;
You, master workman, and your men, I mean:

89.

"For if the Devil, so late my trusty friend,
Should get one hint where I am laid, from you,
Not with my soul content, he'd seek to find
That mouldering mass of bones, my body, too!

90.

"Of hardest ebon let the plank be found,
With clamps and ponderous bars secur'd around,
That if the box by Satan should be storm'd,
It may be able for resistance found."

91.

"Yes, said the master workman, noble Death,
Your coffin shall be strong--that leave to me--
But who shall these your funeral dues discharge?
Nor friends nor pence you have, that I can see."

92.

To this said Death--"You might have ask'd me too,
Base caitiff, who are my executors,
Where my estate, and who the men that shall
Partake my substance, and be called my heirs.

93.

"Know, then, that hell is my inheritance,
The devil himself my funeral dues must pay--
Go--since you must be paid--go, ask of him,
For he has gold, as fabling poets say."

94.

Strait they retir'd--when thus he gave me charge
Pointing from the light window to the west,
"Go three miles o'er the plain, and you shall see
A burying ground of sinners dead, unblest.

95.

"Amid the graves a spiry building stands
Whose solemn knell resounding through the gloom
Shall call thee o'er the circumjacent lands
To the dull mansion destin'd for my tomb.

96.

"There, since 'tis dark, I'll plant a glimmering light
Just snatch'd from hell, by whose reflected beams
Thou shalt behold a tomb-stone, full eight feet,
Fast by a grave, replete with ghosts and dreams.

97.

"And on that stone engrave this epitaph
Since Death, it seems, must die like mortal men;
Yes--on that stone engrave this epitaph,
Though all hell's furies aim to snatch the pen.

98.

"Death in this tomb his weary bones hath laid,
Sick of dominion o'er the human kind--
Behold what devastations he hath made;
Survey the millions by his arm confin'd.

99.

"Six thousand years has sovereign sway been mine;
None, but myself, can real glory claim;
Great Regent of the world I reign'd alone,
And princes trembled when my mandate came.

100.

"Vast and unmatch'd throughout the world my fame
Takes place of gods, and asks no mortal date--
No: by myself, and by the heavens, I swear,
Not Alexander's name is half so great.

101.

"Nor swords nor darts my prowess could withstand,
All quit their arms, and bow'd to my decree,
Even mighty JULIUS died beneath my hand,
For slaves and Cesars were the same to me!

102.

"Traveller, wouldst thou his noblest trophies seek,
Search in no narrow spot obscure for those;
The sea profound, the surface of all land
Is moulded with the myriads of his foes."

103.

Scarce had he spoke, when on the lofty dome
Rush'd from the clouds a hoarse resounding blast--
Round the four caves so loud and sad it play'd
As though all musick were to breathe its last.

104.

Warm was the gale, and such as travellers say
Sport with the winds on Zaara's barren waste;
Black was the sky, a mourning carpet spread,
Its azure blotted, and its stars o'ercast!

105.

Lights in the air like burning stars were hurl'd,
Dogs howl'd, heaven mutter'd, and the tempest blew;
The red half-moon peep'd from behind a cloud
As if in dread the amazing scene to view.

106.

The mournful trees that in the garden stood
Bent to the tempest as it rush'd along;
The elm, the myrtle, and the cypress sad
More melancholy tun'd its bellowing song.

107.

No more that elm its noble branches spread;
The yew, the cypress, or the myrtle tree,
Rent from the roots, the tempest tore them down,
And all the grove in wild confusion lay.

108.

Yet, mindful of his dread command, I part
Glad from the magic dome--nor found relief;
Damps from the dead hung heavier round my heart,
While sad remembrance rous'd her stores of grief.

109.

O'er a dark field I held my dubious way
Where Jack-lanthorn walk'd his lonely round,
Beneath my feet substantial darkness lay,
And screams were heard from the distemper'd ground.

110.

Nor look'd I back, till to a far off wood,
Trembling with fear, my weary feet had sped--
Dark was the night, but at the inchanted dome
I saw the infernal windows flaming red.

111.

And from within the howls of Death I heard,
Cursing the dismal night that gave him birth,
Damning his ancient sire, and mother sin,
Who at the gates of hell, accursed, brought him forth. [18]

112.

(For fancy gave to my enraptur'd soul
An eagle's eye, with keenest glance to see,
And bade those distant sounds distinctly roll
Which, waking, never had affected me.)

113.

Oft his pale breast with cruel hand he smote,
And tearing from his limbs a winding sheet
Roar'd to the black skies, while the woods around,
As wicked as himself, his words repeat.

114.

Thrice tow'rd the skies his meagre arms he rear'd,
Invok'd all hell, and thunders on his head,
Bid lightnings fly, earth yawn, and tempests roar,
And the sea wrap him in its oozy bed.

115.

"My life for one cool draught!--O, fetch your springs;
Can one unfeeling to my woes be found!
No friendly visage comes to my relief,
But ghosts impend, and spectres hover round.

116.

"Though humbled now, dishearten'd and distrest,
Yet, when admitted to the peaceful ground,
With heroes, kings, and conquerors I shall rest,
Shall sleep as safely, and perhaps as sound."

117.

Dim burnt the lamp, and now the phantom Death
Gave his last groans in horror and despair--
"All hell demands me hence"--he said, and threw
The red lamp hissing through the midnight air.

118.

Trembling, across the plain my course I held,
And found the grave-yard, loitering through the gloom,
And, in the midst, a hell-red, wandering light,
Walking in fiery circles round the tomb.

119.

Among the graves a spiry building stood,
Whose tolling bell resounding through the shade
Sung doleful ditties to the ancient wood,
And many a dismal drowsy thing it said.

120.

This fabrick tall, with towers and chancels grac'd,
Was rais'd by sinners hands, in ages fled;
The roof they painted, and the beams they brac'd,
And texts from scripture o'er the walls they spread:

121.

But wicked were their hearts, for they refus'd
To aid the helpless orphan, when distrest;
The shivering, naked stranger they mis-used,
And banish'd from their doors the starving guest.

122.

By laws protected, cruel and prophane,
The poor man's ox these monsters drove away;--
And left Distress to attend her infant train,
No friend to comfort, and no bread to stay.

123.

But heav'n look'd on with keen, resentful eye,
And doom'd them to perdition and the grave,
That as they felt not for the wretch distrest
So heaven no pity on their souls would have.

124.

In pride they rais'd this building tall and fair,
Their hearts were on perpetual mischief bent,
With pride they preach'd, and pride was in their prayer,
With pride they were deceiv'd, and so to hell they went.

125.

At distance far approaching to the tomb,
By lamps and lanthorns guided through the shade,
A coal-black chariot hurried through the gloom,
Spectres attending, in black weeds array'd,

126.

Whose woeful forms yet chill my soul with dread;
Each wore a vest in Stygian chambers wove,
Death's kindred all--Death's horses they bestrode,
And gallop'd fiercely, as the chariot drove.

127.

Each horrid face a grizly mask conceal'd;
Their busy eyes shot terror to my soul
As now and then, by the pale lanthorn's glare,
I saw them for their parted friend condole.

128.

Before the herse Death's chaplain seem'd to go,
Who strove to comfort, what he could, the dead;
Talk'd much of Satan, and the land of woe,
And many a chapter from the scriptures read.

129.

At last he rais'd the swelling anthem high;
In dismal numbers seem'd he to complain;
The captive tribes that by Euphrates wept,
Their song was jovial to his dreary strain.

130.

That done, they plac'd the carcase in the tomb,
To dust and dull oblivion now resign'd,
Then turn'd the chariot tow'rd the House of Night,
Which soon flew off, and left no trace behind.

131.

But as I stoop'd to write the appointed verse,
Swifter than thought the airy scene decay'd;
Blushing the morn arose, and from the east
With her gay streams of light dispell'd the shade.

132.

What is this <u>Death</u>, ye deep read sophists, say?
Death is no more than one unceasing change;
New forms arise, while other forms decay,
Yet all is LIFE throughout creation's range.

133.

The towering <u>Alps</u>, the haughty <u>Appenine,</u>
The <u>Andes</u> wrapt in everlasting snow,
The <u>Apalachian</u> and the <u>Ararat</u>
Sooner or later must to ruin go.

134.

Hills sink to plains, and man returns to dust;
That dust supports a reptile or a flower;
Each changeful atom by some other nurs'd
Takes some new form, to perish in an hour.

135.

Too nearly join'd to sickness, toils and pains,
(Perhaps for former crimes imprison'd here)
True to itself the immortal soul remains,
And seeks new mansions in the starry sphere.

136.

When Nature bids thee from the world retire,
With joy thy lodging leave, a fated guest,
In Paradise, the land of thy desire,
Existing always, always to be blest.

The Beauties of Santa Cruz[19]

1776

Sweet orange grove, the fairest of the isle,
In thy soft shade luxuriously reclin'd,
Where, round my fragrant bed, the flowrets smile,
In sweet delusions I deceive my mind.

But Melancholy's glooms assail my breast,
For potent nature reigns despotic here;--
A nation ruin'd, and a world oppress'd,
Might rob the boldest Stoic of a tear.

1.

Sick of thy northern glooms, come, shepherd, seek
More equal climes, and a serener sky:
Why shouldst thou toil amid thy frozen ground,
Where half year's snows, a barren prospect lie,

2.

When thou mayst go where never frost was seen,
Or north-west winds with cutting fury blow,
Where never ice congeal'd the limpid stream,
Where never mountain tipt its head with snow?

3.

Twice seven days prosperous gales thy barque shall bear
To isles that flourish in perpetual green,
Where richest herbage glads each shady vale,
And ever verdant plants on every hill are seen.

4.

Nor dread the dangers of the billowy deep,
Autumnal winds shall safely waft thee o'er;
Put off the timid heart, or, man unblest,
Ne'er shalt thou reach this gay enchanting shore.

5.

Thus Judah's tribes beheld the promis'd land,
While Jordan's angry waters swell'd between;
Thus trembling on the brink I see them stand,
Heav'n's type in view, the Canaanitish green.

6.

Thus, some mean souls, in spite of age and care,
Are so united to this globe below,
They never wish to cross death's dusky main
That parting them and happiness doth flow.

7.

Though reason's voice might whisper to the soul
That nobler climes for man the gods design--
Come, shepherd, haste--the northern breezes blow;
No more the slumbering winds thy barque confine.

8.

From the vast caverns of old ocean's bed
Fair SANTA CRUZ, arising, laves her waist;
The threat'ning waters roar on every side,
For every side by ocean is embrac'd.

9.

Sharp, craggy rocks repell the surging brine,
Whose cavern'd sides by restless billows wore,
Resemblance claim to that remoter isle[20]
Where once the winds' proud lord the sceptre bore.

10.

Betwixt old Cancer and the mid-way line
In happiest climate lies this envied isle,
Trees bloom throughout the year, streams ever flow,
And fragrant Flora wears a lasting smile.

11.

Cool, woodland streams from shaded clifts descend;
The dripping rock no want of moisture knows,
Supply'd by springs that on the skies depend,
That fountain feeding as the current flows.

12.

Such were the isles which happy Flaccus sung,
Where one tree blossoms while another bears,
Where spring forever gay, and ever young,
Walks her gay round through her unwearied years.

13.

Such were the climes which youthful Eden saw
Ere crossing fates destroy'd her golden reign--
Reflect upon thy loss, unhappy man,
And seek the vales of Paradise again.

14.

No lowering skies are here--the neighbouring sun
Clear and unveil'd, his brilliant journey goes,
Each morn emerging from the ambient main,
And seeking there each evening to repose.

15.

In June's fair month the spangled traveller gains
The utmost limits of his northern way,
And blesses with his beams cold lands remote,
Sad Greenland's coast, and Hudson's frozen bay.

16.

The shivering swains of those unhappy climes
Behold the side-way monarch through the trees;
We feel his fiercer heat, his vertic beams,
Temper'd with cooling winds and trade-wind breeze.

Yet, though so near heav'n's blazing lamp doth run,
We court the beam that sheds the golden day,
And hence are called the children of the sun,
Who, without fainting, bear his downward ray.

18.
No threatening tides upon our island rise,
Gay Cynthia scarce disturbs the ocean here;
No waves approach her orb, and she, as kind,
Attracts no water to her silver sphere.

19.
The happy waters boast, of various kinds,
Unnumber'd myriads of the scaly race;
Sportive they glide above the delug'd sand,
Gay as their clime, in ocean's ample vase.

20.
Some streak'd with burnish'd gold, resplendent glare;
Some cleave the limpid deep, all silver'd o'er;
Some, clad in living green, delight the eye;
Some red, some blue; of mingled colours more.

21.
Here glides the spangled Dolphin through the deep,
The giant-carcas'd whales at distance stray;
The huge green turtles wallow through the wave;
Well pleas'd alike with land or water, they.

22.
The <u>Rainbow</u> cuts the deep, of varied green;
The well fed <u>Grouper</u> lurks remote, below;
The swift <u>Bonetta</u> coasts the watry scene;
The diamond coated <u>Angels</u> kindle as they go,

23.
Delicious to the taste, salubrious food,
Which might some temperate studious sage allure
To curse the fare of his abstemious school,
And turn, for once, a cheerful Epicure.

24.
Unhurt may'st thou this luscious food enjoy,
To fulness feast upon the scaly kind;
These, well selected from a thousand more,
Delight the taste, and leave no plague behind.

25.

Nor think Hygeia[21] is a stranger here.
To sensual souls the clime may fatal prove,
Anguish and death attend, and pain severe,
The midnight revel, and licentious love.

26.

Full many a swain, in youth's serenest bloom, [22]
Is borne untimely to this alien clay,
Constrain'd to slumber in a foreign tomb,
Far from his friends, his country far away.

27.

Yet, if devoted to a sensual soul,
If fondly their own ruin they create,
These victims to the banquet and the bowl
Must blame their folly only, not their fate.

28.

But thou, who first drew breath in northern air,
At early dawn ascend the sloping hills,
And oft' at noon to lime tree shades repair,
Where some soft stream from neighbouring groves distils.

29.

And with it mix the liquid of the lime,
The old ag'd essence of the generous cane,
And sweetest syrups of the liquorish clime,
And drink, to cool thy thirst, and drink again.

30.

This happy beverage, joy inspiring bowl,
Dispelling far the shades of mental night,
Wakes bright ideas on the enraptur'd soul,
And sorrow turns to pleasure and delight.

31.

Sweet verdant isle, through thy dark woods I rove,
And learn the nature of each native tree,
The fustick hard, the poisonous manchineel
Which for its fragrant apple pleaseth thee:

32.

Alluring to the smell, fair to the eye,
But deadliest poison in the taste is found--
O shun the dangerous tree, nor taste, like Eve,
This interdicted fruit in Eden's ground.

33.

The lowly mangrove, fond of watery soil,
The white bark'd gregory, rising high in air,
The mastick in the woods you may descry;
Tamarind, and lofty plumb-trees flourish there.

34.

Sweet orange groves in lonely vallies rise
And drop their fruits, unnotic'd and unknown;
The cooling acid limes in hedges grow;
The juicy lemons swell in shades their own.

35.

Once in these groves divine Aurelia stray'd--!
Then, conscious nature, smiling, look'd more gay;
But soon she left the dear delightful shade;
The shade, neglected, droops and dies away,

36.

And pines for her return, but pines in vain;
In distant isles belov'd Aurelia died,
Pride of the plains, ador'd by every swain,
Sweet warbler of the woods, and of the woods the pride.

37.

Philander early left this rural maid,
Nor yet return'd by fate compell'd to roam,
But absent from the heavenly girl he stray'd,
Her charms forgot, forgot his native home.

38.

O fate severe, to seize the nymph so soon,
The nymph, for whom a thousand shepherds sigh,
And in the space of one revolving moon
To doom the fair one and her swain to die!

39.

Sweet, spungy plumbs on trees wide spreading hang;
Bell-apples here, suspended, shade the ground;
Plump grenadilloes and guavas grey,
With melons in each plain and lawn abound.

40.

The conic form'd cashew, of juicy kind,
Which bears at once an apple and a nut;
Whose poisonous coat, indignant to the lip,
Doth in its cell a wholesome kernel shut.

41.

The prince of fruits, whom some <u>jayama</u> call,
<u>Anana</u> some, the happy flavour'd <u>pine</u>;
In which unite the tastes and juices all
Of apple, peach, quince, grape, and nectarine,

42.

Grows to perfection here, and spreads his crest;
His diadem toward the parent sun;
His diadem, in fiery blossoms drest,
Stands arm'd with swords from potent nature won.

43.

Yon' cotton shrubs with bursting knobs behold,
Their snow white locks these humble groves array;
On slender trees the blushing coffee hangs
Like thy fair cherry, and would tempt thy stay.

44.

Safe from the winds, in deep retreats, they rise;
Their utmost summit may thy arm attain;
Taste the moist fruit, and from thy closing eyes
Sleep shall retire, with all his drowsy train.

45.

The spicy berry, they <u>guava</u> call,
Swells in the mountains on a stripling tree:
These some admire, and value more than all
My humble verse, besides, unfolds to thee.

46.

The smooth white cedar, here, delights the eye;
The bay-tree, with its aromatic green,
The sea-side grapes, sweet natives of the sand,
And pulse, of various kinds, on trees are seen.

47.

Here mingled vines their downward shadows cast;
Here, cluster'd grapes from loaded boughs depend,
Their leaves no frosts, their fruits no cold winds blast,
But, rear'd by suns, to time alone they bend.

48.

The plantane and banana flourish here,
Of hasty growth, and love to fix their root
Where some soft stream of ambling water flows
To yield full moisture to their cluster'd fruit.

49.

No other trees so vast a leaf can boast,
So broad, so long--through these refresh'd I stray,
And though the noon-sun all his radiance shed,
These friendly leaves shall shade me all the way,

50.

And tempt the cooling breeze to hasten there,
With its sweet odorous breath to charm the grove;
High shades and verdant seats, while underneath
A little stream by mossy banks doth rove,

51.

Where once the Indian dames slept with their swains,
Or fondly kiss'd the moon-light eves away;
The lovers fled, the tearful stream remains,
And only I console it with my lay.

52.

Among the shades of yonder whispering grove
The green palmittoes mingle, tall and fair,
That ever murmur, and forever move,
Fanning with wavy bough the ambient air.

53.

Pomegranates grace the wild, and sweet-sops there
Ready to fall, require thy helping hand;
Nor yet neglect the papaw or mamee,
Whose slighted trees with fruits unheeded stand.

54.

Those shaddocks juicy shall thy taste delight,
And yon' high fruits, the richest of the wood,
That cling in clusters to the mother tree,
The cocoa-nut; rich, milky, healthful food.

55.

O grant to me, gods, if yet condemn'd to stray,
At least to spend life's sober evening here,
To plant a grove where winds yon' shelter'd bay,
And pluck these fruits that frost nor winter fear.

56.

Cassada shrubs abound--transplanted here
From every clime, exotic blossoms blow;
Here Asia plants her flowers, here Europe seeds,
And hyperborean plants, un-winter'd grow.

57.

Here, a new herbage glads the generous steed,
Mules, goats, and sheep enjoy these pastures fair,
And for thy hedges, nature has decreed,
Guards of thy toils, the date and prickly pear.

58.

But chief the glory of these Indian isles
Springs from the sweet, uncloying sugar-cane;
Hence comes the planter's wealth; hence commerce sends
Such floating piles to traverse half the main.

59.

Whoe'er thou art that leav'st thy native shore
And shall to fair West India climates come,
Taste not the enchanting plant--to taste forbear,
If ever thou wouldst reach thy much lov'd home.

60.

Ne'er through the Isle permit thy feet to rove,
Or, if thou dost, let prudence lead the way;
Forbear to taste the virtues of the cane;
Forbear to taste what will complete thy stay.

61.

Whoever sips of this enchanting juice,
Delicious nectar, fit for Jove's own hall,
Returns no more from his lov'd Santa Cruz,
But quits his friends, his country, and his all,

62.

And thinks no more of home--Ulysses so
Dragg'd off by force his sailors from that shore
Where <u>lotos</u> grew, and, had not strength prevail'd,
They never would have sought their country more.

63.

No annual toil inters this thrifty plant;
The stalk lopt off, the strengthening showers prolong,
To future years, unfading and secure,
The root so vigorous, and the juice so strong.

64.

Unnumber'd plants, besides, these climates yield,
And grass peculiar to the soil that bears;
Ten thousand varied herbs array the field;
This glads thy palate, that thy health repairs.

65.

Along the shore a wondrous flower is seen,
Where rocky ponds receive the surging wave,
Some drest in yellow, some array'd in green;
Beneath the water, their gay branches lave.

66.

This mystic plant, with its bewitching charms,
Too surely springs from some enchanted bower:
Fearful it is, and dreads impending harms,
And Animal the natives call the flower.

67.

From the smooth rock its little branches rise,
The objects of thy view, and that alone;
Feast on its beauties with thy ravish'd eyes,
But aim to touch it, and--the flower is gone.

68.

Nay, if thy shade but intercept the beam
That gilds their boughs beneath the briny lake,
Swift they retire, like a deluding dream,
And even a shadow for destruction take.

69.

Warn'd by experience, seek not thou to gain
The magic plant thy curious hand invades;
Returning to the light, it mocks thy pain,
Deceives all grasp, and seeks its native shades.

70.

On yonder sleepy hill, fresh harvests rise,
Where the dark tribe from Afric's sun burnt plain
Oft o'er the ocean turn their wishful eyes
To isles remote, high looming o'er the main,

71.

And view soft seats of ease and fancied rest,
Their native groves new painted on the eye,
Where no proud misers their gay hours molest,
Nor lordly despots pass unsocial by.

72.

See, yonder slave that slowly bends this way,
With years, and pain, and ceaseless toil opprest;
Though no complaining words his woes betray,
The eye dejected proves the heart distrest.

73.

Perhaps in chains he left his native shore;
Perhaps he left a helpless offspring there,
Perhaps a wife, that he must see no more,
Perhaps a father, who his love did share.

74.

Curs'd be the ship that brought him o'er the main,
And curs'd the hands who from his country tore;
May she be stranded, ne'er to float again;
May they be shipwreck'd on some hostile shore--

75.

O gold accurst, of every ill the spring,
For thee compassion flies the darken'd mind,
Reason's plain dictates no conviction bring,
And passion only sways all human kind.

76.

O gold accurst! for thee we madly run
With murderous hearts across the briny flood,
Seek foreign climes beneath a foreign sun,
And there exult to shed a brother's blood.

77.

But thou who own'st this sugar-bearing soil,
To whom no good the great FIRST CAUSE denies,
Let freeborn hands attend thy sultry toil,
And fair harvests to thy view shall rise.

78.

The teeming earth shall mightier stores disclose
Than ever struck thy longing eyes before,
And late content shall shed a soft repose,
Repose, so long a stranger at thy door.

79.

Give me some clime, the favourite of the sky,
Where cruel slavery never sought to reign--
But shun the theme, sad muse, and tell me why
These abject trees lie scatter'd o'er the plain?

80.

These isles, lest nature should have prov'd too kind,
Or man have sought his happiest heaven below,
Are torn with mighty winds, fierce hurricanes,
Nature convuls'd in every shape of woe.

81.

Nor scorn yon' lonely vale of trees to rest;
There plantane groves late grew of lively green,
The orange flourish'd, and the lemon bore;
The genius of the isle dwelt there unseen.

82.

Wild were the skies, affrighted nature groan'd
As though approach'd her last decisive day,
Skies blaz'd around, and bellowing winds had nigh
Dislodg'd these cliffs, and tore yon' hills away.

83.

O'er the wild main, dejected and afraid,
The trembling pilot lash'd his helm a-lee,
Or, swiftly scudding, ask'd thy potent aid,
Dear pilot of the Gallilean sea.

84.

Low hung the glooms; distended with the gale
The clouds, dark brooding, wing'd their circling flight;
Tremendous thunders join'd the hurricane,
Daughter of chaos, and eternal night.

85.

And how, alas! could these fair trees withstand
The wasteful madness of so fierce a blast,
That storm'd along the plain, seiz'd every grove,
And delug'd with a sea this mournful waste.

86.

That plantane grove, where oft I fondly stray'd,
Thy darts, dread Phoebus, in those glooms to shun,
Is now no more a refuge or a shade,
Is now with rocks and deep sands over-run.

87.

Those late proud domes of splendour, pomp, and ease
No longer strike the view, in grand attire;
But, torn by winds, flew piece-meal to the seas,
Nor left one nook to lodge the astonish'd 'squire.

88.

But other groves the hand of Time shall raise;
Again shall nature smile, serenely gay;
So soon each scene revives, why should I leave
These green retreats, o'er the dark seas to stray?

89.

For I must go where the mad pirate roves, [23]
A stranger on the inhospitable <u>main,</u>
Torn from the scenes of Hudson's sweetest groves,
Led by false hope, and expectation vain.

90.

<u>There</u> endless plains deject the wearied eye,
And hostile winds incessant toil prepare;
And should loud bellowing storms all art defy,
The manly heart alone must conquer there.

91.

On these blue hills to pluck the opening flowers
Might yet awhile the unwelcome task delay,
And these gay scenes prolong the fleeting hours
To aid bright Fancy on some future day.

92.

Thy vales, <u>Bermuda,</u> and thy sea-girt groves
Can never like these southern forests please;
And, lash'd by stormy waves, you court in vain
The northern shepherd to your cedar trees.

93.

Not o'er those isles such equal planets rule;
All, but the cedar, dread the wintry blast;
Too well thy charms the banish'd <u>Waller</u> sung:[24]
Too near the <u>pilot's star</u> thy doom is cast.

94.

Far o'er the waste of yonder surgy field
My native climes in fancied prospect lie,
Now hid in shades, and now by clouds conceal'd,
And now by tempests ravish'd from my eye.

95.

There, triumphs to enjoy, are, Britain, thine;
There, thy proud navy awes the pillag'd shore;
Nor sees the day when nations shall combine
That pride to humble and our rights restore.

96.

Yet o'er the globe shouldst thou extend thy reign,
Here may thy conquering arms one grotto spare;
Here--though they conquest vex--in spite of pain,
I quaff the enlivening glass, in spite of care.

97.

What, though we bend to a <u>tyrannic crown</u>;
Still Nature's charms in varied beauty shine--
What though we own the proud imperious <u>Dane,</u>
Gold is his sordid care, the Muses mine.

98.

Winter, and winter's glooms are far remov'd;
Eternal spring with smiling summer join'd;--
Absence, and death, and heart-corroding care,
Why should they cloud the sun-shine of the mind?

99.

But, shepherd, haste, and leave behind thee far
Thy bloody plains, and iron glooms above,
Quit the cold northern star, and here enjoy,
Beneath the smiling skies, this land of love. [25]

100.

The drowsy pelican wings home his way, [26]
The misty eve sits heavy on the sea,
And though yon' sail drags slowly o'er the main,
Say, shall a moment's gloom discourage thee?

101.

To-morrow's sun now paints the faded scene;
Though deep in ocean sink his western beams,
His spangled chariot shall ascend more clear,
More radiant from the drowsy land of dreams.

102.

Of all the isles the neighbouring ocean bears,
None can with this their equal landscape boast:
What could we do on SABA'S cloudy height;
Or what could please on 'STATIA'S barren coast? [27]

103.

Couldst thou content on rough TORTOLA stray,
Confest the fairest of the <u>Virgin</u> train;
Or couldst thou on these rocky summits play
Where high St. JOHN stands frowning o'er the main?

104.

Haste, shepherd, haste--Hesperian fruits for thee,
And cluster'd grapes from mingled boughs depend--
What pleasure in thy forests can there be
That, leafless now, to every tempest bend?

105.

To milder stars, and skies of clearer blue,
Sworn foe to arms, at least a-while repair,
And, till to mightier force proud Britain bends,
Despise her triumphs, and deceive thy care.

106.

Soon shall the genius of the fertile soil
A new creation to thy view unfold;
Admire the works of Nature's magic hand,
But scorn that vulgar bait, all potent gold.

107.

Yet, if persuaded by no lay of mine,
You still admire your climes of frost and snow,
And pleas'd, prefer above our southern groves
The darksome forests, that around thee grow;

108.

Still there remain--thy native air enjoy,
Repel the tyrant, who thy peace invades,
While, pleas'd, I trace the vales of Santa Cruz,[28]
And sing with rapture her inspiring shades.

The British Prison Ship[29]

CANTO I.   The CAPTURE.

Assist me, CLIO! while in verse I tell
The dire misfortunes that a ship befell,
Which outward bound, to St. Eustatia's shore,
Death and disaster through the billows bore.

From Philadelphia's crowded port she came;
For there the builder plann'd her lofty frame;
With wond'rous skill, and excellence of art
He form'd, dispos'd, and order'd every part,
With joy beheld the stately fabric rise
To a stout bulwark of stupendous size,
'Till launch'd at last, capacious of the freight,
He left her to the Pilots, and her fate.

First from her depths the tapering masts ascend,
On whose firm bulk the transverse yards depend;

By shrouds and stays secur'd from side to side
Trees grew on trees, suspended o'er the tide,
Firm to the yards extended, broad and vast
They hung the sails susceptive of the blast;
Far o'er the prow the lengthy bowsprit lay,
Supporting on the extreme the taut Gib-stay;
Twice ten six pounders at their port holes plac'd
And rang'd in rows, stood hostile in the waist:
Thus all prepar'd, impatient for the seas,
She left her station with an adverse breeze,
This her first outset from her native shore,
To seas a stranger, and untry'd before.

From the bright radiance that his glories spread
Ere from the east gay Phoebus lifts his head,
From the sweet morn, a kindred name she won,
AURORA call'd, the offspring of the sun,
Whose form projecting, the broad prow displays,
Far glittering o'er the wave, a mimic blaze.

The gay ship now, in all her pomp and pride,
With sails expanded, flew along the tide;
'Twas thy deep stream, O Delaware, that bore
This pile intended for a southern shore,
Bound to those isles where endless summer reigns,
Fair fruits, gay blossoms, and enamell'd plains;
Where sloping lawns the roving swain invite,
And the cool morn succeeds the breezy night,
Where each glad day a heaven unclouded brings
And sky-topt mountains teem with golden springs.

From Cape HENLOPEN, urg'd by favouring gales,
When morn emerg'd, we sea-ward spread our sails,
Then east-south-east explor'd the briny way,
Close to the wind, departing from the bay;
No longer seen the hoarse resounding strand,
With hearts elate we hurried from the land,
Escap'd the dangers of that shelvy ground
To sailors fatal, and for wrecks renown'd--

The gale increases as we stem the main;
Now scarce the hills their sky-blue mist retain;
At last they sink beneath the rolling wave
That seems their summits, as they sink, to lave;
Abaft the beam the freshening breezes play,
No mists advancing to deform the day,
No tempests rising o'er the splendid scene,
A sea unruffled, and a heaven serene.

Now Sol's bright lamp, the heav'n born source of light,
Has pass'd the line of his meridian height,
And westward hung--retreating from the view
Shores disappear'd, and every hill withdrew,
When, still suspicious of some neighbouring foe,
Aloft the Master bade a Seaman go,
To mark if, from the mast's aspiring height
Through all the round a vessel came in sight.

Too soon the Seaman's glance, extending wide,
Far distant in the east a ship espy'd;
Her lofty masts stood bending to the gale,
Close to the wind was brac'd each shivering sail;
Next from the deck we saw the approaching foe,
Her spangled bottom seem'd in flames to glow
When to the winds she bow'd in dreadful haste
And her lee-guns lay delug'd in the waste:
From her top-gallant glow'd an <u>English Jack</u>;
With all her might she strove to gain our tack,
Nor strove in vain--with pride and power elate,
Wing'd on by hell, she drove us to our fate;
No stop, no stay her bloody crew intends,
(So flies a comet with its host of fiends);
Nor oaths, nor prayers arrest her swift career,
Death in her front, and ruin in her rear.

Struck at the sight, the Master gave command
To change our course, and steer toward the land--
Swift to the task the ready sailors run,
And while the word was utter'd, half was done;
As from the south the fiercer breezes rise
Swift from her foe alarm'd AURORA flies;
With every sail extended to the wind
She fled the unequal foe that chac'd behind;
Along her decks dispos'd in close array,
Each at its port, the grim artillery lay,
Soon on the foe with brazen throat to roar;
But, small their size, and narrow was their <u>bore</u>;
Yet faithful they their destin'd station keep
To guard the barque that wafts them o'er the deep,
Who now must bend to steer a homeward course
And trust her swiftness rather than her force,
Unfit to combat with a powerful foe;
Her decks too open, and her <u>waist</u> too low.

While o'er the wave with foaming prow she flies,
Once more emerging, distant landscapes rise;

84

High in the air the <u>starry</u> streamer plays,
And every sail its various tribute pays:
To gain the land we bore the weighty blast;
And now the wish'd for <u>cape</u> appear'd at last;
But the vext foe, impatient of delay,
Prepar'd for ruin, press'd upon her prey;
Near, and more near, in aweful grandeur came
The frigate IRIS, not unknown to fame;
IRIS her name, but HANCOCK once she bore,
Fram'd, and completed on NEW ALBION'S shore,
By MANLEY lost, the swiftest of the train
That fly with wings of canvas o'er the main.

    Now, while for combat some with zeal prepare,
Thus to the heavens the Boatswain sent his prayer;
"List' all ye powers that rule the skies and seas!
Shower down perdition on such thieves as these;
Fate strike their hearts with terror and dismay,
And sprinkle on their powder salt-sea spray!
May bursting cannon, while his aim he tries,
Destroy the Gunner, and be-damn his eyes--
The chief who awes the quarter-deck, may he,
Tripp'd from his stand, be tumbled in the sea.
May they who rule the <u>round-top's</u> giddy height
Be canted headlong to perpetual night;
May fiends torment them on a leeward coast,
And help forsake them when they want it most--
From their wheel'd engines torn be every gun--
And now, to sum up every curse in one,
May latent flames, to save us, intervene,
And hell-ward drive them from their magazine!"--

    The Frigate, now, had every sail unfurl'd,
And rush'd tremendous o'er the wat'ry world;
Thus fierce <u>Pelides</u>, eager to destroy,
Chac'd the proud Trojan to the gates of Troy--
Swift o'er the waves while hostile they pursue,
As swiftly from their fangs AURORA flew;
At length HENLOPEN'S cape we gain'd once more,
And vainly strove to force the ship ashore;
Stern fate forbade the barren shore to gain,
Denial sad, and source of future pain!
For then the inspiring breezes ceas'd to blow,
Lost were they all, and smooth the seas below;
By the broad cape becalm'd, our lifeless sails
No longer swell'd their bosoms to the gales;
The ship, unable to pursue her way,

Tumbling about, at her own guidance lay;
No more the helm its wonted influence lends,
No oars assist us, and no breeze befriends;
Mean time the foe, advancing from the sea,
Rang'd her black cannon, pointed on our lee;
Then up she luff'd, and blaz'd her entrails dire,
Bearing destruction, terror, death, and fire.

Vext at our fate, we prim'd a piece, and then
Return'd the shot, to shew them we were men.
Dull night at length her dusky pinions spread,
And every hope to 'scape the foe was fled;
Close to thy cape, Henlopen, though we press'd,
We could not gain thy desert, dreary breast;
Though ruin'd trees beshroud thy barren shore
With mounds of sand half hid, or cover'd o'er,
Though ruffian winds disturb thy summit bare,
Yet every hope and every wish was there;
In vain we sought to reach the joyless strand;
Fate stood between, and barr'd us from the land.

All dead becalm'd, and helpless as we lay,
The ebbing current forc'd us back to sea,
While vengeful IRIS, thirsting for our blood,
Flash'd her red lightnings o'er the trembling flood;
At every flash a storm of ruin came
'Till our shock'd vessel shook through all her frame--
Mad for revenge, our breasts with fury glow
To wreak returns of vengeance on the foe;
Full at his hull our pointed guns we rais'd;
His hull resounded as the cannon blaz'd;
Through his main-topsail one a passage tore,
His sides re-echo'd to the dreadful roar,
Alternate fires dispell'd the shades of night--
But how unequal was this daring fight!
Our stoutest guns threw but a six-pound ball,
Twelve pounders from the foe our sides did maul,
And, while no power to save him intervenes,
A bullet struck our captain of Marines;
Fierce, though he bid defiance to the foe,
He felt his death and ruin in the blow;
Headlong he fell, distracted with the wound,
The deck distain'd, and heart blood streaming round.
Another blast, as fatal in its aim,
Wing'd by destruction, through our rigging came,
And, whistling tunes from hell upon its way,
Shrouds, stays, and braces tore at once away;

Sails, blocks, and oars in scatter'd fragments fly--
Their softest language was--SUBMIT, OR DIE.

Repeated cries throughout the ship resound;
Now every bullet brought a different wound;
'Twixt wind and water, one assail'd the side;
Through this aperture rush'd the briny tide--
'Twas then the Master trembled for his crew,
And bade thy shores, O Delaware, adieu!--
And must we yield to yon' destructive ball,
And must our colours to these ruffians fall!--
They fall!--his thunders forc'd our pride to bend,
The lofty topsails with their yards descend,
And the proud foe, such leagues of ocean pass'd,
His wish completed in our woe at last.

Convey'd to YORK, we found, at length, too late,
That Death was better than the prisoner's fate;
There doom'd to famine, shackles and despair,
Condemn'd to breathe a foul, infected air
In sickly hulks, devoted while we lay,
Successive funerals gloom'd each dismal day--
But what on captives British rage can do,
Another Canto, friend, shall let you know.

CANTO II.   The PRISON SHIP.

The various horrors of these hulks to tell,
These Prison Ships where pain and horror dwell,
Where death in tenfold vengeance holds his reign,
And injur'd ghosts, yet unaveng'd, complain;
This be my task--ungenerous Britons, you
Conspire to murder those you can't subdue.--

Weak as I am, I'll try my strength to-day
And my best arrows at these hell-hounds play,
To future years one scene of death prolong,
And hang them up to infamy, in song.

That Britain's rage should dye our plains with gore,
And desolation spread through every shore,
None e'er could doubt, that her ambition knew,
This was to rage and disappointment due;
But that those monsters whom our soil maintain'd,
Who first drew breath in this devoted land,
Like famish'd wolves, should on their country prey,

87

Assist its foes, and wrest our lives away,
This shocks belief--and bids our soil disown
Such friends, subservient to a bankrupt crown;
By them the widow mourns her partner dead,
Her mangled sons to darksome prisons led;
By them--and hence my keenest sorrows rise,
My friend, my guardian, my Orestes dies;
Still for that loss must wretched I complain,
And sad Ophelia mourn her favourite swain.

Ah! come the day when from this bloody shore
Fate shall remove them to return no more--
To scorch'd Bahama shall the traitors go
With grief and rage, and unremitting woe,
On burning sands to walk their painful round,
And sigh through all the solitary ground,
Where no gay flower their haggard eyes shall see,
And find no shade but from the cypress tree.

So much we suffer'd from the tribe I hate,
So near they shov'd me to the brink of fate,
When two long months in these dark hulls we lay
Barr'd down by night, and fainting all the day
In the fierce fervours of the solar beam,
Cool'd by no breeze on Hudson's mountain-stream;
That not unsung these threescore days shall fall
To black oblivion that would cover all!

No masts or sails these crowded ships adorn,
Dismal to view, neglected and forlorn!
Here, mighty ills oppress the imprison'd throng;
Dull were our slumbers, and our nights too long--
From morn to eve along the decks we lay
Scorch'd into fevers by the solar ray;
No friendly awning cast a welcome shade;
Once was it promis'd, and was never made;
No favours could these sons of death bestow;
'Twas endless cursing, and continual woe:
Immortal hatred doth their breasts engage,
And this lost empire swells their souls with rage.

Two hulks on Hudson's stormy bosom lie,
Two, farther south, affront the pitying eye--
There, the black SCORPION at her mooring rides;
There, STROMBOLO swings, yielding to the tides;
Here, bulky JERSEY fills a larger space,
And HUNTER, to all hospitals disgrace--
Thou, Scorpion, fatal to thy crowded throng,

Dire theme of horror and Plutonian song,
Requir'st my lay--thy sultry decks I know,
And all the torments that exist below!
The briny wave that Hudson's bosom fills
Drain'd through her bottom in a thousand rills;
Rotten and old, replete with sighs and groans,
Scarce on the waters she sustain'd her bones;
Here, doom'd to toil, or founder in the tide,
At the moist pumps incessantly we ply'd;
Here, doom'd to starve, like famish'd dogs we tore
The scant allowance, that our tyrants bore.

Remembrance shudders at this scene of fears--
Still in my view some English brute appears;
Some base-born Hessian slave walks threat'ning by;
Some servile Scot with murder in his eye
Still haunts my sight, as vainly they bemoan
Rebellions manag'd so unlike their own!
O may I never feel the poignant pain
To live subjected to such fiends again,
Stewards and Mates that hostile Britain bore,
Cut from the gallows on their native shore;
Their ghastly looks and vengeance-beaming eyes
Still to my view in dismal colours rise--
O may I ne'er review these dire abodes,
These piles for slaughter, floating on the floods, --
And you, that o'er the troubled ocean go,
Strike not your standards to this miscreant foe;
Better the greedy wave should swallow all,
Better to meet the death-conducted ball,
Better to sleep on ocean's deepest bed
At once destroy'd and number'd with the dead,
Than thus to perish in the face of day
Where twice ten thousand deaths one death delay.

When to the ocean dives the western sun,
And the scorch'd Tories fire their evening gun,
"Down, rebel, down!" the angry Scotchmen cry,
"Damn'd dogs, descend, or by our broad swords die!"

Hail, dark abode! what can with thee compare--
Heat, sickness, famine, death, and stagnant air--
Pandora's box, from whence all mischief flew,
Here real found, torments mankind anew!--
Swift from the guarded decks we rush'd along,
And vainly sought repose, so vast our throng:
Three hundred wretches here, denied all light,
In crowded mansions pass the infernal night;

Some for a bed their tatter'd vestments join,
And some on chests, and some on floors recline;
Shut from the blessings of the evening air,
Pensive we lay with mingled corpses there;
Meagre and wan, and scorch'd with heat, below,
We loom'd like ghosts, ere death had made us so--
How could we else, where heat and hunger join'd
Thus to debase the body and the mind,
Where cruel thirst the parching throat invades,
Dries up the man, and fits him for the shades?

No waters laded from the bubbling spring
To these dire ships the British monsters bring--
By planks and ponderous beams completely wall'd,
Invain for water, and invain, I call'd--
No drop was granted to the midnight prayer,
To Dives in these regions of despair!
The loathsome cask a deadly dose contains,
Its poison circling through the languid veins;
"Here, generous Britain, generous, as you say,
To my parch'd tongue one cooling drop convey;
Hell has no mischief like a thirsty throat,
Nor one tormentor like your David Sproat. "30

Dull flew the hours, till, from the East display'd,
Sweet morn dispells the horrors of the shade;
On every side dire objects meet the sight,
And pallid forms, and murders of the night;
The dead were past their pain; the living groan,
Nor dare to hope another morn their own;
But what to them is morn's delightful ray,
Sad and distressful as the close of day?
O'er distant streams appears the dewy green,
And leafy trees on mountain tops are seen,
But they no groves nor grassy mountains tread,
Mark'd for a longer journey to the dead.

Black as the clouds that shade St. Kilda's shore,
Wild as the winds that round her mountains roar,
At every post some surly vagrant stands,
Pick'd from the British or the Irish bands,
Some slave from Hesse, some hangman's son at least
Sold and transported, like his brother beast--
Some miscreant Tory, puff'd with upstart pride,
Led on by hell to take the royal side;
Dispensing death triumphantly they stand,
Their musquets ready to obey command;

Wounds are their sport, as ruin is their aim;
On their dark souls compassion has no claim,
And discord only can their spirits please:
Such were our tyrants here, and such were these.

Ingratitude! no curse like thee is found
Throughout this jarring world's extended round;
Their hearts with malice to our country swell
Because in former days we us'd them well--!
This pierces deep, too deeply wounds the breast;
We help'd them naked, friendless, and distrest,
Receiv'd their vagrants with an open hand,
Bestow'd them buildings, privilege, and land--
Behold the change!--when angry Britain rose,
These thankless tribes became our fiercest foes,
By them devoted, plunder'd, and accurst,
Stung by the serpents whom ourselves had nursed.

But such a train of endless woes abound,
So many mischiefs in these hulks are found,
That on them all a poem to prolong
Would swell too high the horrors of my song--
Hunger and thirst to work our woe combine,
And mouldy bread, and flesh of rotten swine,
The mangled carcase, and the batter'd brain,
The doctor's poison, and the captain's cane,
The soldier's musquet, and the steward's debt,
The evening shackle, and the noon-day threat.

That juice destructive to the pangs of care
Which Rome of old, nor Athens could prepare,
Which gains the day for many a modern chief
When cool reflection yields a faint relief,
That charm, whose virtue warms the world beside,
Was by these tyrants to our use denied;
While yet they deign'd that healthy juice to lade,
The putrid water felt its powerful aid;
But when refus'd--to aggravate our pains--
Then fevers rag'd and revel'd through our veins;
Throughout my frame I felt its deadly heat;
I felt my pulse with quicker motions beat:
A pallid hue o'er every face was spread;
Unusual pains attack'd the fainting head;
No physic here, no doctor to assist,
My name was enter'd on the sick man's list;
Twelve wretches more the same dark symptoms took,
And these were enter'd on the doctor's book;

The loathsome HUNTER was our destin'd place,
The HUNTER, to all hospitals disgrace;
Joyful we left the SCORPION'S dire abode;
Some tears we shed for the remaining crew,
Then curs'd the hulk, and from her sides withdrew.

CANTO III.   The HOSPITAL PRISON SHIP.

Now tow'rd the HUNTER'S gloomy sides we came,
A slaughter-house, yet hospital in name;
For none came there (to pass through all degrees)
'Till half consum'd, and dying with disease;--
But when too near with labouring oars we ply'd
The Mate with curses drove us from the side;
That wretch who, banish'd from his navy crew,
Grown old in blood, did here his trade renew;
His serpent's tongue, when on his charge let loose,
Utter'd reproaches, scandal, and abuse,
Gave all to hell who dar'd his king disown,
And swore mankind were made for George alone:
Ten thousand times, to irritate our woe,
He wish'd us founder'd in the gulph below;
Ten thousand times he brandish'd high his stick,
And swore as often that we were not sick--
And yet so pale!--that we were thought by some
A freight of ghosts from Death's dominions come--
But calm'd at length--for who can always rage,
Or the fierce war of endless passion wage?
He pointed to the stairs that led below
To damp, disease, and varied shapes of woe--
Down to the gloom I took my pensive way;
Along the decks the dying captives lay;
Some struck with madness, some with scurvy pain'd,
But still of putrid fevers most complain'd!
On the hard floors these wasted objects laid,
There toss'd and tumbled in the dismal shade;
There no soft voice their bitter fate bemoan'd,
And Death trode lately, while the victims groan'd;
Of leaky decks I heard them long complain,
Drown'd as they were in deluges of rain,
Deny'd the comforts of a dying bed,
And not a pillow to support the head--
How could they else but pine, and grieve, and sigh,
Detest a wretched life--and wish to die?

Scarce had I mingled with this dismal band
When a thin spectre seiz'd me by the hand--
"And art thou come, (death heavy on his eyes)
And art thou come to these abodes, he cries;
Why didst thou leave thy damp infected cell?
If that was purgatory, this is hell--
We too grown weary of that horrid shade
Petitioned early for the doctor's aid;
His aid denied, more deadly symptoms came;
Weak, and yet weaker, glow'd the vital flame;
And when disease had worn us down so low
That few could tell if we were ghosts, or no,
And all asserted, death would be our fate--
Then to the doctor we were sent--too late.
Here wastes away Autolycus the brave;
Here, gay Alcander, gay, alas, no more,
Dies far sequester'd from his native shore;
He late, perhaps, too eager for the fray,
Chac'd the vile Briton o'er the wat'ry way
'Till fortune jealous, bade her clouds appear,
Turn'd hostile to his fame, and brought him here.

"Thus do our warriors, thus our heroes fall;
Imprison'd here, base ruin meets them all,
Or, sent afar to Britain's barbarous shore,
There die neglected, and return no more:
Ah rest in peace, poor, injur'd, parted shade,
By cruel hands in death's dark weeds array'd,
But happier climes, where suns unclouded shine,
Light undisturb'd, and endless peace are thine."--

From Brookland groves a Hessian doctor came,
Not great his skill, nor greater much his fame;
Fair Science never call'd the wretch her son,
And Art disdain'd the stupid man to own;--
Can you admire that Science was so coy,
Or Art refus'd his genius to employ!--
Do men with brutes an equal dullness share,
Or cuts yon' groveling mole the midway air--
In polar worlds can Eden's blossoms blow,
Do trees of God in barren desarts grow,
Are loaded vines to Etna's summit known,
Or swells the peach beneath the torrid zone--?
Yet still he doom'd his genius to the rack,
And, as you may suppose, was own'd a quack.

He on his charge the healing work begun
With antimonial mixtures, by the tun,
Ten minutes was the time he deign'd to stay,
The time of grace allotted once a day--
He drencht us well with bitter draughts, 'tis true,
Nostrums from hell, and cortex from Peru--
Some with his pills he sent to Pluto's reign,
And some he blister'd with his flies of Spain;
His cream of Tartar walk'd its deadly round,
Till the lean patient at the potion frown'd,
And swore that hemlock, death, or what you will,
Were nonsense to the drugs that stuff'd his bill.--
On those refusing he bestow'd a kick,
Or menac'd vengeance with his walking stick;
Here uncontroul'd he exercis'd his trade,
And grew experienced by the deaths he made;
By frequent blows we from his cane endur'd
He kill'd at least as many as he cur'd,
On our lost comrades built his future fame,
And scatter'd fate, where 'er his footsteps came.

Some did not seem obedient to his will,
And swore he mingled poison with his pill,
But I acquit him by a fair confession:
He was no Englishman--he was a Hessian--
Although a dunce, he had some sense of sin,
Or else the Lord knows where we now had been;
Perhaps in that far country sent to range
Where never prisoner meets with an exchange--
Then had we all been banish'd out of time
Nor I return'd to plague the world with rhyme.

Fool though he was, yet candour must confess
Not chief Physician was this dog of Hesse--
One master o'er the murdering tribe was plac'd;
By him the rest were honour'd or disgrac'd;--
Once, and but once, by some strange fortune led
He came to see the dying and the dead--
He came--but anger so deform'd his eye,
And such a faulchion glitter'd on his thigh,
And such a gloom his visage darken'd o'er,
And two such pistols in his hands he bore!
That, by the gods!--with such a load of steel
He came, we thought, to murder, not to heal--
Hell in his heart, and mischief in his head,
He gloom'd destruction, and had smote us dead,
Had he so dar'd--but fate with-held his hand--
He came--blasphem'd--and turn'd again to land.

94

From this poor vessel, and her sickly crew,
An English ruffian all his titles drew,
Captain, esquire, commander, too, in chief,
And hence he gain'd his bread, and hence his beef,
But, sir, you might have search'd creation round
Ere such another miscreant could be found--
Though unprovok'd, an angry face he bore;
We stood astonish'd at the oaths he swore;
He swore, till every prisoner stood aghast,
And thought him Satan in a brimstone blast;
He wish'd us banish'd from the public light;
He wish'd us shrouded in perpetual night!
That were he king, no mercy would he show,
But drive all <u>rebels</u> to the world below;
That if we <u>scoundrels</u> did not scrub the decks
His staff should break our damn'd <u>rebellious</u> necks;
He swore, besides, that if the ship took fire
We too should in the pitchy flame expire;
And meant it so--this tyrant I engage
Had lost his breath to gratify his rage.--

If where he walk'd a captive carcase lay,
Still dreadful was the language of the day--
He call'd us <u>dogs</u>, and would have us'd us so,
But vengeance check'd the meditated blow,
The vengeance from our injur'd nation due
To him, and the base, unmanly crew.

Such food they sent, to make complete our woes,
It look'd like carrion torn from hungry crows;
Such vermin vile on every joint were seen,
So black, corrupted, mortified, and lean
That once we try'd to move our flinty chief,
And thus address'd him, holding up the beef:

"See, captain, see! what rotten bones we pick;
What kills the healthy cannot cure the sick:
Not dogs on such by <u>Christian</u> men are fed,
And see, good master, see, what lousy bread!"

"Your meat or bread (this man of flint replied)
Is not my care to manage or provide--
But this, damn'd rebel dogs, I'd have you know,
That better than you merit we bestow;
Out of my sight!"--nor more he deign'd to say,
But whisk'd about, and frowning, strode away.

Each day, at least three carcases we bore,
And scratch'd them graves along the sandy shore;
By feeble hands the shallow graves were made,
No stone memorial o'er the corpses laid;
In barren sands, and far from home, they lie,
No friend to shed a tear, when passing by;
O'er the mean tombs insulting Britons tread,
Spurn at the sand, and curse the rebel dead.

When to your arms these fatal islands fall,
(For first or last they must be conquer'd all)
Americans! to rites sepulchral just,
With gentlest footsteps press this kindred dust,
And o'er the tombs, if tombs can then be found,
Place the green turf, and plant the myrtle round.

Americans! a just resentment shew,
And glut revenge on this detested foe;
While the warm blood exults the glowing vein
Still shall resentment in your bosoms reign;
Can you forget the greedy Briton's ire,
Your fields in ruin, and your domes on fire,
No age, no sex from lust and murder free,
And black as night, the hell born refugee!
Must York forever your best blood entomb,
And these gorg'd monsters triumph in their doom,
Who leave no art of cruelty untry'd;
Such heavy vengeance, and such hellish pride!
Death has no charms, except in British eyes;
See, arm'd for death, the infernal miscreants rise;
See how they pant to stain the world with gore,
And, millions murder'd, still would murder more;
This selfish race, from all the world disjoin'd,
Perpetual discord spread throughout mankind,
Aim to extend their empire o'er the ball,
Subject, destroy, absorb, and conquer all,
As if the power that form'd us did condemn
All other nations to be slaves to them--
Rouse from your sleep, and crush the thievish band;
Defeat, destroy, and sweep them from the land;
Ally'd like you, what madness to despair;
Attack the ruffians while they linger there;
There Tryon sits, a monster all complete;
See Clinton there with vile Knyphausen meet,
And every wretch whom honour should detest
There finds a home--and Arnold with the rest.
Ah! traitors, lost to every sense of shame,

Unjust supporters of a tyrant's claim,
Foes to the rights of freedom and of men,
Flush'd with the blood of thousands you have slain,
To the just doom the righteous skies decree
We leave you, toiling still in cruelty,
Or on dark plans in future herds to meet,
Plans form'd in hell, and projects half complete:
The years approach that shall to ruin bring
Your lords, your chiefs, your miscreant of a king,
Whose murderous acts shall stamp his name accurs'd,
And his last triumphs more than damn the first.

On the Memorable Victory[31]

1.

O'er the rough main with flowing sheet
The guardian of a numerous fleet,
    <u>Seraphis</u> from the Baltic came;
A ship of less tremendous force
Sail'd by her side the self-same course,
    <u>Countess of Scarb'ro'</u> was her name.

2.

And now their native coasts appear,
Britannia's hills their summits rear
    Above the German main;
Fond to suppose their dangers o'er,
They southward coast along the shore,
    Thy waters, gentle Thames, to gain.

3.

Full forty guns Seraphis bore,
And Scarb'ro's Countess twenty-four,
    Mann'd with Old England's boldest tars--
What flag that rides the Gallic seas
Shall dare attack such piles as these,
    Design'd for tumults and for wars!

4.

Now from the top-mast's giddy height
A seaman cry'd--"Four sail in sight
    Approach with favouring gales;"
Pearson, resolv'd to save the fleet,
Stood off to sea these ships to meet,
    And closely brac'd his shivering sails.

5.

With him advanc'd the Countess bold,
Like a black tar in wars grown old:
    And now these floating piles drew nigh;
But, muse, unfold what chief of fame
In th'other warlike squadron came,
    Whose standards at his mast head fly.

6.

'Twas JONES, brave JONES, to battle led
As bold a crew as ever bled
    Upon the sky surrounded main;
The standards of the Western World
Were to the willing winds unfurl'd,
    Denying Britain's tyrant reign.

7.

The Good Man Richard led the line;
The Alliance next: with these combine
    The Gallic ship they Pallas call:
The Vengeance, arm'd with sword and flame,
These to attack the Britons came--
    But two accomplish'd all.

8.

Now Phoebus sought his pearly bed:
But who can tell the scenes of dread,
    The horrors of that fatal night!
Close up these floating castles came;
The Good Man Richard bursts in flame;
    Seraphis trembled at the sight.

9.

She felt the fury of her ball;
Down, prostrate down, the Britons fall;
    The decks were strew'd with slain:
JONES to his foe his vessel lash'd;
And, while the black artillery flash'd,
    Loud thunders shook the main.

10.

Alas! that mortals should employ
Such murdering engines, to destroy
    That frame by heav'n so nicely join'd;
Alas! that e'er the god decreed
That brother should by brother bleed,
    And pour'd such madness in the mind.

11.

But thou, brave JONES, no blame shalt bear;
The rights of men demand thy care:
    For these you dare the greedy waves--
No tyrant on destruction bent
Has plann'd thy conquests--thou art sent
    To humble tyrants and their slaves.

12.

See!--dread Seraphis flames again--
And art thou, JONES, among the slain,
    And sunk to Neptune's caves below--
He lives--though crowds around him fall,
Still he, unhurt, survives them all;
    Almost alone he fights the foe.

13.

And can thy ship these strokes sustain?
Behold thy brave companions slain,
    All clasp'd in ocean's dark embrace.
STRIKE, OR BE SUNK--the Briton cries--
SINK, IF YOU CAN--the chief replies,
    Fierce lightnings blazing in his face.

14.

Then to the side three guns he drew,
(Almost deserted by his crew)
    And charg'd them deep with woe:
By Pearson's flash he aim'd the balls;
His main-mast totters--down it falls--
    Tremendous was the blow.

15.

Pearson as yet disdain'd to yield,
But scarce his secret fears conceal'd,
    And thus was heard to cry--
"With hell, not mortals, I contend;
What art thou--human, or a fiend,
    That dost my force defy?

16.

"Return, my lads, the fight renew."
So call'd bold Pearson to his crew;
    But call'd, alas! in vain;
Some on the decks lay maim'd and dead;
Some to their deep recesses fled,
    And more were bury'd in the main.

17.

Distress'd, forsaken, and alone,
He haul'd his tatter'd standard down,
   And yielded to his gallant foe;
Bold Pallas soon the Countess took,
Thus both their haughty colours struck,
   Confessing what the brave can do.

18.

But, Jones, too dearly didst thou buy
These ships possest so gloriously,
   Too many deaths disgrac'd the fray:
Thy barque, that bore the conquering flame,
That the proud Briton overcame,
   Even she forsook thee on thy way;

19.

For when the morn began to shine,
Fatal to her, the ocean brine
   Pour'd through each spacious wound;
Quick in the deep she disappear'd:--
But JONES to friendly Belgia steer'd,
   With conquest and with glory crown'd.

20.

Go on, great man, to daunt the foe,
And bid the haughty Britons know
   They to our Thirteen Stars shall bend;
Those Stars that, veil'd in dark attire,
Long glimmer'd with a feeble fire,
   But radiant now ascend.

21.

Bend to the Stars that flaming rise
In western, not in eastern, skies,
   Fair Freedom's reign restor'd--
So when the magi, come from far,
Beheld the God-attending Star,
   They trembled and ador'd.

To His Excellency General Washington[32]

Accept, great chief, that share of honest praise
A grateful people to your merit pays:
Verse is too mean your merit to display,
And words too weak our meaning to convey.

When first proud Britain rais'd her heavy hand
With claims unjust to bind your native land,
Transported armies, and her millions spent
To enforce the mandates that a tyrant sent;
"Resist! resist!" was heard through every state,
You heard the call, and mourn'd your country's fate;
Then rising fierce her sons in arms array'd,
And taught to vanquish those who dar'd invade.

Those British chiefs whom former wars had crown'd
With conquest--and in every clime renown'd;
Who forc'd new realms to own their monarch's law
And whom even George beheld with secret awe,
Those mighty chiefs, compell'd to fly or yield,
Scarce dar'd to meet you on the embattled field:
To Boston's town you chas'd the trembling crew;
Quick, even from thence the British ruffians flew--
Through wint'ry waves they fled, and through the sea
With all its storms less terrible than thee!

What chief like you our armies could command,
And bring us safely to the promis'd land?--
Not Clinton-like, with victory elate--
'Tis in misfortune you are doubly great:
When Howe victorious thy weak army chas'd,
And, sure of conquest, laid Cesarea waste,
When prostrate bleeding at his feet she lay
And the proud victor tore her wreaths away,
You undismay'd put forth your warlike hand
And rais'd the drooping genius of the land,
Repell'd the foe, their choicest warriors slain,
And drove them howling to their ships again.

While others kindle into martial rage
Whom fierce ambition urges to engage,
An iron race by angry heav'n design'd
To conquer first and then enslave mankind;
In HIM a hero more humane we see;
He ventures life that others may be free.

O! May you live to hail that glorious day
When Britain homeward shall pursue her way--
That race subdu'd, who fill'd the world with slain
And rode tyrannic o'er the subject main!--
What few presum'd, you boldly have atchiev'd,
A tyrant humbled, and a world reliev'd.

Rome's boasted chiefs, who, to their own disgrace,
Prov'd the worst scourges of the human race,
Pierc'd by whose darts a thousand nations bled,
Who captive princes at their chariots led;
Born to enslave, to ravage and subdue--
Return to nothing when compar'd to you;
Throughout the world thy growing fame has spread;
In every country are thy virtues read;
Remotest India hears thy deeds of fame;
The hardy Scythian stammers at thy name;
The haughty Turk, now longing to be free,
Neglects his Sultan to enquire of thee;
The barbarous Briton hails thee to his shores,
And calls him Rebel, whom his heart adores.

Still may the heavens prolong thy vital date,
And still may conquest on thy banners wait:
Whether afar to ravag'd lands you go,
Where wild Potowmac's rapid waters flow,
Or where Saluda laves the fertile plain
And swoln by torrents rushes to the main;
Or if again to Hudson you repair
To smite the cruel foe that lingers there--
Revenge their cause, whose virtue was their crime,
The exil'd hosts from Carolina's clime.

Late from the world in quiet may'st thou rise
And, mourn'd by millions, reach thy native skies--
With patriot kings and generous chiefs to shine,
Whose virtues rais'd them to be deem'd divine:
May LOUIS only equal honours claim,
Alike in merits and alike in fame. [33]

To the Memory of the Brave Americans [34]

At Eutaw springs the valiant died:
    Their limbs with dust are cover'd o'er--
Weep on, ye springs, your tearful tide;
    How many heroes are no more!

102

If in this wreck of ruin, they
    Can yet be thought to claim a tear,
O smite thy gentle breast, and say
    The friends of freedom slumber here!

Thou, who shalt trace this bloody plain,
    If goodness rules thy generous breast,
Sigh for the wasted rural reign;
    Sigh for the shepherds sunk to rest!

Stranger, their humble graves adorn;
    You too may fall, and ask a tear:
'Tis not the beauty of the morn
    That proves the evening shall be clear--

They saw their injur'd country's woe;
    The flaming town, the wasted field;
Then rush'd to meet the insulting foe;
    They took the spear--but left the shield. [35]

Led by thy conquering standards, GREENE,
    The Britons they compell'd to fly:
None distant view'd the fatal plain;
    None griev'd in such a cause to die--

But, like the Parthian, fam'd of old,
    Who, flying, still their arrows threw;
These routed Britons, full as bold,
    Retreated, and retreating slew.

Now rest in peace, our patient band;
    Though far from nature's limits thrown,
We trust they find a happier land,
    A brighter Phoebus of their own.

Philosophical Reflections [36]

Still round the world triumphant discord flies;
Still angry kings to bloody contest rise,
Hosts bright with steel in dreadful order plac'd,
And ships contending on the wat'ry waste;
Distracting demons every breast engage,
Unwearied nations glow with mutual rage;
Still to the charge the routed Briton turns,
The war still rages and the battle burns;
See, man with man in deadly combat join;

See, the black navy form the flaming line;
Death smiles alike at battles lost or won--
Art does for him what nature would have done.

Can scenes like these delight the human breast?--
Who sees with joy humanity distrest?
Such tragic scenes fierce passions might prolong,
But slighted Reason says, they must be wrong.

Curs'd be the day, how bright soe'er it shin'd,
That first made kings the masters of mankind;
And curs'd the wretch who first with regal pride
Their equal rights to equal men deny'd;
But curs'd, o'er all, who first to slav'ry broke,
Submissive bow'd and own'd a monarch's yoke;
Their servile souls his arrogance ador'd
And basely own'd a brother for a lord;
Hence wrath and blood, and feuds and wars began,
And man turn'd monster to his fellow-man.

Not so that age of innocence and ease
When men, yet social, knew no ills like these;
Then dormant yet, ambition (half unknown)
No rival murder'd to possess a throne;
No seas to guard, no empires to defend--
Of some small tribe the father and the friend.
The hoary sage beneath his sylvan shade
Impos'd no laws but those which reason made;
On peace not war, on good not ill intent,
He judg'd his brethren by their own consent;
Untaught to spurn those brethren to the dust,
In virtue firm, and obstinately just,
For him no navies rov'd from shore to shore,
No slaves were doom'd to dig the glitt'ring ore;
Remote from all the vain parade of state,
No slaves in diamonds saunter'd at his gate,
Nor did his breast the guilty passions tear;
He knew no murder and he felt no fear.

Was this the patriarch sage?--Then turn thine eyes
And view the contrast that our age supplies;
Touch'd from the life, I trace no ages fled;
I draw no curtain that conceals the dead;
To distant Britain let thy view be cast,
And say the present far exceeds the past;
Of all the plagues that e'er the world have curs'd,
Name George the tyrant, and you name the worst!

What demon, hostile to the human kind,
Planted these fierce disorders in the mind?
All urg'd alike, one phantom we pursue,
But what has war with HAPPINESS to do?
In death's black shroud this gem can ne'er be found;
Who deals for that, the life-destroying wound,
Or pines with grief to see a brother live,
That life dissolving which he cannot give?

'Tis thine, Ambition!--Thee these honors suit:
Lost to the human, she assumes the bruit;
She proudly vain or insolently bold,
Her heart revenge, her eye intent on gold,
Sway'd by the madness of the present hour,
Mistakes for happiness EXTENT OF POWER,
That shining bait which, dropt in folly's way,
Tempts the weak mind, and leads the heart astray!

Thou happiness! still sought but never found,
We, in a circle, chase thy shadow round,
Meant all mankind in different forms to bless,
Which yet possessing we no more possess:--
Thus far remov'd and painted on the eye,
Smooth verdant fields seem blended with the sky;
But where they both in fancied contact join
In vain we trace the visionary line;
Still as we chase, the empty circle flies,
Emerge new mountains or new oceans rise.

Verses made at Sea, in a Heavy Gale[37]

Happy the man who, safe on shore,
Now trims, at home, his evening fire;
Unmov'd, he hears the tempests roar,
That on the tufted groves expire:
    Alas! on us they doubly fall;
    Our feeble barque must bear them all.

Now to their haunts the birds retreat;
The squirrel seeks his hollow tree;
Wolves in their shaded caverns meet;
All, all are blest but wretched we--
    Foredoom'd a stranger to repose,
    No rest the unsettled ocean knows.

While o'er the dark abyss we roam,
Perhaps, whate'er the pilots say,
We saw the Sun descend in gloom,
No more to see his rising ray,
But bury'd low, by far too deep,
On coral beds, unpitied, sleep!

But what a strange, uncoasted strand
Is that, where death permits no day--
No charts have we to mark that land,
No compass to direct that way--
What pilot shall explore that realm,
What new Columbus take the helm?

While death and darkness both surround,
And tempests rage with lawless power,
Of friendship's voice I hear no sound,
No comfort in this dreadful hour--
What friendship can in tempests be,
What comfort on this angry sea?

The barque, accustom'd to obey,
No more the trembling pilots guide;
Alone she gropes her trackless way,
While mountains burst on either side--
Thus, skill and science both must fall,
And ruin is the lot of all.

The Literary Plunderers[38]

The head, whose tolling concave teems
With millions of unfinish'd schemes,
Plans that in shapeless embrio ly,
Or projects form'd, the Lord knows why,
Had better far those whims resign,
And aid this humble theme of mine,
Contrive some means to crush the power
Of MICE, that every art devour,
Check, with success, their hostile rage,
And slay these Vandals of the age.

Fame says that Wales did first contrive
To seize the unwary mice alive,
And they who scorn'd all locks and keys
Were caught by means of toasted cheese--

Vain scheme! for still these fiends annoy,
And dare my favourite books destroy--
No cares of mine their rage defeat;
The Welchman's trap is incomplete!--
See Homer there, the bard renown'd,
His Iliad one perpetual wound--
Each chief, by their infernal teeth,
Once more was doom'd to suffer death;
Even Helen's charms they dar'd to gnaw
Great Ajax' carcase fill'd their maw,
And half the gods that crowd his strain,
In mangled morsels, scarce remain.

But, wretch, who taught thee to engage
A poet of a later age?
Alas! thy cruel weapons tore
The only genius I adore--
Is SHAKESPEARE thus disgrac'd by you
Who look'd the world of nature through,
Who soaring high, where others fail'd,
Invention's brightest heav'n assail'd,
And saw beyond the dark disguise
What lay too deep for vulgar eyes!

Is this the end of human wit;
Must mice untouch'd such spoils commit!
Must all these fine ideas die
That warm'd the heart, or fill'd the eye--
Must reptiles thus our shelves molest,
Insects that Nature made in jest,
Who, when their learned feast is o'er,
Shrink from the light--to rise no more?

Yes--fates like these our toils attend,
And goths have serv'd no other end.

Vex'd tho' I am, 'tis vain to frown,
I sigh--and lay my cudgel down:
'Tis worse than mad to arm for fight
When not a mouse appears in sight--
Yet, here they stood in dark array;
Their tragic footsteps I survey!
Here--for no cat the plunderers chac'd--
They laid the lands of learning waste,
Made war with wit, such havock there
As scarce the ages can repair!--
Like British hosts, where'er they go,

They leave their vestiges of woe,
Towns half destroy'd, polluted shades,
Fields robb'd of fence, and ruin'd maids.

Why, Susan, couldst not thou defend
These shelves that did with learning bend?
One mew of thine had put to flight
These children of congenial night.
Where wast thou when these cruel teeth
Spread through my leaves untimely death?--
See! how my MONTESQUIEU is torn--
See! RABELAIS, the mices scorn.
See, how they tore the MANTUAN SWAIN,
Who wrote in so divine a strain--
MILTON, whose fancy soar'd so high,
No more delights my tearful eye,
And SWIFT, so late a fund of wit,
No longer prompts the laughing fit.

Ah, Susan, such neglect was hard--
I fear you kept a careless guard,
Or gadded o'er the neighbouring plain
To seek some favourite bright ey'd swain--
Had but those eyes fail'd in their art,
To tell their language to your heart,
I should not thus have lost repose,
Nor sigh'd in vain to crush my foes.

My mezzotintos--ah behold--
The beauties fam'd in days of old!
She, who for Tarquin's lawless love
In her own breast the dagger drove,
These fiends of night have made their prey
And gnaw'd her charming face away.

And here in ragged robes is seen
Bright Cleopatra, Egypt's queen;
With cruel fangs those eyes they tore
That warm'd a gazing world of yore;
With hostile tooth they gnaw'd that breast
Which robb'd a Roman prince of rest,
He who for crowns and conquest strove,
'Till honour was disgrac'd by love.

And here, in vile condition, lies
What once had charm'd a hermit's eyes--
This picture art can ne'er restore,

This VENUS, that shall bloom no more;
Art form'd her such as angels are,
Beyond all mortal beauty fair;--
But time can every charm displace,
And MICE have spoil'd the finest face!

But must that soft, bewitching eye
With meaner shreds neglected by--
Must all those lovely colours fade,
By nicest art so lavish laid
On her fair face--to soothe my pain,
I sigh, and look, and sigh again.

Yes--miscreant, though thy venom tore
The painting art can ne'er restore,
Still in the dreams of fancy blest,
I steal her image to my breast,
By fancy's aid that form repair,
And, miser-like, retain it there.

Good captain Mouse, what mov'd thine ire,
To mangle what I most admire?--
Could not this chief have led his band[39]
Where yonder brainless authors stand--
To those that deal in forms and modes,
To laureat Whitehead's New Year odes,
To verses wrote on puppies dead,
To elegies that ne'er were read,
To Whaycum's tale, that brings repose,
To Wesley's hymns, or Whitefield's prose;--
Why didst thou not attack the train
Who teize us with their frothy strain,
The tribe who female honour blast,
In sniveling rhimes, at random cast,
Or those who fly to domes of state,
At folly's door submissive wait,
And servile still, where wealth appears,
Their works inscribe to financiers?

To arms, to arms! ye chosen few
Who science love, and arts pursue;
Or, if your arms should nought avail,
(Since mice may over men prevail)
Put on some wise, inventive cap,
AND FIND US A COMPLETER TRAP.

Columbus at Valladolid[40]

1.

How sweet is sleep, when gain'd by length of toil:[41]
No dreams disturb the slumbers of the dead--
To snatch existence from this scanty soil,
Were these the hopes deceitful fancy bred;
And were her painted pageants nothing more
Than this life's phantoms by delusion led?

2.

The winds blow high: one other world remains;
Once more without a guide I find the way,
In the dark tomb to slumber with my chains--
Prais'd by no poet on my funeral day,
Nor even allow'd one dearly purchas'd claim--
My new found world not honor'd with my name.

3.

Yet, in this joyless gloom while I repose,
Some comfort will attend my pensive shade
When memory paints, and golden fancy shows
My toils rewarded, and my woes repaid,
When empires rise where lonely forests grew,
Where Freedom shall her generous plans pursue.

4.

To shadowy forms, and ghosts and sleepy things,
Columbus, now with dauntless heart repair;
You liv'd to find new worlds for thankless kings;
Write this upon my tomb--yes--tell it there--
Tell of those chains that sullied all my glory-- [42]
Not mine but theirs--ah, tell the shameful story.

On the Folly of Writing Poetry[43]

Of all the fools that haunt our coast,
The scribbling tribe I pity most:
Theirs is a standing scene of woes,
And theirs no prospect of repose.

Then, Sylvius, why this eager claim
To light your torch at CLIO'S flame!
To few she shows sincere regard,
And none from her should hope reward.

A garret high (dark, dismal room)
Is still the pensive poets' doom;
Hopes rais'd to heaven must be their lot,
Yet bear the curse, to be forgot.

Boldly they tell of things above,
And trace their tribe from Grecian Jove,
Yet stand abash'd, with all their fire
When brought to face some snuffling 'squire.

To mend the world is still their aim--
The world, alas! remains the same,
And so must stand to every age,
Proof to the morals of the page.

The wight that keeps a tippling inn,
The red-nos'd boy, that deals out gin,
If aided by some paltry skill,
May both be statesmen when they will.

The man that mends the beggar's shoes,
The quack that heals your negro's bruise,
The wretch that turns a cutler's stone--
Have wages that they call their own:

The head that plods in trade's domains
Gets something to rewards its pains;
But WIT--that does the world beguile--
With pain attracts an empty smile.

Yet each presumes his verse shall rise
And gain a place beyond the skies--
From earth and cold oblivion freed,
Immortal in the poets' creed.

Can Reason in that breast remain,
Which fondly feeds a hope so vain,
When every age, that passes by,
Beholds a tribe of poets die!

Poor Sappho's fate shall Milton know--
His scenes of grief, and tales of woe,
Fame scarce shall save from death's domain
When Goths, once more, shall have their reign.

To all that write, and all that read,
Death shall, with hasty step, succeed;

Even Shakespeare's page of mirth and tears
Shall sink beneath this flood of years.

Ned Spenser's doom shall, Pope, be thine!
The music of each moving line
Shall bribe an age or two to stay,
Admire thy strain--then flit away.

The people of old Chaucer's times
Were once in raptures with his rhymes;
But Time, that over verse prevails,
To other ears tells other tales:

Why then so sad, dear rhyming friends?
One common fate on both attends;
The bards that please a monarch's ear
And them who rhyme for bread,--or beer.

Mere structures, form'd of common earth,
Not they from Jove derive their birth,
Or why, like empty bubbles pass
To mingle with the meaner mass.--

Of all the souls from dust that came
To animate this mortal frame,
Of all the millions on the wing,
How few can taste the muses' spring!

Sejanus, of mercantile skill,
Without whose aid the world stands still,
And by whose wonder working play
Great things are done, (his flatterers say)

Sejanus has, in house, declar'd
"These States, as yet, have borne no bard,
And all the sing-song of our clime
Is only nonsense--tagg'd with rhyme."--

With such a bold, conceited air
When such assume the critic's chair,
Low in the dust is genius laid--
The Muses with the man in trade.

Then, Sylvius, come--let you and I
On Neptune's breast new gambols try;
Perhaps the muse may still impart
Her balm, to ease the aching heart.

Tho' cold might chill, and storms dismay,
Yet <u>Zoilus</u> will be far away--
With me, at least, depart, and share
No garret--but a cabbin there. 44

The Wild Honey Suckle [45]

Fair flower, that dost so comely grow,
Hid in this silent dull retreat,
Untouch'd thy honey'd blossoms blow;
Unseen thy little branches greet:
   No roving foot shall find thee here,
   No busy hand provoke a tear.

By Nature's self in white array'd,
She bade thee shun the vulgar eye,
And planted here the guardian shade,
And sent soft waters murmuring by;
   Thus quietly thy summer goes,
   Thy days declining to repose.

Smit with these charms, that must decay,
I grieve to see thy future doom;
They died--nor were those flowers less gay,
(The flowers that did in Eden bloom)
   Unpitying frosts and Autumn's power
   Shall leave no vestige of this flower.

From morning suns and evening dews
At first, thy little being came:
If nothing once, you nothing lose,
For when you die, you are the same;
   The space between is but an hour,
   The mere idea of a flower.

An Author's Soliloquy [46]

My leaves bound up, compact and fair,
In neat array at length prepare:
To pass their hour on time's broad stage,
To meet the surly critic's rage,
The statesman's slight, the pedant's sneer--
Alas! were these my only fear,
I should be quiet and resigned--

113

What most torments my boding mind
Is that no critic will be found
To read my works and give the wound!

   Thus, when one fleeting year is pass'd,
With dead men's work my book is class'd;
With some to praise, but more to blame,
The soul returns from whence it came,
And I must wear the marks of time
Who hardly flourish'd in my prime.

   Thrice happy DRYDEN, who could meet
Some rival bard on every street:
When all were bent on writing well,
It was some credit to excel,
While those condemn'd to stand alone
Can only by themselves be known:
Thrice happy DRYDEN, who could find
A Milbourne, for his sport design'd,
And POPE, who saw the harmless rage
Of Dennis bursting o'er his page,
Might well despise the critic's aim,
Who only help'd to swell his fame.

   On these bleak climes by Fortune thrown
Where rigid reason reigns alone,
Where mimic fancy holds no sway
Nor golden forms around her play,
Nor Nature takes her magic hue--
Alas, what has the Muse to do!
An age employ'd in pointing steel
Can no poetic raptures feel:
No fabled Love's enchanting power,
Nor tale of Flora's painted bower,
Nor woodland haunt, or murmuring grove
Can their prosaic bosoms move.

   The Muse of Love in no request,
I'll try my fortune with the rest,
Which of the Nine shall I engage
To suit the humour of the age: [47]
On one, alas, my choice must fall,
The least engaging of them all!
So late she does her wreaths prepare,
I hardly think them worth my care:
Her visage stern, severe her stile,
A clouded brow, a cruel smile,

A mind on murder'd victims plac'd--
She, only she can suit the taste.

Lines Occasioned by
A Visit to an Old Indian Burying Ground[48]

In spite of all the learn'd have said,
I still my old opinion keep;
The posture that we give the dead
Points out the soul's eternal sleep.

Not so the ancients of these lands;--
The Indian, when from life releas'd,
Again is seated with his friends,
And shares again the joyous feast.

His imag'd birds, and painted bowl,
And ven'son, for a journey drest,
Bespeak the nature of the soul,
Activity, that wants no rest.

His bow for action ready bent,
And arrows, with a head of bone,
Can only mean that life is spent,
And not the finer essence gone.

Thou, stranger, that shalt come this way,
No fraud upon the dead commit;
Yet mark the swelling turf and say,
They do not lie, but here they sit.

Here, still a lofty rock remains,
On which a curious eye may trace
(Now wasted half by wearing rains)
The fancies of a ruder race.

Here, still an aged elm aspires,
Beneath whose far projecting shade
(And which the shepherd still admires)
The children of the forest play'd.

There oft a restless Indian queen,
(Pale Marian with her braided hair)
And many a barbarous form is seen
To chide the man that lingers there.

115

By midnight moons, o'er moistening dews,
In vestments for the chace array'd,
The hunter still the deer pursues, 49
The hunter and the deer--a shade.

And long shall timorous Fancy see
The painted chief and pointed spear,
And reason's self shall bow the knee
To shadows and delusions here.

The Jug of Rum 50

Within these earthen walls confin'd,
The ruin lurks of human kind;
More mischiefs here, united, dwell,
And more diseases haunt this dell
Than ever plagu'd the Egyptian flocks,
Or ever curs'd Pandora's box.

Within these prison-walls repose
The seeds of many a bloody nose,
The chattering tongue, the horrid oath,
The fist for fighting, nothing loth,
The passion quick, no words can tame,
That bursts like sulphur into flame,
The nose with diamonds glowing red,
The bloated eye, the broken head!

Forever fastened be this door--
Confin'd within, a thousand more
Destructive fiends, of hateful shape,
Even now are plotting an escape.

Here, only by a cork controul'd,
And slender walls of earthen mould,
In all their pomp of death reside
Revenge, that ne'er was satisfy'd;
The Tree, that bears the deadly fruit
Of murder, maiming, and dispute;
ASSAULT, that innocence assails,
The IMAGES of gloomy jails,
The GIDDY THOUGHT, on mischief bent,
The midnight hour, in folly spent,
ALL THESE within this jug appear,
And JACK, the hangman, in the rear.

116

Thrice happy he, who early taught
By Nature, ne'er this poison sought;
Who, friendly to his own repose,
Treads under foot this worst of foes, --
He, with the purling stream content,
The beverage quaffs that Nature meant;
In Reason's scale his actions weigh'd,
His spirits want no foreign aid--
Not swell'd too high, or sunk too low,
Placid, his easy minutes flow;
Long life is his, in vigour pass'd,
Existence welcome to the last,
A spring that never yet grew stale;
Such virtue lies in--ADAM'S ALE!

The Dish of Tea[51]

Let some in grog place their delight,
O'er bottled porter waste the night,
   Or sip the rosy wine:
A dish of TEA more pleases me,
Yields softer joys, provokes less noise,
   And breeds no base design.

From China's groves, this present brought
Enlivens every power of thought,
   Riggs many a ship for sea:
Old maids it warms, young widows charms;
And ladies' men, not one in ten
   But courts them for their TEA.

When throbbing pains assail my head,
And dullness o'er my brain is spread,
   (The muse no longer kind)
A single sip dispels the hyp:
To chace the gloom fresh spirits come,
   The flood-tide of the mind.

When worn with toil, or vext with care,
Let Susan but this draught prepare,
   And I forget my pain.
This magic bowl revives the soul,
With gentlest sway, bids care be gay,
   Nor mounts, to cloud the brain. --

If learned men the truth would speak
They prize it far beyond their GREEK,
    More fond attention pay;
No HEBREW root so well can suit,
More quickly taught, less dearly bought,
    And studied twice a day.

This leaf, from distant regions sprung,
Puts life into the female tongue,
    And aids the cause of love.
Such power has TEA o'er bond and free,
Which priests admire, delights the 'squire,
    And Galen's sons approve.

The Distrest Theatre[52]

Health to the Muse!--and fill the glass,--
Heaven grant her soon some better place
Than earthen floor and fabric mean,
Where disappointment shades the scene:

There as I came, by rumour led,
I sigh'd, and almost wish'd her dead,
Her visage stain'd with many a tear,
No HALLAM and no HENRY here!

But what could all their art attain?--
When pointed laws the stage restrain,
The prudent Muse obedience pays
To sleepy squires, that damn all plays.

Like thieves they hang beyond the town;
They shove her off--to please the gown;--
Tho' Rome and Athens own'd it true,
The stage might mend our morals too.

See, Mopsus all the evening sits
O'er bottled beer, that drowns his wits;
Were PLAYS allow'd, he might at least
Blush--and no longer act the beast.

See Marcia, now from guardian free,
Retailing scandal o'er her tea;
Might she not come, nor danger fear
From Hamlet's sigh, or Juliet's tear.

118

The world but acts the Players' part--[53]
(So says the motto of their art)
That world in vice great lengths is gone
That fears to see its picture drawn.

Mere vulgar actors ne'er can please;
The streets supply enough of these;
And what can wit or beauty gain
When sleepy dullness joins their train?

A State betrays a homely taste
By which the stage is thus disgrac'd,
Where, drest in all the flowers of speech,
True virtue might her precepts teach.

Let but a dancing bear arrive,
A pig that counts you four or five--
And Cato, with his moral strain,
Shall strive to mend the town in vain.

The American Soldier[54]

Deep in a vale, a stranger now to arms,
Too poor to shine in courts, too proud to beg,
He, who once warr'd on Saratoga's plains,
Sits musing o'er his scars, and wooden leg.

Remembering still the toil of former days,
To other hands he sees his earnings paid;--
They share the due reward--he feeds on praise,
Lost in the abyss of want, misfortune's shade.

Far, far from domes where splendid tapers glare,
'Tis his from dear bought peace no wealth to win,
Remov'd alike from courtly cringing 'squires,
The great-man's Levee, and the proud man's grin.

Sold are those arms which once on Britons blaz'd,
When, flush'd with conquest, to the charge the came;
That power repell'd, and Freedom's fabrick rais'd,
She leaves her soldier--famine and a name!

The Lost Louisa⁵⁵

Within the drear and silent gloom,
  The lost Louisa pines, unknown.
Fate shrouds her in a living tomb;
  And heaven, relentless, hears her groan;
    Yet 'midst the murky shade of woe,
    The tears of fond regret shall flow.

Yon' lofty wall, that mocks my grief,
  Still echoes with my evening pray'r;
The gale that fans the trembling leaf
  Shall waft it through the realms of air
    Till prostrate at the throne of heaven,
    Unpitied love shall be forgiven.

Or if to endless sorrow born--
  If doom'd to fade a victim here:
Still pining, friendless, and forlorn,
  Ah! let religion drop one tear:
    Like holy incense shall it prove,
    To heal the wounds of hopeless love.

Ye blackening clouds that sail along,
  Oh hide me in your shade profound;
Ye whispering breezes, catch my song
  And bear it to the woods around;
    Perchance some hapless Petrarch's feet
    May wander near this dear retreat.

Ah! tell him love's delicious strain
  No rapture yields, no joys inspires
Where fell seclusion's icy chain
  Has long subdued its quivering fires;
    No ray of comfort gilds the gloom
    That marks the hopeless vestal's tomb.

The ruby gem within my breast
  Now faintly glows with vital heat;
Each warring passion sinks to rest;
  My freezing pulses slowly beat;
    Soon shall these languid eye balls close
    And death's stern mandate seal my woes.

Then when the virgin's matin song
  Shall 'midst the vaulted roof resound,
Haply the tuneful seraph's throng

Shall whisper gentle pity round,
  While VIRTUE, sighing o'er my bier,
  Shall drop unseen--A SAINTED TEAR.

On Superstition[56]

Implanted in the human breast,
Religion means to make us blest;
On reason built, she lends her aid
To help us through life's sickening shade.

But man, to endless error prone,
And fearing most what's most unknown,
To phantoms bows that round him rise,
To angry gods, and vengeful skies.

Mistaken race, in error lost,
And foes to them who love you most,
No more fictitious gods revere,
Nor worship what engenders fear.

O Superstition! to thy sway
If man has bow'd and will obey,
Misfortune still must be his doom
And sorrow through the days to come.

Hence, ills on ills successive grow
To cloud our day of bliss below;
Hence wars and feuds, and deadly hate,
And all the woes that on them wait.

Here moral virtue finds its bane;
Hence, ignorance with her slavish train;
Hence, half the vigor of the mind
Relax'd, or lost in human kind.

The social tie by this is broke
When we some tyrant god invoke:
The bitter curse from man to man
From this infernal fiend began.

The reasoning power, celestial guest,
The stamp upon the soul impress'd,
When Superstition's awe degrades,
Its beauty fails, its splendor fades.

121

O! turn from her detested ways,
Unhappy man! her fatal maze;
The reason which he gave, improve,
And venerate the power above.

On the Abuse of Human Power, as Exercised over Opinion[57]

What human power shall dare to bind
The mere opinions of the mind?[58]
Must man at that tribunal bow
Which will no range to thought allow,
But his best powers would sway or sink,
And idly tells him what to THINK?

Yes! there are such, and such are taught
To fetter every power of thought,
To chain the mind, or bend it down
To some mean system of their own,
And make religion's sacred cause
Amenable to human laws.

Has human power the simplest claim
Our hearts to sway, our thoughts to tame;
Shall she the rights of heaven assert;
Can she to falsehood truth convert,
Or truth again to falsehood turn,
And at the test of reason spurn?

All human sense, all craft must fail,
And all its strength will nought avail,
When it attempts with efforts blind
To sway the independent mind,
Its spring to break, its pride to awe,
Or give to private judgment, law.

Oh impotent! and vile as vain,
They, who would native thought restrain!
As soon might they arrest the storm
Or take from fire the power to warm,
As man compel, by dint of might,
Old darkness to prefer to light.

No! leave the mind unchain'd and free,
And what they ought, mankind will be,

No hypocrite, no lurking fiend,
No artist to some evil end,
But good and great, benign and just,
As God and nature made them first.

On the Uniformity and Perfection of Nature[59]

On one fix'd point all nature moves,
Nor deviates from the track she loves;
Her system drawn from reason's source,
She scorns to change her wonted course.

Could she descend from that great plan
To work unusual things for man,
To suit the insect of an hour--
This would betray a want of power,

Unsettled in its first design
And erring, when it did combine
The parts that form the vast machine,
The figures sketch'd on nature's scene.

Perfections of the great first cause
Submit to no contracted laws,
But all-sufficient, all-supreme,
Include no trivial views in them.

Who looks through nature with an eye
That would the scheme of heaven descry
Observes her constant, still the same[60]
In all her laws, through all her frame.

No imperfection can be found
In all that is, above, around, --
All nature made, in reason's sight,
Is order all, and all is right.

On the Universality and Other Attributes of the God of Nature[61]

All that we see, about, abroad,
What is it all but nature's God?
In meaner works discover'd here
No less than in the starry sphere.

In seas, on earth, this God is seen;
All that exist upon him lean;
He lives in all, and never stray'd
A moment from the works he made:

His system fix'd on general laws
Bespeaks a wise creating cause;
Impartially he rules mankind
And all that on this globe we find.

Unchanged in all that seems to change,
Unbounded space is his great range;
To one vast purpose always true,
No time, with him, is old or new.

In all the attributes divine
Unlimited perfections shine;
In these enwrapt, in these complete,
All virtues in that centre meet.

This power who doth all powers transcend,
To all intelligence a friend, [62]
Exists, the greatest and the best
Throughout all worlds, to make them blest.

All that he did he first approved;
He all things into being loved;
O'er all he made he still presides,
For them in life, or death provides.

On the Religion of Nature[63]

The power that gives with liberal hand
    The blessings man enjoys while here,
And scatters through a smiling land
    The abundant products of the year,

124

That power of nature, ever bless'd,
Bestow'd religion with the rest.

Born with ourselves, her early sway
    Inclines the tender mind to take
The path of right, fair virtue's way
    Its own felicity to make.
        This universally extends
        And leads to no mysterious ends.

Religion, such as nature taught,
    With all divine perfection suits;
Had all mankind this system sought,
    Sophists would cease their vain disputes,
        And from this source would nations know
        All that can make their heaven below.

This deals not curses to mankind,
    Or dooms them to perpetual grief;
If from its aid no joys they find,
    It damns them not for unbelief;
        Upon a more exalted plan
        Creatress nature dealt with man--

Joy to the day when all agree
    On such grand systems to proceed,
From fraud, design, and error free,
    And which to truth and goodness lead:
        Then persecution will retreat
        And man's religion be complete.

On the Evils of Human Life[64]

To him who rules the starry spheres,
No evil in his works appears:
Man with a different eye surveys
The incidents in nature's maze,
    And all that brings him care or pain
    He ranks among misfortune's train.

The ills that God or nature deal,
The ills we hourly see or feel,
The sense of wretchedness and woe
To man may be sincerely so,

And yet these springs of tears and sighs
Be heaven's best blessings in disguise.

Some favorite late in anguish lay
And agonized his life away:
You grieved--to be consoled refused,
And heaven itself almost accused
    Of cruelty, that could dispense
    Such tortures to such innocence.

Could you but lift the dreary veil,
And see with eyes or mind less frail
The secrets of the world to come,
You would not thus bewail <u>his</u> doom
    To find on some more happy coast
    More blessings, far, than all he lost.

The seeming ills on life that wait
And mingle with our best estate,
Misfortune on misfortune grown,
And heaviest most when most alone,
    Calamities and heart oppress'd--
    These all attend us for the best.

Learn hence, ye mournful, tearful race,
On a sure ground your hopes to place;
Immutable are nature's laws,
And hence the soul her comfort draws
    That all that God allots to man
    Proceeds on one unerring plan.

Hold to the moral system, true,
And heaven will always be in view:
O man! by heaven this law was taught
To reconcile you to your lot,
    To be your friend, when friendship fails,
    And nature a new being hails.

Belief and Unbelief [65]

What some believe, and would enforce
Without reluctance or remorse,
Perhaps another may decry,
Or call a fraud, or deem a lie.

Must he for that be doom'd to bleed,
And fall a martyr to some creed
By hypocrites or tyrants framed,
By reason damn'd, by truth disclaim'd?

On mere belief no merit rests,
As unbelief no guilt attests:
Belief, if not absurd and blind,
Is but conviction of the mind;

Nor can conviction bind the heart
Till evidence has done its part:
And when that evidence is clear,
Belief is just and truth is near.

In evidence belief is found;
Without it none are fairly bound
To yield assent, or homage pay
To what confederate worlds might say.

They who extort belief from man
Should, in the out-set of their plan,
Exhibit, like the mid-day sun,
An evidence denied by none.

From this great point, o'erlook'd or miss'd,
Still unbelievers will exist;
And just their plea, for how absurd
For evidence, to take your word!

Not to believe, I therefore hold
The right of man, all uncontrol'd
By all the powers of human wit,
What kings have done or sages writ,

Not criminal in any view,
Nor--man!--to be avenged by you
Till evidence of strongest kind
Constrains assent and clears the mind.

Stanzas to the Memory of Gen. Washington[66]

Departing with the closing age
    To virtue, worth and freedom true,
The chief, the patriot, and the sage

127

To Vernon bids his last adieu:
    To reap in some exalted sphere
    The just rewards of virtue here.

Thou, Washington, by heaven design'd
    To act a part in human things
That few have known among mankind,
    And far beyond the task of kings,
        We hail you now to heaven received,
        Your mighty task on earth achieved.

While sculpture and her sister arts
    For thee their choicest wreaths prepare,
Fond gratitude her share imparts
    And begs thy bones for burial there,
        Where, near Virginia's northern bound,
        Swells the vast pile on federal ground.

To call from their obscure abodes
    The Grecian chief, the Roman sage,
The kings, the heroes, and the gods
    Who flourish'd in time's earlier age
        Would be to class them not with you, --
        Superior far, in every view.

Those ancients of ferocious mould,
    Blood their delight, and war their trade,
Their oaths profaned, their countries sold,
    And fetter'd nations prostrate laid;
        Could these, like you, assert their claim
        To honor and immortal fame?

Those monarchs, proud of pillaged spoils,
    With nations shackled in their train,
Returning from their desperate toils
    With trophies, --and their thousands slain,
        In all they did no traits are known
        Like those that honor'd Washington.

Who now will save our shores from harms,
    The task to him so long assign'd?
Who now will rouse our youth to arms,
    Should war approach to curse mankind?
        Alas! no more the word you give,
        But in your precepts you survive.

Ah, gone! and none your place supply,
    Nor will your equal soon appear;
But that great name can only die
    When memory dwells no longer here,
        When man and all his systems must
        Dissolve, like you, and turn to dust.

Lines Addressed to Mr. Jefferson on his Retirement[67]

To you, great sir, our heart felt praise we give,
And your ripe honors yield you--while you live.

At length the year, which marks his course, expires,
And JEFFERSON from public life retires,
That year, the close of years which own his claim
And give him all his honors, all his fame.
Far in the heavens of fame I see him fly,
Safe in the realms of immortality:
On EQUAL WORTH his honor'd mantle falls,
HIM, whom Columbia her true patriot calls,
Him whom we saw her codes of freedom plan,
To none inferior in the ranks of man.

When to the helm of state your country call'd,
No danger awed you and no fear appall'd;
Each bosom, faithful to its country's claim,
Hail'd JEFFERSON, that long applauded name;
All then was dark, and wrongs on wrongs accrued,
Our treasures wasted and our strength subdued;
What seven long years of war and blood had gain'd
Was lost, abandon'd, squander'd, or restrain'd:
Britannia's tools had schemed their easier way
To conquer, ruin, pillage, or betray;
Domestic traitors, with exotic, join'd
To shackle this last refuge of mankind;
Wars were provoked, and FRANCE was made our foe,
That George's race might govern all below
O'er this wide world, uncheck'd, unbounded reign,
Seize every clime and subjugate the main.

All this was seen--and rising in your might,
By genius aided, you reclaim'd our right,
That RIGHT which conquest, arms, and valor gave
To this young nation--not to live a slave.

129

And what but toil has your long service seen?
Dark tempests gathering o'er a sky serene--
For wearied years no mines of wealth can pay,
No fame, nor all the plaudits of that day,
Which now returns you to your rural shade,
The sage's heaven, for contemplation made,
Who, like the ROMAN, in their country's cause
Exert their valor, or enforce its laws,
And late retiring, every wrong redress'd,
Give their last days to solitude and rest.

This great reward a generous nation yields--
REGRET attends you to your native fields,
Their grateful thanks for every service done
And hope your thorny race of care is run.

From your sage counsels what effects arise!
The vengeful Briton from our waters flies;
His thundering ships no more our coasts assail,
But seize the advantage of the western gale.
Though bold and bloody, warlike, proud, and fierce,
They shun your vengeance for a MURDERED PEARCE,[68]
And starved, dejected, on some meagre shore,
Sigh for the country they shall rule no more.

Long in the councils of your native land,
We saw you cool, unchanged, intrepid stand;
When the firm CONGRESS, still too firm to yield,
Stay'd masters of the long contested field,
Your wisdom aided what their counsels framed--
By you the murdering savages were tamed--
That INDEPENDENCE we had sworn to gain,
By you asserted (nor DECLARED in vain)
We seized, triumphant, from a tyrant's throne;
And Britain totter'd when the work was done.

You, when an angry faction vex'd the age,
Rose to your place at once and check'd their rage;
The envenom'd shafts of malice you defied
And turn'd all projects of revolt aside:--
We saw you libell'd by the worst of men,[69]
While hell's red lamp hung quivering o'er his pen
And fiends congenial every effort try
To blast that merit which shall never die--

These had their hour, and traitors wing'd their flight
To aid the screechings of distracted night.

Vain were their hopes--the poison'd darts of hell
Glanced from your flinty shield and harmless fell.

All this you bore--beyond it all you rose,
Nor ask'd despotic laws to crush your foes.
Mild was your language, temperate though severe,
And not less potent than ITHURIEL'S spear
To touch the infernals in their loathsome guise,
Confound their slanders and detect their lies.

All this you braved--and now what task remains
But silent walks on solitary plains:
To bid the vast luxuriant harvest grow,
The slave be happy and secured from woe--
To illume the statesmen of the times to come
With the bold spirit of primeval Rome,
To taste the joys your long tried service brings,
And look, with pity, on the cares of kings:--
Whether, with NEWTON, you the heavens explore
And trace through nature the creating power,
Or if with morals you reform the age,
(Alike in all the patriot and the sage)
May peace and soft repose attend you still,
In the long vale or on the cloud-capp'd hill,
While smiling plenty decks the abundant plain
And hails ASTREA to the world again. [70]

On the Capture of the Guerriere [71]

Long the tyrant of our coast
 Reign'd the famous Guerriere;
Our little navy she defy'd,
 Public ship and privateer:
On her sails in letters red
To our captains were display'd
Words of warning, words of dread,
 All who meet me, have a care!
 I am England's Guerriere. [72]

On the wide Atlantic deep
 (Not her equal for the fight) [73]
The CONSTITUTION on her way
 Chanced to meet these men of might:
On her sails was nothing said,
But her waist the teeth displayed

131

That a deal of blood could shed,
　　Which, if she would venture near,
　　Would stain the decks of the Guerriere.

Now our gallant ship they met--
　　And to struggle with John Bull--
Who had come, they little thought,
　　Strangers yet to Isaac Hull,
Better soon to be acquainted:
<u>Isaac</u> hail'd the lord's anointed--
While the crew the cannon pointed,
　　And the balls were so directed
　　With a blaze so unexpected;

Isaac did so maul and rake her
That the decks of captain Dacres
Were in such a woful pickle
As if death, with scythe and sickle,
　　With his sling, or with his shaft
　　Had cut his harvest fore and aft.
Thus in thirty minutes ended,
Mischiefs that could not be mended:
Masts and yards and ship descended,
　　All to David Jones's locker--
　　Such a ship in such a pucker!

Drink a bout to the Constitution!
　　She perform'd some execution,
Did some share of retribution
　　For the insults of the year
When she took the Guerriere.
　　May success again await her,
Let who will again command her,
　　Bainbridge, Rodgers, or Decatur--
Nothing like her can withstand her
　　With a crew like that on board her,
Who so boldly call'd "to order"
　　One bold crew of English sailors,
Long, too long our seamen's jailors,
　　Dacres and the Guerriere!

To a Caty-Did [74]

　　In a branch of willow hid
Sings the evening Caty-did:

132

From the lofty locust bough,
Feeding on a drop of dew,
In her suit of green array'd,
Hear her singing in the shade,
     Caty-did, Caty-did, Caty-did!

    While upon a leaf you tread,
Or repose your little head,
On your sheet of shadows laid,
All the day you nothing said:
Half the night your cheery tongue
Revell'd out its little song,
    Nothing else but Caty-did.

    From your lodgings on the leaf,
Did you utter joy or grief--?
Did you only mean to say,
I have had my summer's day,
And am passing soon away
To the grave of Caty-did:--
    Poor, unhappy Caty-did!

    But you would have utter'd more,
Had you known of nature's power--
From the world when you retreat,
And a leaf's your winding sheet,
Long before your spirit fled,
Who can tell but nature said,
Live again, my Caty-did!
    Live, and chatter Caty-did.

    Tell me, what did Caty do?
Did she mean to trouble you?--
Why was Caty not forbid
To trouble little Caty-did?--
Wrong indeed at you to sling,
Hurting no one while you sing
    Caty-did! Caty-did! Caty-did!

    Why continue to complain?
Caty tells me, she again
Will not give you plague or pain:--
Caty says you may be hid;
Caty will not go to bed
While you sing us Caty-did.
    Caty-did! Caty-did! Caty-did!

But while singing, you forgot
To tell us what did Caty <u>not</u>:
Caty-did not think of cold,
Flocks retiring to the fold,
Winter, with his wrinkles old,
Winter, that yourself foretold
     When you gave us Caty-did.

  Stay securely in your nest;
Caty now will do her best,
All she can, to make you blest;
But you want no human aid--
Nature, when she form'd you, said,
"Independent you are made,
My dear little Caty-did:
Soon yourself must disappear
With the verdure of the year,"--
And to go we know not where
     With your song of Caty-did.

The Battle of Lake Erie[75]

"To clear the lake of <u>Perry's</u> fleet
And make his flag his winding sheet,
This is my object--I repeat--"
  --Said Barclay, flush'd with native pride,
To some who serve the British crown:--
But <u>they</u> who dwell beyond the moon
Heard this bold menace with a frown,
    Nor the rash sentence ratified.

Ambition so bewitch'd his mind,
And royal smiles had so combined
With skill, to act the part assign'd,
  He for no contest cared a straw;
The ocean was too narrow far
To be the seat of naval war;
He wanted lakes and room to spare,
    And all to yield to Britain's law.

And thus he made a sad mistake;
Forsooth he must possess the lake,
As merely made for England's sake,
  To play her pranks and rule the roost,
Where she might govern, uncontrol'd,

An unmolested empire hold,
And keep a fleet to fish up gold,
    To pay the troops of George Provost.

The ships approach'd of either side;
And Erie, on his bosom wide,
Beheld two hostile navies ride,
    Each for the combat well prepared:
The lake was smooth, the sky was clear,
The martial drum had banish'd fear,
And death and danger hover'd near,
    Though both were held in disregard.

From lofty heights their colors flew,
And Britain's standard all in view
With frantic valor fired the crew
    That mann'd the guns of Queen Charlotte.
"And we must Perry's squadron take,
And England shall command the lake;--
And you must fight for Britain's sake,
    (Said Barclay) sailors, will you not?"

Assent they gave with heart and hand,
For never yet a braver band
To fight a ship forsook the land
    Than Barclay had on board that day;--
The guns were loosed the game to win,
Their muzzles gaped a dismal grin,
And out they pull'd their tompion pin,
    The bloody game of war to play.

But Perry soon, with flowing sail,
Advanced, determined to prevail,
When from his bull-dogs flew the hail
    Directed full at Queen Charlotte.
His wadded guns were aim'd so true,
And such a weight of ball they threw
As, Barclay said, he never knew
    To come before, so scalding hot!

But still, to animate his men,
From gun to gun the warrior ran
And blazed away and blazed again--
    Till Perry's ship was half a wreck:
They tore away both tack and sheet,--
Their victory might have been complete

135

Had <u>Perry</u> not, to shun defeat,
    In lucky moment left his deck.

Repairing to another post,
From another ship he fought their host
And soon regain'd the fortune lost;
    And down his flag the Briton tore:
With loss of arm and loss of blood,
Indignant on his decks he stood
To witness Erie's crimson flood
    For miles around him, stain'd with gore!

Thus for dominion of the lake
These captains did each other rake,
And many a widow did they make;--
    Whose is the fault, or who to blame?--
The Briton challenged with his sword;
The Yankee took him at his word,
With spirit laid him close on board--
    They're ours--he said--and closed the game.

Stanzas on the Decease of Thomas Paine[76]

    Princes and kings decay and die
        And, instant, rise again:
    But this is not the case, trust me,
        With men like THOMAS PAINE.

    In vain the democratic host
        His <u>equal</u> would attain:
    For years to come they will not boast
        A second Thomas Paine.

    Though many may his name assume,
        Assumption is in vain,
    For every man has not <u>his</u> plume[77]
        Whose name is <u>Thomas Paine.</u>

    Though heaven bestow'd on all its sons
        Their <u>proper</u> share of brain,
    It gives to few, ye simple ones,
        The mind of Thomas Paine.

    To tyrants and the tyrant crew,
        Indeed he was the bane;

He writ, and gave them all their due,
    And signed it, --THOMAS PAINE.

Oh! how we loved to see him write
    And curb the race of Cain!
They hope and wish that Thomas P----
    May never rise again.

What idle hopes!--yes--such a man
    May yet appear again. --
When they are dead, they are for aye:
    --Not so with Thomas Paine.

The Military Ground[78]

The Hills remain!--but scarce a man remains
    Of all who once paraded on these lands;
Yet the rough soil some vestiges retains
    Of camps, and crowds, and military bands.
I mark, I trace a spot renowned in fame;
    And something still may Fancy's pencil claim.

Here walked the man[79] to live to distant times,
    Born to a world its freedom to restore,
While 'midst a war of rancour and of crimes
    Fell at his feet the shafts of foreign power;
And they, who trod this verge of Hudson's stream,
    Won all he wished, with duty, love, esteem.

To raise such scenes, pourtray such crimes again,
    To draw the picture of a land distressed,
Another Gage should cross the Atlantic main,
    Another Navy float on Hudson's breast,
Some new Cornwallis to the charge return,
    Burgoyne arrive, and Howe for conquest burn.

Here flamed the fires that flash'd beyond the wave
    And struck with anguish, terror, and despair
The Chiefs who little to their monarch gave
    But sky built castles and the brow of care:
Manhattan's island saw their rise and fall
    To dine on wormwood, and to sup on gall.

Ambition's aims, with hateful avarice join'd,
    Would worlds subdue, if worlds could yet be found,

137

Bend to one Yoke the myriads of mankind,
  Debase their tribes & chain them to the ground:
To such the muse her offerings will disdain,
  Nor shall they live in her celestial strain.

This vision, life!--how cheerly, once, was trod
  This glittering field when all was mirth and glee,
Their views accomplished and their fame abroad,
  And Patriots still, though curs'd with Poverty.
Naught are they now--all decomposed to clay,
  Or wrecks of men and hastening to decay.

The vulture screams!--approaching night I see;
  This scene of Soldiers soon will be concealed
Where once, perhaps, they met at yonder tree,
  Where once, no doubt, my friend, like us they smiled
To think that George, the terror of mankind,
  Here to another George a world resign'd.

Philosophical Fortitude[80]

Though Vice and Folly dread that final day
Which takes us from this dying world away,
Yet no weak fears of mingling with the dust
Alarm the Virtuous or disturb the Just;
Let systems fail, or systems be restored,
Still active Virtue meets a due reward. --
Though Vice and Folly dread that debt to pay
Required by Nature on the funeral day,
Yet conscious goodness soars above the clod
And life, well spent, secures the path to God.

  The Wise at Nature's laws will ne'er repine,
Nor think to scan or mend the grand design.
Ills from ourselves, and not from Nature flow;
And true Religion never leads to woe:
What Nature gives, receive--her laws obey;
If you must die to morrow, live to day:
'Tis ours to improve this life, not ours to know
From whence this meteor comes, or where shall go;
This mind, this spark that animates our frame
Directs, impels, and still remains the same. --
As o'er some fen, when heaven is wrapt in night,
An ignus fatuus waves its trembling light;
Now up, now down, the mimic taper plays,

As varying winds affect the trembling blaze;
Soon the light phantom spends its magic store,
Dies into darkness and is seen no more:
Thus flows our life! but is that life secure?--
Heaven trusts no mortal's fortune in his power;
Nor serve those prayers, importunate, we send
To alter fate or Providence to mend;
As well in Judgement as in mercy kind,
Heaven hath for both the fittest state designed;
The fools on life, the wise on death depend,
Waiting, with sweet reverse, their toils to end,
Quit the vain scene, where few have found or know
The first grand purpose--why we live below.

Shakespeare's Bermuda [81]

This Island Shakespear made the haunt
   Of spirits from the vasty deep,
Where PROSPER waved his magic wand
   Or in his cavern fell asleep,
While Calyban contrived a plot,
   With sharpened steel, to cut his throat.

Maranda there, his daughter fair,
   Still lives in one bright nymph I see;
Her cherry lip, her auburn hair
   Might tempt one to idolatry:
And yet 'tis true, 'tis surely true,
(Revealed to me, but known to few)
She has one fault, but not first rate;
She wants Bermuda made a STATE.

Had she the power, no monarch here
   Would dare to exercise command;
She would some Congress-men prefer
   For Legislators to the land,
Had they but ships and boats and oars
To storm the isle, or seize its shores.

Alas, alas! I grieve to say,
   Kind nymph, they have no ships to spare!!
You must submit, you must obey--
   Two cock-boats and a sloop of war,
At best, would only raise a smile,
Scarce guard yourself, not guard the isle!

Bold Britons still must be your guard;
Obey them, tho' you think it hard:

If rapine half supports their reign,
    Yet Time an awful change prepares;
Not theirs shall be the subject maine,
    Nor every shore it circles, theirs. --

But who comes here, approaching near,
    What blue-eyed hag, mis-shapen form?
'Tis Sycorax, [82] by all that's good;
    She comes, the fury in the storm. --
I know her step; I know her wiles;
She once possessed these stormy isles,
    A witch of Endor's ghastly brood. --
Say, madam, what your errand is;
And why exhibit such a phiz?

SYCORAX.

"From shaded cliffs and rocky reefs
I shaped my course on borrowed wings
    To fetch some dew, to fetch some due;
A sail appears on yond' deep sea
That brings some welcome news to me;
    May it prove true, may it prove true!--
The fires that stream through that red sky
Portend some brilliant changes nigh,
New men, new men to hold the helm,
To steer the barque on oceans dark,
And be good sailors in a calm.

"The times arrive when I alone
    Should have these islands in my care;
But now, too old to mount a throne,
    I name a Regent--'tis but fair,
And Calyban shall govern here!
My Calyban shall govern here!
His cousin, too, shall near him wait
And be--FIRST MINISTER OF STATE!"

    Sept. 1778   F.

                    140

"Now what avails it to be brave?--
  On liquid precipices hung,
Around us fierce tornadoes rave;
Beneath us yawn'd a sea-deep grave
  And silenced every tongue."

What ruling force, what active power
  That bids the winds and waves obey
Will now appear to soothe the roar
  Of nature in her agony?

Does lightning's flash announce our doom!--
  Do thunders, rattling through the sky?--
Strange fires the watery wave illume
  That inlet to eternity!

The creaking yards, the laboring masts
  Proclaimed distress, not distant far:
No sail endures these rugged blasts,
  Engaged in elemental roar.

Ah me! what waves assail the ship,
  What bursting seas, what floods of spray!
Scarce nimble Jack retains his grip
  When up the shrouds he gropes his way.

What yet avails, what yet remains
  But anxious hearts and toil severe--
The clanking pumps--incessant rain
  Descends, another deluge here!

How feeble are the strongest hands,
  How weak all human efforts prove!--
He who obeys, and who commands
  Must await a mandate from above.

'Tis done!--we view in western skies
  The clouds dispersed, and stars appear;
Before the blast the vapour flies,
  The waves subside their awful swell,
    The starboard watch hails, All is well!
  And from the land again we steer.

The Dying Prophecy of Tecumseh[84]

TECUMSEH-- commonly called King of the woods, the noted Indian Priest, Prophet, warrior, and fanatic, who, about the year 1811, began, it was said, under the influence of British bribery, to excite large bodies of Savages to unite in the destruction of our frontier settlements, which finally occasioned the battle of Tippecanoe, in which the enemy was routed by General Harrison and his militia, although with some loss on the side of the Americans. Tecumseh lost his life on the borders of Canada in a skirmish with a body of Vermont militia towards the close of the year 1813. --The following prophecy of this king of the woods, as he was called, is supposed to be addressed to the King of Great Britain, George the third.

"Great monarch, of unequalled sway,
Whose nod the subject seas obey,
Whose rule o'er countries far away
    Extends almighty and supreme:
Great king, attend my last address--
A savage of the wilderness
Whom death assails, and wounds oppress,
    Too late repents his idle dream.

"A Prophet born, if I foretold
Some deeds atchieved, sublime and bold,
Of right was I with them enrolled
    Who thirteen fires to death decreed.
Your presents came; the gun, the sword,
The scalping knife our strength restored;
Our aid your warlike chiefs implored
    To bid Columbia's warriors bleed.

"Then from our huts we rush'd abroad;
The white man's town was overawed,
And scalps were had, by force and fraud,
    And these you bought--for these you paid.
For every scalp we, yelling, took,
You gave us credit in your book;
Humanity our hearts forsook
    And nature's laws were prostrate laid!

"We joined the potent Iroquoi;
We rushed to battle, man and squaw;
Not Christian blood escaped the maw
    Of Christian men with Indian joined.
And there I met my fatal wound;
A rifle brought me to the ground--
I now must go, O king renowned,
    To the land of shades, my joys to find:

"But ere I go--for go I must,
And soon be mingled with the dust,
I'll tell the event, and true, I trust,
    Of this sad war and what remains:
Your warlike hosts will melt away;
Our nations will their league betray;
Your ships will burn on every sea,
    Your armies faint on Indian plains.

"Your flag will from the mast be torn,
The jest of malice and of scorn;
Your every hope will be forlorn;
    Our hearts will sink to meet the foe.
On lake Champlain your hosts will die,
On Erie's waves your squadrons fly;
The Ontarian sea will not supply
    One conquest, you are brought so low.

"On southern plains your warriors fail,
Where Jackson's prowess will prevail--
In vain you come, with oar and sail,
    All Mississippi to defy.
Your thousands there in vain unite:
In vain they form; in vain they fight;
The mists of death, the glooms of night
    Involve them half; they faint and die!

"From northern hills, the rugged waste,
I see the flower of thousands haste--
What power has yet their vengeance faced
    Those sons of valor, all in arms.
They rush, indignant, to the shore,
To conquer or return no more,
To swell the flood with British gore;
    Such spirits every bosom warms!

"Touched with a madness, half divine,
They load the gun; they man the line--

O chief[85] of chiefs! What fate is thine
    My dreams forbode--I will not tell.
Or shall I tell what I forsee,
Oh Packenham!--the destiny,
The doom the Gods prepare for thee;
    Thy bold advances they repel.

"Kentucky pours her legions down;
Wild Tennessee, with martial frown,
Drains forest, mountain, field, and town
    To join where Jackson holds command.
Nor shall his vengeance be withstood,
Nor unattended with a flood
Of English and Creolian blood
    To dye the saturated strand.

"Heroes and chiefs he will entomb,
Nor shall your boldest powers presume
To pull one feather from his plume,
    That waves above the brow of Mars.
O what a flame and what a heat,
And how the men and horses sweat,
Happy, thrice happy to retreat
    And curse the white man's spangled stars.

"Cockburne, himself, they will pursue--
He may invade, but not subdue;
And he may fall by Yankees too
    That swear to aid the Orleans' cause.
Who can oppose their ardent rage!
Who can with men of fire engage
That now command the western stage, --
    What deer resists the tiger's claws!

"Your noblest chiefs will faint or fall;
The blast of death pursues them all
From rifle, sword, or cannon ball,
    Who do not haste a quick retreat,
Unless they quit the fatal spot
Where Fortune's smile awaits them not--
Where old renown will be forgot
    In disappointment and defeat.

"The drum of death has beat to arms!
The forest with its thousands swarms;
The Event of battle has no charms
    For some that I in dreams behold.

144

In dreams I see them march away;
In dreams I see the infernal play,
And thousands marching in array
　　Whom now you deem to England sold.

"I now must die!"--Tecumseh said,
And to the ground he dropt his head--
His kindred bore him to that bed
　　From which Tecumseh cannot rise!
Death on his eyes hung heavy, cold--
Tecumseh was to Britain sold--
And now she owns, as we are told, [86]
　　All his predictions--were not lies.

Modern Greece [87]

In modern Greece the attentive eye may find
What woes Mahomet brought on human kind:
Dire superstition first his flag unfurled,
Which, for three centuries, awed the Christian world.
There, to the source, despotic empire trace,
The worst of mischiefs, Reason's worst disgrace.

See ancient Greece in every age distressed,
Deceived, enslaved, deluded, and oppressed;
See modern Greece, as high renowned in fame,
Her sons as nervous, but her fate the same.

'Tis but too true, when Public Virtues failed,
Then tyrants rose and tyranny prevailed;
Too late the few, who morals prized, essayed
To attract deluded millions to their aid,
To excite the nations to a generous strife
And Liberty prefer to servile life--
All sunk, bewildered, in the general doom,
While tyrants trampled on the Athenian tomb.

Virtue despised, and vicious paths pursued,
While private avarice governed public good;
All this--and more--a fatal stroke prepared
To crush the fabric that with toil was reared;
In sad mistakes were long misfortunes sown,
--Kings were their tyrants--but the fault their own.

145

When heaven, in man, did soul and body join,
Infused in torpid clay the flame divine
And formed a creature on a different plan
From brutal shapes--and called that creature man,
One glimmering light the Almighty lent below,
In this dark world to guide us safely through;
That heaven born light who follows must be blest,
The lamp of reason in the human breast.

Contemning this and warped to error's way,
What wars have cursed, what falshoods had their day;
From such contempt despotic empire rose,
And fiends to triumph in a nation's woes!

On the Battle of Monmouth[88]

On the green fields of Monmouth, since WASHINGTON fought,
What years have elapsed & what changes are wrought!
An age has departed, so time runs away,
And few the survivors who witness'd that day.

Where a house was demolished, another is built;
And harvests have sprung from the blood that was spilt:
Where once was displayed on the soil we now tread
The combat of arms and the bones of the dead,
The ploughman's long furrow has travers'd the plain
And the soil been inverted again and again.

Where a Tavern once flourished is opened a Store,
And the landlord that kept it sells whiskey no more!
The sign-post, the eagle suspended on high,
And there was the Lass of the languishing eye,
The toast of the Lads and the pride of the town
When she flirted the street in her calico gown.

Dear females who lived in that season of strife,
Ye few, very few yet remaining in life,
It is a sad truth that with age and with care,
If unhurt by the war, you're the worse for the wear.

Where now the young farmer is raking his hay,
Two armies encountered in battle array;
Where now pretty Fanny is turning her wheel,
Arm'd parties were stationed to plunder and steal;
Where late the bold planter his fabric has rais'd,

With the roar of Mount Aetna artillery blazed,
And vomited death on that desperate band
Who came to subdue or to ravage the land.

On the day that preceded Sir Harry's retreat,
The sky was on fire with a mid-summer heat;
The <u>wells</u> were exhausted; no fountains were seen,
Nor a drop from the brook to recruit the canteen.

The Sun, when he rose in his march from the east,
Announced the destruction of man and of beast;
With a blaze so unusual he traversed the sky,
And such was the ardour that flamed from on high,
All nature lay drooping beneath his control,
Unnerving the body, oppressing the soul.

At the dawn of the day, what a scene of distress!
What a bustle there was, we may easily guess:
No female but shed her abundance of tears,
Confessing her doubts and revealing her fears. --
The aid of the skies to our arms was implored,
And they often look'd out for the MAN they adored:
No farmers but quitted the care of their farms
When the trumpet was heard, & the drum beat to arms:
They never suspected what <u>now</u> we can say,
It would be but a battle of----slap and away.

Now woe to the soldier subjected to fear!
The matches are lighted and red-coats are near;
If we take a sure aim at the slaves of the throne,
By the sword of St. Gideon, the day is our own!--

When orders arrived and the battle began,
Not a musket was levelled but brought down its man;
Not a cannon exploded, its aim was so just,
But Hessians and Britons were hurled in the dust:--
Let them sleep, let them sleep in the fields where they bled
'Till the lands and the ocean shall give up their dead.

If others advanced, they were glad to retire
In whirlwinds of smoke and a torrent of fire:--
All the message we sent or the notice we gave
Was that of the drum and the march of the brave.

FAYETTE, with the front of a lion, came on;
In the view of six thousand his sabre was drawn;
With the stars and the stripes, & the lillies of France,

The Royalists trembled to see him advance.
His legion beheld him with rapture and awe;
To all he directed they gave the huzza!
Such a man as the <u>Marquis</u> was seen on our stage
But rarely, too rarely,--scarce twice in an age!

    Hark! the drums how they beat, and the fifes how they play!
What a harvest of men will be cut down this day!
With the sun in the west, what a lesson it brings
To the sons of the Yankees and subjects of Kings!

    Then WASHINGTON rode at the head of his line
And rush'd on the foe with a courage divine:
He spurr'd up his <u>charger</u> and gallop'd the plain,
Determin'd to conquer again and again.
All cool and collected, himself was a host;
At the glance of a moment each flew to his post;
The heart that was fainting, to life he restored;
And heroes sprung up at the gleam of his sword.
No check of disaster his valor depress'd,
So great was the spirit that govern'd his breast;
With the arm of a giant, a legion he broke,
And AMERICA heard him whenever he spoke.

    In the course of experience how often we find
What chances direct the affairs of mankind;
So often prevented from acting aright
By the faults of a day or mistakes of a night!--
Yes, often, too often--we cannot tell why,
The finger of Fortune is seen in the pie.

    To capture an army, their total defeat,
And take from Sir Harry all hopes of retreat
Was his purpose, 'tis certain; and thousands agree
That purpose was lost by one blunder of LEE.

    To act, on occasion, with might and with main,
Sir Harry 'till midnight had puzzled his brain:
The <u>Hessians</u> by hundreds were snoring around
And slept very safely, but not very sound:
They relish'd no doses of WASHINGTON'S pills,
And long'd for a prospect of <u>Neversink Hills</u>.

    To crush a <u>rebellion</u>, they stupidly came
Where <u>rebels</u> were hot, as they found to their shame;
But the <u>blood</u> was as black, that ran in their veins,
As the rivers of hell that antiquity feigns:--

148

The can and the bottle went cheerly about,
And regiments snapp'd at a dish of sour-krout;--
How they curs'd the vile supper, I will not repeat,
The best to be had, but the worst to be eat.

Strict orders were issued to keep a look out,
But the captains made love to their jugs & brown stout:
The word was repeated, to mount a strong guard;
But the majors were weary and soldiers drank hard,
Knyphausen[89] exclaiming, as drunk as a lord,
"When I gives up my bottle, I gives up my sword."

Sir Harry, unwilling much longer to stay,
Press'd loyal conductors to shew them the way;
Through fields and through forests they hastened their flight,
And halted but once till the sea was in sight.
He made a retreat with a flea in his ear
By the light of the moon, in confusion and fear;
Some thousands retreated, as still as the grave;
And the bravest among them no longer were brave.
The drums were all muffled; no music was play'd;
The fate of Burgoyne was their fate if they stay'd;
A farewell to Jersey forever they took,
And hardly look'd back at the Point of the Hook.

*   *   *   *   *   *   *   *   *   *

Young soldiers! may Peace be forever your lot,
But be not the Battle of Monmouth forgot.
If wars are an evil and heroes a curse,
Like a wife you must take them for better or worse.
The times may arrive when a foe will appear;
Take care to be ready when danger is near:
If Britons, or Russians, or be who they will,
Your business is only to capture or kill;
At least you must promise, if ever you meet,
To give them the tune of--Harry's Retreat.

Winter[90]

The Sun hangs low!--So much the worse, we say,
For those whose pleasure is a Summer's day;
Few are the joys which stormy Nature yields
From blasting winds and desolated fields;
Their only pleasure in that season found
When orchards bloom and flowers bedeck the ground.

149

But are no Joys to these cold months assign'd?
Has winter nothing to delight the Mind?
No friendly Sun that beams a distant ray,
No Social Moons that light us on our way?--
Yes, there are Joys that may all storms defy,
The chill of Nature and a frozen Sky.

Happy with wine we may indulge an hour,
The noblest beverage of the mildest power.
Happy, with Love, to solace every care,
Happy with sense and wit an hour to share,
These to the mind a thousand pleasures bring
And give to winter's frosts the smiles of spring;
Above all praise pre-eminence they claim,   91
Nor leave a sting behind--remorse and shame.

Ye Nymphs and Swains on Hudson's quiet shore,
Blest in your Village, who would wish for more?
Compare your state with thousands of our kind;
How happy are you in the lot you find!--
While others shiver in the cheerless hut
And freeze o'er charcoal, or a peck of Soot,
Scarce on their beds a blanket or a sheet,
With little left to hope and less to eat,
You sit conversing by your hickory fires,
For social purpose Met, that never tires.

Contrast the Scene with Greenland's wastes of Snow,
Where darkness rules and oceans cease to flow,

[Ms. ends here.]

POLITICAL VERSE[92]

To Shylock Ap-Shenkin[93]

When round the barque the howling tempest raves,
Toss'd in the conflict of a thousand waves,
The lubber landsmen weep, complain and sigh,
And on the pilot's skill or heaven rely,
Lurk in their holds, astonish'd and aghast,
Dreading the moment that must be their last--
The tempest o'er--their terror also ceases;
And up they come and show their shameless faces,
At once grow brave and tell the pilot too,
"He did no more than they themselves could do."

A FOE TO TYRANTS!--One thy heart restores--
There is a Tyrant that thy soul adores;
And every stupid line too plainly shows
Your heart is hostile to that tyrant's foes.

What mighty malice urg'd this Genius dull
With Churchill's[94] wreathes to shade his barren scull?
So utter darkness union claims with light;
So oil and water in one mass unite:
No more thy rage in borrow'd rhimes repeat;
Sneak into prose--the dunce's last retreat!
REED'S patriot fame to distant times shall last
When these base reptiles to the dogs are cast,
Or where Oblivion spreads her dreary wings,
Lost in the slumber of forgotten things;
And none shall ask, nor wish to know, nor care
Who--what their names--or when they liv'd, or where.

To the Foe to Tyrants on his Farewell[95]

Since ink, thank heaven, is all the blood you spill,
Health to the driver of the true goose quill;
Such war shall leave no widow in despair,
Nor curse one orphan with the public care.

'Tis the worst wound the heart of man can feel,
Thus to be wounded by an ass's heel:
With generous satire give me all my due;
Nay, give me more, and call me scoundrel too;
Make me as black as hell's remotest gloom,
But still to genius let me owe my doom:
By Jove's red lightnings 'tis no shame to bleed,
But by a grovelling swine--is death indeed.

Now, by the laurels of your yellow crew,
I felt no shame 'till I engag'd with you;
But such an odour scented from your song,
I stopt my nose and quickly pass'd along,
Blush'd for the wretch that could such filth display,
His guts disgorging in the public way.

Arm'd as I stand, unusual tumults rise;
And all my soul comes swelling through my eyes,
To think that in the skirmish of a day
This bard must perish and his fame decay,

151

So quick retire to black oblivion's clime,
Turn'd, chas'd, and routed by the power of rhime!

    I wish'd him still <u>unhandled</u> and unhurt;
I wish'd no evils to this man of dirt;
I thought to leave him swelt'ring in his den,
Not with such rotten hash to stain my pen;
But his base labours wrought his utter woe,
And his own efforts now shall lay him low:--
Before his eyes the sexton's spade appears,
And bells unceasing ring within his ears;
Already is his span of being fled;
Sense, wit, and reason all proclaim him <u>dead</u>;
In his own lines he toll'd his funeral knell,
And when he could not <u>sing</u>, he <u>stunk</u>
                      FAREWELL.

Ode III[96]

    Since the day we attempted the NATION'S GAZETTE,
Pomposo's dull printer does nothing but fret,
         Now preaching
         And screeching,
         Then nibbling
         And scribbling,
         Remarking
         And barking,
         Repining
         And whining,
         And still in a pet
From morning to night with the Nation's Gazette.

    Instead of whole columns our page to abuse,
Your readers would rather be treated with news
         While wars are a-brewing
         And kingdoms undoing,
         While monarchs are falling
         And princesses squalling,
         While France is reforming
         And Irishmen storming--
In a glare of such splendour, what nonsense to fret
At so humble a thing as--the Nation's Gazette!

    No <u>favours</u> we ask'd from <u>your friends</u> in the east;
On your wretched soup-meagre I left them to feast--

So many base lies you have sent them in print
That scarcely a man at our paper will squint:
                    And now you begin
                    With a grunt and a grin,
                    With the bray of an ass
                    And a visage of brass,
With a quill in your hand and a lie in your mouth,
To play the same trick on the men of the south.

One National Paper, you think, is enough
To flatter and lie, to pallaver and puff,
To preach up in favour of monarchs and titles,
And garters and ribbons, to prey on our vitals:
Who knows but our Congress will give it in fee
And make Mr. Fenno the grand patentee!
                    Then take to your scrapers
                    Other national papers--
                    No rogue shall go snacks,
                    And the NEWSPAPER-TAX
                    Shall be puffed to the skies
                    As a measure most wise--
So a spaniel, when master is angry and kicks it,
Sneaks up to his shoe and submissively licks it.

                To the National Gazette[97]

Nine months are now elaps'd, dear rambling paper,
Since first on this world's stage you cut your caper
With spirit still of democratic proof,
And still despising Whaacum's canker'd hoof--
What doom the fates decree is hard to say,
Whether to live to some far distant day,
                    Or sickening in your prime
                    In this news-taxing clime,
Take pet, make wings, say prayers, and flit away.

                        AIR.[98]
                "Virtue, Order, and Religion,
                Haste and seek some other region:
Your plan is fix'd, to hunt them down,
                Destroy the mitre, rend the gown,"
And that vile b-tch-h--Philosophy--restore--
                Did ever paper plan so much before!

                            153

For nine months past, a host of busy foes
        Have buzz'd about your nose,
            White, black, and gray,
            By night and day,
            Garbling, lying,
            Singing, sighing:--
These eastern gales a cloud of insects bring
That fluttering, snivelling, whimpering on the wing,
And wafted still as Discord's demon guides,
Flock round the flame that yet must scorch their hides.

Well--let the fates decree whate'er they please;
Whether you're doom'd to drink Oblivion's cup
        Or Praise-God-Bare-Bones eats you up,
This we can say, you've spread your wings afar,
Hostile to garter, ribbon, crown, and star,
Still on the people's, still on freedom's side,
          With full determin'd aim
          To baffle every claim
Of well-born wights that aim to mount & ride.

          To Duncan Doolittle,
        A "half-Starved" Democrat[99]

DUNCAN, with truth it may be said,
Your mouth was made for rye or barley bread;
What claim have you to halls of state,
Whose business is to stand and wait,
    Subservient to command?
What right have you to white-bread, superfine,
Who were by nature destin'd for "a swine"--
    As said good Edmund Burke,
    The drudge of Britain's dirty work,
Whose mighty pamphlets rous'd the royal band!

When passing by a splendid dome of pride,
    By speculation built (and built so vast
That there a standing army might reside)
    Say, Duncan, stood you not aghast
When gazing up (like fox that look'd for grapes)
You saw so many things in curious shapes,
    Trees rang'd along the table
    And sugar-columns, far above the rabble,
    With roses blooming in October
    And wisdom's figure--dull and sober.

Ah! how you smack'd your lips and look'd so wishful
When pigs and poultry--many a lovely dish-full,
Imparted to your nose the savoury scent
For royal noses--not for Duncan's--meant.

For things like these you, caitiff, were not born--
    A pewter spoon was for your chops intended;
Some hints of beef, and garlands made of thorn--
    On things like these has Freedom's feast depended.
Though in the days of fight you musquet carried,
    Or wandered up and down, a cannon-hauling,
Better you might in Jericho have tarried
    And rebel-starving made your loyal calling.
Among our far-famed chieftains that are dead
(Like beer set by in mug without a lid,
    And sure, a half-jill glass I'll put it all in)
I'll toast your health--yes, to the very brim,
And to the little gaping world proclaim
    You are a Hero fallen:
One of the wights who dar'd all death or wound,
And warr'd for two and sixpence in the pound.

Of public virtue you're a rare example--
    Go, mind your hoe, your pick-ax, or your spade;
A hut of six foot square shall be your "temple,"
    And all your honour--strutting on parade.
        But pray, beware of public good;
        It will not always find you food;
        And if your son should any thing inherit,
        Bequeath him not your public spirit,
But six pence, to be train'd to SAWING WOOD.

Lines Extempore on the Spur of the Occasion[100]

    The daring Feds have try'd, but all in vain,
    To hold the sword of power another reign;
But better stars determined the event,
And JEFFERSON'S elected President.
    In spite of fraud, chicane, and every art
    That could be practis'd on the human heart,
The man of Science, Morals, and good will
Must the first station in the Union fill.
    'Tis welcome news to every freeman's heart
    Altho' Aristocratic feds must smart;
Their insolence demands retaliation,

155

But patriots disdain such degradation.
    They can look down with scorn, and yet forgive
    When feds wou'd cry, "don't let a patient live."
Fam'd Jefferson can both forgive and rule,
When every monarchist will look a fool.
    Now wheel about, ye sycophantic feds,
    Or, like the stinking lentil, hang your heads;
Slink home from whence you came and tell the story,
That honesty alone has claim to glory.

Notes

1.   From "The American Village, A Poem." To which are added, Several other original Pieces in Verse. By Philip Freneau, A.B. New York, 1772. This is a pamphlet of 28 pages, and is Freneau's first collection. "The American Village" imitates Goldsmith's "Deserted Village," but with a cheerful philosophy, faith in the American future, in rebuke to Goldsmith's melancholy attitude. The poem takes up 400 lines and 18 pages, and describes America as a refuge from European wars, another Atlantis. It mentions the Indians' happiness, then the arrival of Columbus and Cabot, and war by "rav'nous nations." A tale is told of the Indian Caffraro, his wife Colma, their love and tragic death. The conclusion emphasizes the poet's yearning for retirement in an atmosphere of happiness with the great English poets' works. Republished in facsimile, Providence, 1906, edited by Harry L. Koopman and Victor H. Paltsits.

2.   From the 1786 "Poems." Has "Written 1770" beneath the title, indicating that the poem was composed while Freneau was still in college. It is one of his better lyrics, and rather deistic, especially in the idea that the stars are fancies and ideas, products of God's mind and reason, a Hegelian idea, almost a precursor of the idealist fashion in philosophy. Note the resemblance in form and tone to Milton's "L'Allegro" and "Il Penseroso."

3.   Milton's Paradise Lost, B. II v. 1052. [Freneau's note.]

4.   From the 1786 "Poems." The subscription indicates, as Freneau's footnote explains, that the Freneau-Brackenridge version had been revised to make the poem wholly Freneau's. The original version was separately published

in Philadelphia in 1772; it glorified General William Johnson, an early leader in New York, and did not consider American independence. This version glorifies Washington and independence.

5.   Genesis x. 25. [Freneau's note.]

6.   Hor. Epod. 16. [Freneau's note.]

7.   Hom. Odyss. B. 24. [Freneau's note.]

8.   Newton. [Freneau's note.]

9.   The massacre at Boston, March 5th, 1770, is here more particularly glanced at.   [Freneau's note.]

10.   Colonial governor of Massachusetts, who, in 1768, dissolved the General Court.

11.   St. John is said to have been exiled to this island.

12.   Typical of the patriotic poems Freneau wrote in 1775. Beneath title is "Published in New York, August 1775." The "conqueror" was General Thomas Gage.   From the 1786 "Poems."

13.   Pattee calls his "the first distinctly romantic note heard in America," the poem that made Freneau "One of the earliest pioneers in that dimly lighted region which was soon to be exploited by Coleridge and Poe." Freneau himself, however, apparently grew ashamed of it, published only a fragment of it in the 1795 "Poems," and omitted it from the 1809 "Poems," perhaps as too romantic for his classic tastes.   Yet in some ways it is remarkable--a product of sheer imagination, with a weird supernatural atmosphere, yet with references to American flowers and trees, even the whippoorwill.   Like Coleridge in the "Ancient Mariner," Freneau moralizes at the close.   The poem in 73 stanzas appeared in Brackenridge's "United States Magazine" for August, 1779.

14.   Note that the stanza form is that of Gray in "Elegy Written in a Country Churchyard."

15.   A Bird peculiar to America, of a solitary nature, who never sings but in the night.   Her note resembles the name given to her by the country people.   [Freneau's note.]

16. NOTES.) Verse 21. "Anchylosis--a morbid contraction of the joints.

Verse 21--"Os Femoris"--the thigh bone.

Verse 21--"Trochanters--two processes in the upper part of the thigh bones, otherwise called, "rotator major et minor," in which the tendons of many muscles terminate. [Freneau's notes.]

17. NOTE.) Verse 49. --"Calenture"--an inflammatory fever, attended with a delirium common in long voyages at sea, in which the diseased persons fancy the sea to be green fields and meadows, and, if they are not hindered, will leap overboard. [Freneau's note.]

18. See Milton's "Paradise Lost," II, 11. 649 ff.

19. From the 1786 "Poems." The motto is evidently by Freneau. Early in 1776 Freneau sailed to Santa Cruz (now St. Croix) Island as the guest of John Hanson, on whose estate he lived for over two years. The poem, in 52 stanzas, appeared in Brackenridge's "United States Magazine" for February, 1779, with an essay describing the island. The poem is addressed to a resident of the United States, presumably suffering from the cold climate and a cruel war, who is invited to desert them for the mild climate and peace of Santa Cruz. Yet the poet expands on two faults of the island, slavery and the hurricane. Here again he uses the form of Gray's "Elegy," also its tone.

20. (Eolia) Freneau inserted.

21. Goddess of Health. [Freneau's note.]

22. Note the resemblance here to Gray's "Elegy," stanza 14.

23. A confession of Freneau's insatiable wanderlust.

24. Probably a reference to Waller's "Battle of the Summer Islands," a mock epic on an attempt to capture two whales.

25. Evidence that Freneau knew about the Revolutionary War.

26. Note the close resemblance to the first stanza of Gray's "Elegy."

27.   These names probably refer to Saba and Saint Eusta-
tius, Dutch islands in the West Indies.

28.   Here is further evidence that Freneau was deliberately
avoiding a participation in the Revolutionary War.   Some
commentators have thought he was unaware of its existence.

29.   From the 1786 "Poems."   Based on actual voyage,
capture, and imprisonment of six weeks in ships off New
York Harbor, in the summer of 1780.   Under the title is
"Written 1780."   Freneau was a passenger on the "Aurora,
an American privateer, when it was taken.   "Canto I" is
better than the rest, which is dominated by hatred for the
British.   See Freneau's "Some Account of the Ship 'Aurora',"
edited by Jay Milles, New York, 1899.   Milles says Freneau built the ship for himself, but there is no good evidence
to support the statement.   And in the prose account, he refers to himself as a passenger who has paid his fare.

30.   Commissary of Prisoners at New-York.   [Freneau's
note.]

31.   1786 "Poems."   The rest of the title is "obtained by
the gallant captain PAUL JONES, of the "Good Man Richard,"
over the "Seraphis," &c. under the command of captain
PEARSON."   Beneath is "Written August, 1781."   Then
Freneau was in Philadelphia, helping to edit "The Freeman's
Journal," in which it appeared on August 8, 1781.   The poem is typical of several on sea battles by Freneau, usually
exaggerated in patriotic bias.   The battle took place on September 23, 1779, off the east coast of England.   The British ships were guarding a convoy of merchant vessels.

32.   1786 "Poems."   Despite his later editorial criticisms
of Washington as a tool of the Federalists, Freneau always
admired him as a man.   This poem is one of several on the
same subject, all eulogies.   Under the title is "Written September, 1781."   In "The Freeman's Journal," September 5,
1781.

33.   In 1793, Freneau, editing the "National Gazette," was
to condemn King Louis as heartily as he praises him here.

34.   1786 "Poems." Full title, "To the Memory of the
Brave Americans, under General Greene, who fell in the ac-
tion of September 8, 1781."   Popularly called "Eutaw
Springs" and generally regarded as one of Freneau's best.

It sounds very like Collins's "Ode Written in the Beginning of the Year 1746," which begins thus:

> How sleep the brave who sink to rest
> By all their country's wishes blest!

35. This line borrowed by Scott in "Marmion," Canto III, line 4.

36. 1786 "Poems." Freneau liked to philosophize on current events and figures, comparing them with those of the ancient past, in both editorials and poems. Here he follows the Rousseau-Paine line of thought on monarchy.

37. 1786 "Poems." Later titled "The Hurricane." The storm occurred near Jamaica, July 30, 1784. Note the facile first lines. Freneau endured several terrible storms at sea.

38. 1786 "Poems." Beneath the title is "1785." Good example of Freneau's humor, also revealing his worship of Shakespeare.

39. Freneau, after using the depredations of mice to lament his favorite authors (Shakespeare, Virgil, Milton, Swift, Montesquieu), now points to a favorite scorn--the uninspired and sycophantic writers. William Whitehead was poet laureate from 1757 to 1785. Freneau had little liking for solemn hymns and sermons, and the novels of seduction, then very popular.

40. After he found himself in disgrace with the Court of Spain, he retired to Valladolid, a town of Old Castile, where he died, it is said, more of a broken heart than any other disease, on the 20th of May 1506. [Freneau's note.]

41. "Miscellaneous Works," 1788. This is "Picture XVIII" and the last of poems under "The Pictures of Columbus, the Genoese," a biography of Columbus from the time when he made maps and conceived the earth to be round, to his retirement in disgrace at Valladolid. Freneau greatly admired the admiral, and wrote also "Columbus to Ferdinand" (1786 "Poems"), a plea for supporting his project.

42. History agrees that Columbus, once a national hero, titled "admiral of the ocean sea" and made governor general of all the lands he discovered, was neglected and ignored in his last years. Freneau feels the tragedy keenly.

160

43. "Miscellaneous Works," 1788. Dated 1785 and addressed "To Sylvius." Freneau also used "Sylvius" as a pseudonym. The subject is a familiar one in Freneau's prose and poetry--the futility of seeking literary success in America. "Robert Slender" in the same volume, under "Advice to Authors," presents a pessimistic view of prospects for writers.

44. Zoilus (400-320 B.C.) was a Greek rhetorician and critic of Homer; and a "Zoilus" came to be known as a harsh critic. Who was "Sylvius?" Possibly Andrew Brown, genial Philadelphia teacher and editor.

45. "Miscellaneous Works," 1788. Generally regarded as Freneau's best poem. Leary (page 144) says it "placed Freneau... chronologically at the head of America's procession of poets." It is evidence that Freneau was the precursor of the nature poets, Burns and Wordsworth. He used the agreeable stanza form in a number of other poems, but never with quite the same success.

46. "Miscellaneous Works," 1788. This poem illustrates the complaint of Freneau and other American writers--that the proper atmosphere for literary creation did not exist on the west side of the Atlantic. It remains an interesting speculation what sort of career Freneau might have found in London.

47. This melancholy conclusion--the necessity of choosing Melpomene, the muse of tragedy--correctly forecasts the tone of much of Freneau's serious poetry, one of sadness. Nevertheless, many of his best poems are optimistic.

48. "Miscellaneous Works," 1788. Usually called "The Indian Burying Ground." Next to "The Wild Honey Suckle," it is regarded most highly by Freneau's admirers, and appears in modern anthologies as representative of Freneau's "noble savage" view of the Indian. That he changed from this romantic attitude to a realistic one may be seen in the "Old Soldier" essays on the Indian problem in Freneau's old age. The latter half of the poem is a delightful fantasy.

49. Thomas Campbell borrowed this line for his "O'Connor's Child"--stanza IV, line 8. Evidently Freneau's first two collections circulated rather widely among the English romanticists.

50. 1795 "Poems." Freneau's most popular poem in its time. Leary lists thirty republications after its first appearance in the New York "Daily Advertiser" in 1791.

51. 1795 "Poems." A popular poem in its time--Leary lists about a dozen reprintings in newspapers.

52. 1795 "Poems." Freneau defended the stage against Puritan-Quaker opposition, but believed in "republican" plays, and felt that aristocracy should not be favorably portrayed.

53. "Totus Mundus agit Histrionem." [Freneau's note.]

54. 1795 "Poems." Beneath the title is "(A Picture from the Life.)" One of Freneau's deepest sympathies was that for the neglected veteran, in an age of no pensions or hospital care for the wounded soldier. Many of his essays and editorials were written on behalf of the "old soldier." Washington's weekly levee, a stiffly formal reception, was resented by Freneau and other Jeffersonians as too aristocratic.

55. "Time Piece," Sept. 15, 1797, with editorial introduction condemning monasteries and other religious houses, as parasites on the people, enforcing an unnatural celibacy. The poem was written about a girl imprisoned in "the monastery of Santa Clara, in the island of Madeira." Ignored by Leary. Note the stanza--same as used in "The Wild Honey Suckle."

56. 1815 "Poems." This is one of several deistic poems in this edition, a sales failure, very likely in part because of them. Americans were in no mood for deism, in fact tended to confuse it with atheism, and thought Paine and Jefferson were atheists, though they were deists.

57. 1815 "Poems." Characteristic of Freneau, who was an independent thinker, and had rejected the Calvinism under which he was reared for deism. Probably intended to rebuke Presbyterians, Puritans, and all who insisted on conformity in religion.

58. Freneau was, here, using "mere" in its old sense--complete.

59. 1815 "Poems." Another deistic poem. Note the closing lines' resemblance to Pope's deistic "Essay on Man."

60. "Still" is probably here used in its old meaning--always.

61. 1815 "Poems." A deistic poem with a pantheistic flavor.

62. ----- Jupiter, optimus, maximus. -----CICERO. [Freneau's note.]

63. 1815 "Poems." Another pantheistic-deistic poem. Note the criticism of orthodoxy. Freneau was reared in a Presbyterian-Huguenot atmosphere, and Princeton was founded by Presbyterians.

64. 1815 "Poems." Typical of the calm philosophy Freneau achieved in his later years--doubtless stemming from deism, which also appears here, with a Christian Science touch.

65. 1815 "Poems." An extension of the title is "Humbly Recommended to the Serious Consideration of Creed Makers" --evidently intended for orthodox believers. Freneau had renounced orthodoxy very early, probably during his college years. This is a plea for freedom in belief, even in doubt, a condemnation of blind faith, and an argument for evidence as the basis of faith.

66. 1815 "Poems." Extension of the title: "who died Dec. 14, 1799." Motto: "Terra tegit, moeret, coelum habet!" Freneau had written several poems in praise of Washington (and some prose satires); but this appears to be his crowning tribute and final opinion.

67. 1815 "Poems." Rest of title --"from the presidency of the United States. --1809." Motto--"Praesenti tibi maturos largimur honores--HOR." Freneau's only known poem in praise of Jefferson, this item calls Hamilton his libeller and "the worst of men."

68. Helmsman John Pierce of the American sloop "Richard," on April 25, 1806, was killed by a shot from the marauding British warship "Leander," seeking prizes and the impressment of American sailors. The unprovoked killing aroused a national wave of indignation. President Jefferson issued a proclamation for the arrest of Captain Henry Whitby of the "Leander" and forbidding it the use of our ports.

69. Evidently Hamilton, who attacked Jefferson in several newspaper essays, under pseudonyms, in 1792.

70. Greek goddess of justice, who withdrew from the world when the Golden Age ended.

71. 1815 "Poems." Beneath the title: "Captain Dacres, August 19, 1812--by the Constitution, American frigate, capt. Hull." Subtitled "An Irregular Ode." This was an important victory, bolstering public morale--the first battle loss of an English frigate. "The Guerriere" was so badly damaged that she had to be blown up.

72. Female warrior, or amazon. [Freneau's note.]

73. The "Constitution" carried 44 guns to the "Guerriere's" 38.

74. A well known insect, when full grown, about two inches in length, and of the exact color of a green leaf. It is of the genus cicada, or grasshopper kind, inhabiting the green foliage of trees and singing such a note as "Caty-did" in the evening, towards autumn. [Freneau's note.] In the 1815 "Poems," and an example of Freneau at his best in a light humorous poem. Note the flexible stanza and the change in the last one.

75. 1815 "Poems." Beneath the title is "September 10, 1813." Probably written, like many other items in the 1815 edition, during the war, but not published until collected. Note the unusual rime scheme and the lilting effect.

76. 1815 "Poems." Title extension--"Who Died at New-York, on the 8th of June, 1809." Freneau always admired Paine, and as editor reprinted much of his work. Like Freneau, Jefferson, and Franklin, Paine was a deist; yet he was abominated as an atheist.

77. Probably a slap at the once popular poet Robert Treat Paine, Jr., whose original name was Thomas Paine.

78. From Leary's "Last Poems of Philip Freneau." Originally in the "True American" (Trenton, N.J.), June 8, 1822. This version from the "Fredonian" (New Brunswick, N.J.), July 18, 1822. About the Revolutionary Army Camp at Newburg, N.Y. Good example of Freneau's reminiscent, philosophical mood.

79.   Washington.

80.   From the "Last Poems." Originally in the "Fredonian," July 18, 1822. Another example of the strongly
philosophical bent of Freneau's mind in old age.

81.   "True American," Aug. 10, 1822. Signed "F." Un-
titled--title supplied. It concludes "3. Recollections of
Past Times and Events," an essay. Leary notes the essay
in "That Rascal Freneau's" bibliography, but not the poem.
But it is one of Freneau's better efforts, and highly interesting in its relation to Shakespeare and the characters of "The
Tempest." Here "Maranda" may have been Frances Bruere,
the governor's daughter, with whom Freneau may have been
in love. Freneau says in an introduction, "This little Poem
is founded on the "Tradition" that these islands, or some
one of them, was the scene of one of "Shakespear's" finest
and most fanciful "Plays" called "the Tempest." Dated
"Sept. 1778."

82.   A Sorceress, mother to Calyban, a deformed savage.
[Freneau's note.]

83.   From the "Last Poems." In the 'Fredonian," Sept. 19,
1822; in "True American" two days later with this added,
"Brig Washington, January 25, 1804." Leary omits a note
under the title--"Written on an outward "bound voyage from"
Charleston to the Canary Islands"-- and quotes around first
stanza, indicating that it was taken from another poem.

84.   "Fredonian," Jan. 30, 1823. Among poems in "Last
Poems" (Appendix) that Leary did not "hesitate to attribute"
to Freneau, though lacking "demonstrable proof." Leary
mostly assigned poems to Freneau that were signed by one
of the letters in FRENEAU. This poem is not so signed,
but in every other way appears to be his work. Apparently
Freneau's last Indian poem.

85.   Sir Edward Packenham. [Freneau's note.]

86.   As can be seen, this is less an Indian poem than a
denunciation of England, Freneau now having the advantage
of hindsight for his predictions. There was a persistent
rumor, not officially denied, that the Canadian British did
pay Indians for American scalps.

87.   Not noted by Leary, yet, by the initials signature,

evidently Freneau's work.   Signed "N.R." and dated "September 15," in the "True American" for Oct. 5, 1822. Illustrates Freneau's lip service to reason, though a highly emotional, and definitely romantic person.   Freneau used "N.R." with "Ode on a Remote Perspective View of Princeton College," in the "Fredonian," Oct. 31, 1822.   See "Last Poems," page 134.

88. Apparently Freneau's last published poem.   Signed "F.," " in the "True American," June 30, 1827.   Not noted by Leary.   Full title: "LINES, (Anniversary forty-ninth,) On the battle of Monmouth and subsequent retreat of Sir Henry Clinton--June 28th, 29th, & 30th, 1778." See P.M. Marsh, "Freneau's Last Published Poem," "American Literature," March, 1958.

89.   The old Hessian General.   [Freneau's note.]

90.   From "Last Poems" and ms. in N.Y. Public Library. Never published in Freneau's time.   The ms. bears the date "November 28, 1827;" so it is Freneau's last known poem.   Note the optimism, the absence of satire; melancholy and ridicule were once characteristic of his verse.

91.   End of Leary's quotation in both "That Rascal Freneau" and "Last Poems."   But there is more; the rest is from the manuscript.

92.   Most of Freneau's political verse is not worth reprinting.   Though Freneau republished many of his political poems in the collections, they were often toned down and made more nearly impersonal.   These quotations are from the original newspaper publications, and thus are more pertinent to the current controversies.

93.   "Freeman's Journal," Aug. 28, 1782.   Marked by Freneau as his in his personal file.   Untitled retort to "A Foe to Tyrants" in "Independent Gazetteer."   Also a defense of Joseph Reed, Whig leader in Philadelphia.   By "A Foe to Malice."   Later title, in the 1795 "Poems," "To Shylock Ap-Shenkin: (An abusive Court-Writer.)"

94.   An English satiric poet.

95.   "Freeman's Journal," Sept. 11, 1782.   Unsigned, but marked by Freneau as his in his personal file.   In 1795 "Poems" titled "To Shylock Ap-Shenkin." (on his Farewell.)

Good example of Freneau at his most vulgar level. By
now the original issue, Joseph Reed, had been forgotten in
a storm of vituperation. The poem is reminiscent of Freneau's satires of the Tories at college.

96. "National Gazette," July 28, 1792. Third in a series
of editorial odes begun as "Odes on Various Subjects," July
14, 1792. Beneath title: "(Note well-the following is to be
sung or said as occasion may require.)" Satire on John
Fenno, rival editor of the "Gazette of the United States,"
to whom it is addressed in the second, third, and fourth
stanzas. "Pomposo" refers to John Adams, whom Freneau
suspected of backing Fenno; it is taken from Churchill, the
English satiric poet, who thus named Samuel Johnson in his
poem "The Ghost."

97. "National Gazette," Aug. 4, 1792. "Ode IV" in the
series of editorial poems, "Odes on Various Subjects." In
the 1795 "Poems," a bit changed, as "To My Book," page
394. Here it is a defiance of Federalism, orthodoxy, and
aristocracy.

98. "The National Gazette is--the vehicle of party spleen
and opposition to the great principles of order, virtue, and
religion." Gaz. U. States. [Freneau's note.]
An article by "Detector" (probably Hamilton) in GUS for
July 28, 1792, had said, referring to NG, "It is only the
tool of a faction, and the prostituted vehicle of party spleen
and opposition to the great principles of order, virtue and
religion."

99. "Time Piece," Oct. 20, 1797. No. III of "The Book
of Odes," a series of twelve poems. Satire on the "royal"
Federalists and American aristocrats, their ways and ideas,
and the neglect of the veteran soldier. Motto above title:
    "Lodge where you must, drink small-beer where you can
    But eat no roast pig, if no federal man."

100. "Aurora," Feb. 20, 1801--probably by Freneau. His
last-of-a-series "Robert Slender" essay appeared in the
"Aurora" the day before, as news of Jefferson's election to
the presidency arrived in Philadelphia. The poem appears
in the editorial column, as if carrying a sort of editorial
message. Freneau probably helped Duane in various editorial duties.

SELECTIONS FROM THE PROSE

Account of the Island of Santa Cruz[1]

As I resided a considerable time on the island of
Santa Cruz, it is but natural I should say something concern-
ing it.   The appearance of this island, as you approach it
from the ocean, is inexpressibly beautiful.   The whole isle
is divided into square plantations cutting each other every
way at right angles.   The verdure of the canes, which are
of a most lively green, affords a pleasure to the eye which
is not so striking in any northern country.   Santa Cruz is
about 28 or 30 miles in length from east to west; and at
most is not more than 4 miles broad, and in general much
less: The latitude of this most delicious island is 17: 50 N.,
its longitude between 63 and 64 West--Although in a clear
sky you may see several other islands from this, yet there
are no soundings between, and when you are but a mile from
the shore the sea appears as blue and bottomless as any
part of the main ocean; but at the distance of half a mile
from the land and inwards you can see the bottom with the
greatest perspicuity, which is of a fine bright sand, and various kinds of fish sporting above it, some the most beautiful
that the eye ever beheld, particularly the angel fish, which
is streaked over with circles near half an inch in breadth,
which glow with all the lustre of the most brilliant diamond.

From this island as I mentioned before, you have a
prospect of several others in clear weather, viz. the east

end of Porto Rico, and in particular Cape Malapasco--2.
St. Thomas, St. John, Tortola, and the Virgin Gorda, these
being some of the Virgin islands--you may also see Bori-
quain, otherwise Crab Island, not far from Porto Rico. --
There are two towns on St. Cruz, Bassend or Bassin, so
called formerly by the French, i.e. Bason, in respect to
the harbour, and a smaller town at the west end called by
the Danes Frederickstadt; at the other is Christianstadt. [2]
Bassend is situate upon a pretty level spot at the foot of a
mountain close to the water side; it may contain 5 or 600
houses, some of them very handsome buildings of stone, but
in general of wood--The harbour is defended from the sea by
a continued reef of rocks upon which the sea breaks with a
continual roar. There are only two narrow passages through
this reef into the harbour, one for ships, the other for
sloops and vessels of a moderate draught of water. This
harbour will contain 2 or 300 sail of vessels, and is always
as smooth as a mill-pond, with excellent anchoring ground
in one, two, three, or four fathoms, but not much more, I
believe. Within the harbour is a small island containing
three or four acres of ground, upon which is built an elegant edifice for the use of the king's pilot, who keeps his
look-out from hence for all vessels that heave in sight. The
pilot is here a man of consequence, being ranked as a
king's officer, and keeps only one small sloop-rigged boat
with a deputy, who, with three or four Negroes, conducts
all the business: There is a town wharf here, but not
water enough for any thing but boats to come along side; all
the shipping are obliged to lie at anchor. Within a stone
throw of this wharf to the eastward stands a handsome fort,
called Christianswaern, which commands the whole harbour.
Bassend is twelve miles from the most eastwardly part of

the island, and as well as Frederickstadt, is situated upon the north side. From this town up to the east end the island is generally laid out in plantations of cotton, or else pasture lands for keeping mules, sheep, neat cattle and the like: But when you travel from Bassend down towards the west, the scene is inexpressibly charming, and even those that have no taste to admire the beauties of nature would at the view be forced to confess that the vales of Paradise were now displayed in their primaeval beauty. From the summits of the hills which rise with an easy ascent, you look forward as far as the eye can reach over the most enchanting plains and little vallies. On the right hand towards the north are high mountains bordering on the sea covered with wood. To use the words of Milton,

"Mountains on whose barren breast,
The labouring clouds do often rest."

Towards the south the land slopes away with a gentle descent towards the sea, which you have in sight all the way. The square plantations of sugar cane with their regular intervals; the tall cocoa-nut trees, with the planters' habitations surrounded with orange and other fruit trees; the exact straightness of the road and the charming mildness of the climate give one the idea of an inchanted island, or such as we read of in romance--Too much cannot be said of the happy climate of this and the neighbouring islands: The sky is ever serene and unclouded in comparison to that of the northern countries; there are never any heavy continued rains; the land is watered by gentle showers, and it is the rarest thing in the world to lose sight of the sun for two hours together after he is above the horizon. The days and nights are pretty equally divided, each never being much more or less than twelve hours. From ten o'clock in the morning till

171

four in the afternoon the heat is somewhat troublesome, but even then you are fanned with a brisk dry wind always from the eastward, which renders it at least tolerable. The evenings and nights are cool and refreshing. The moon and stars shine with an extraordinary brightness, owing I suppose to their reflection on the water of the ocean, which surrounds these happy lands. The town at the west end is but mean and ordinary, consisting of a fort, and perhaps 80 or 90 wooden houses. The harbour is nothing but an open road, where however ships lie in the utmost security at their moorings, the bottom being good for anchorage, and the wind always offshore. About two miles to the eastward of this town along the sea shore is the estate of capt. Hanson, into which the sea has formed a beautiful little bay, called Buttler's Bay, about 100 yards across; it has a sandy shore and an excellent landing, though all the rest of the shore is sharp craggy rocks. My agreeable residence at this place, for above two years off and on during the wars in America, renders the idea of it but too pleasing, and makes me feel much the same anxiety at a distance from it as Adam did after he was banished from the bowers of Eden.

The only disagreeable circumstance attending this island, which it has in common with the rest, is the cruel and detestable slavery of the Negroes. "If you have tears prepare to shed them now." A description of the slavery they endure would be too irksome and unpleasant to me; and to those who have not beheld it, would be incredible. Sufficient be it to say, that no class of mankind in the known world undergo so complete a servitude as the common Negroes in the West-Indies. It casts a shade over the native charms of the country; it blots out the beauties of the eternal spring which Providence has there ordained to reign, and

172

amidst all the profusion of bounties which nature has scattered, the brightness of heaven, the mildness of the air, and the luxuriancy of the vegetable kingdom, it leaves me melancholy and disconsolate, convinced that there is no pleasure in this world without its share of pain. And thus the earth, which, were it not for the lust of pride and dominion, might be an earthly paradise, is, by the ambition and overbearing nature of mankind, rendered an eternal scene of desolation, woe, and horror; the weak goes to the wall, while the strong prevails; and after our ambitious phrenzy has turned the world upside down, we are contented with a narrow spot, and leave our follies and cruelties to be acted over again, by every succeeding generation. But to return: the only natural failing I know of here is the hurricanes, which are storms of wind that blow with an inconceivable fury, and often carry away all before them. They are so much the more dangerous, as they do not blow steadily from one point, but often go round the compass in less than half an hour. There are melancholy remains in Santa Cruz of the havoc they made in 1772. There was also one on Sept. 7, 1776, while I was on the island. It exceeded any thing I had ever seen before, but however did not do much damage, the strongest of it not lasting above six hours. [3]

Some Account of the Capture of the Ship Aurora-- [4]

On the 25. of May in beating down Delaware Bay we unfortunately retook a small sloop from the Refugees loaded with Corn which hindered us from standing out to Sea that night whereby in all probability we should have avoided the Enemy which afterwards captured us--

Friday Morning May 26. The Air very smoky and the

Wind some what faintish, though it afterwards freshened up. the Wind was so that we stood off E. S. E. after putting the Pilot on board the small Sloop Handcuffing the Prisoners, and sending the Prize for Cape May. About three oclock in the afternoon we discovered three Sail bearing from us about E. N. E. they were not more than two $\overline{\text{5}}$ [sic] Leagues from us when we discovered them from the fore top, at the same time we could see them from the Quarter Deck, one appeared to be a pretty large Ship, the other two Brigs. we soon found they were in chase of us: we therefore tacked immediately, set all sail we could croud and stood back for the Bay. My advice to the officers was to stand for Egg Harbour or any part of the Jersey Shore and run the Ship on the flats rather than be taken. but this was disregarded. we continued to stand in till we saw Cape Henlopen the frigate in the mean time gaining on us apace, about Sun half an hour high we were abreast of the Cape close in when the Wind took us aback and immediately after we were becalmed, the tide of Ebb at the same time setting very strong out of the Bay so that we rather drifted out: our Design was if possible to get within Havekill Road round the Point and there run the Ship on shore but want of wind and the tide being against us hindered from putting this in Execution. we were now within 300 Yards of the Shore. the frigate in the mean time ran in the Bay to Leeward of us about one Quarter of a Mile (her Distance from the cape hindering it from becalming her as it did us) and began to bring her Cannon to bear upon us, her two Prizes hove to: one we knew to be the Brig Active Capt. Mesnard the other, as we afterwards learned, was a Salem Brig from the West Indies. the Frigate was the Iris returning from Charlestown to New York with the Express of the former's being taken. we

174

now began to fire on each other at the Distance of about
300 Yards. the frigate hulld us several times. one Shot
went betwixt Wind and Water which made the Ship leak
amazingly, making 24 Inches in 30 minutes; we found our
four Pounders but mere trifles against the frigate so we got
our nine Pounder, the only one we had, pointed from the
Cabbin windows with which we played upon the frigate for
above half an hour: at last a twelve Pown Shot came from
the Frigate and striking a parcel of Oars lashed upon the
Starboard Quarter broke them all in two and continuing its
destructive course struck Capt. Laboyteaux in the right
thigh which it mashed to atoms, tearing part of his belly
open at the same time with the Splinters from the Oars:
he fell from the Quarter Deck close by me and for some
time seemed very busily engaged in setting his Leg to
rights--He died about 11 the same night and next Day was
sewed up in his Hammock and sunk. every shot seemed
now to bring Ruin with it. A Lad named Steel had his Arm
broke and some others complained of Slight wounds. whereupon finding the frigate ready and in a proper Position to
give us a broad side we struck after having held a very unequal contest with her for above an Hour. During the En-
gagement 6 or 7 of our People hoisted out the Yard and
made their Escape to the Shore tho at the most imminent
hazard of their Lives, as we afterwards learned that they
pointed a 12 Pounder at her in the frigate and were unani-
mously for sinking her except Capt. Hawkes whose humanity
would not suffer the Piece to be fired which was loaded with
round, Grape Shot and Langrage. As soon as we struck,
one Squires with some Midshipmen came on board and took
Possession of the Vessell. Squires was Prize Master, they
had a few Sailors with them. I informed the Prize Master

I was a Passenger on board & supposed I might be excused from going on board the Frigate on that account. He then asked me several Questions where I was going &c I satisfied him in every thing and in return was assured I might stay on board our own Vessel till we got to New York where he said he did not doubt but I would get my Liberty immediately. this assurance hindered me from packing up any thing in my chest to carry with me on board the frigate but when the barge came the last time for Prisoners I was cruelly siezed [sic] and driven down the side, in the sight of Squires, into the Barge among the common Sailors and could not even get Liberty to go to my chest to put up any thing so that I had to go on board the frigate in my common Ship cloaths. all the Satisfaction I could get from Squires was that I should have my chest safe and sound next morning who swore that he had no one on board that would meddle with it.   with this Promise I was obliged to be contented and went on board the frigate, it being now dark. I was ranged along with the common Sailors on the Quarter Deck, tho I strongly remonstrated against it to the Master of Arms who seemed to have the Management of us. I represented to him that I was a Passenger, going on my Private business to the Islands and insisted, such usage was cruel inhuman and injust [sic]. He asked me if I was not a Colonist--I told I was an American--then said he You have no right to expect favours more than others.   the List of us was now taken and we were ordered down to be handcuffed two and two. I expected nothing else to have been my fate. when we got between Decks I thought I should have been suffocated with the heat. there were above one hundred Prisoners forward, the Stench of whom was almost intolerable-- So many melancholy Sights and dismal countenances made it

176

a pretty just Representation of the infernal Region. I
marched thro' a torrent of cursing and Blasphemy to my
station, viz. at the Blacksmiths Vice [sic] where the Miserable Prisoners were handcuffed two and two: at last it
came to my turn--Pray said I is it your custom to handcuff
Passengers, the Americans I am confident never use the
English so--Are you a Passenger said the Blacksmith? at
the same happening to look up I saw Hugh Ray looking
steadily at me, who immediately siezed [sic] my hand and
asked me how I did--Do you know him said Holmes, the
master at Arms? then you are free from Irons, come over
among the Gentlemen. this was an unexpected Diliverance
[sic] from such a cursed Disgrace which I hardly knew how
I should get clear of. after this I was used very well by
every body, the next Day I expected my chest on board
hourly, but had the mortification to learn nothing of it and
was suffered to come on deck but twice about 5 Minutes at
a time the whole day; the Day after Squires came on board
and I took that opportunity to renew my applications for my
chest, urging that I could not dress myself so as to appear
decent for want of it. He replied that I must wait till we
got to New York as it would be very inconvenient to hoist
the boats out while we were at Sea. --

Sunday afternoon we entered the Hook and Monday a-
bout 12 oclock Anchored in the North River--Wednesday all
the Prisoners wore sent from the Iris to the Prison Ship
except the Captain, Surgeons and Passengers. Thursday
Hulings the Deputy Commissary came on board And took us
on shore to the commissarys office--I should have observed
that before this Capt. Sutton told me that Capt. Hawkes had
promised him I should have my Liberty to go where I
pleased so that I had no expectation of going on board the

Prison ship--I was much surprized therefore at the Commissarys office when I was denied a Parole especially as Capt. Hawkes and all his officers had promised me repeatedly that at least I should be paroled to Long Island. but Capt. Sutton afterwards informed me that his Second Mate had taken upon to enroll me among those who were stationed at the Guns and he believed this would be some detriment to me--I answered him that as he had been exact enough with regard to my paying my Passage he should have seen that I was not put into any of their inrollments [sic] and added with a good deal of resentment that I wished I had never seen the ship. and immediately walked away. to return. at the Commissarys office as I said before Capt. Mesnard and myself were refused our Paroles. Hulings told me that the Americans so generally disregarded their Paroles that they must take care who they trusted for the future. I told him if he would suffer me to go with the Guard to a friend of mine in Town I would get them Security even to 10,000 £ that I would stay within the Limits of my Parole till I was exchanged--He refused letting me go any where only he said if I would write a Letter he would take it from me the next Day and deliver it to Mr. Gardner. I had writ Mr. Gardner from the Iris by a Person who I am sure delivered the Letter but I recieved [sic] no Answer. after this Viz on Thursday June 1. Capt. Mesnard and myself were conducted on board the Scorpion Prison Ship lying off the College in the North River. at Sundown we were ordered down between Decks to the Number of near 300 of us; the best Lodging I could procure this night was on a chest almost suffocated with the heat and Stench. I expected to die before Morning, but human Nature can bear more than one would at first suppose.   The want of bedding and the

178

loss of all my cloaths rendered me wretched indeed, besides
the uncertainty of being exchanged, for who could assure me
that I should not lye 6 or 8 Months in this horrid Prison?
One Gauzoo was Steward of the Ship one of the most brutal
of mankind who abused us continually. it is impossible for
words to give his character: it seemed as tho' he could not
give any of us a civil word upon the most indifferent occasion, when he was not cursing us he kept in his cabbin in
gloomy reserve, the most idle and detestable of mortals. --

June 3.   About Midnight the weather was very stormy
and the River uncommonly rough. the ship rolled considerably and the water gushed into some of the lower Ports
which made some of the Landsmen who slept in the Cable
tier imagine she was sinking. in a moment the Alarm became general, The ship is sinking, the ship is sinking! was
echoed fore and aft--I expected every minute to feel myself
afloat in the Birth [sic] where I lay but at the same time
considering it would be a folly to drown between Decks when
I might perhaps get on shore somehow jumped up and hurried towards the main Hatchway where was a multitude endeavouring to git [sic] out, the centries at the same time
beating on their Heads with their drawn Swords and Musquets without Mercy, imagining the whole to be a scheme of
an Insurrection--Some Lamented that they should never see
their Wives and children again, others begged by the Love
of God to be let upon Deck and they would bind themselves
Slaves forever on board a Man of war or any other Service
--there was an Italian Gunner who prayed to St Anthony most
heartily and desired the Prayers of his holy father the Pope
in case he should be drowned.   To such ridiculous distress
does the fear of Death reduce the Generality of mankind
when they apprehend it to be nigh. after some trouble we

179

got a light and examining the Pump-well, found the Ship dry
and tight. the Mistake of the water coming in the port was
soon detected and the same shut and Corked. indeed it was
a dismal night. But upon the next night we were doomed
to experience more real Dangers. about 35 of our People
formed a design of making their escape in which they were
favoured by a large Schooners accidentally driving alongside
of us: she was one that was destined for the expedition to
Elizabeth Town and anchored just a stern of us. We were
then suffered to continue upon Deck, if we so chose, till
Nine o clock. We were all below by that time except the
Insurgents. who rushed upon the centries and disarmed
them in a moment. one they tyed by his neck to the Quarter rails and carried off his Musquet with them (they were
all Hessians) the rest they drove down with their arms into
the Cabbin and rammed the Centry box down the companion
in such a manner that no one could get up or down. one
Murphy possessed himself of Gauzoos silver hilted Sword
and carried it off with him. when the Centries were all
Silent they manned the Ship's boat and boarded the Schooner
tho' the People on board attempted to keep them off with
Hand spikes, the Wind blowing fresh at South and the tide of
flood being made they hoisted Sail and were out of sight in
a few minutes. these Particulars we learned from some
who were on deck but were unsuccessful in getting into the
Boat. As soon as the Centries got Possession of the Vessel
again which they had no difficulty in doing as there was no
resistance made they posted themselves at each Hatchway
and most basely and cowardly fired fore and aft among us
Pistols and musquets for a full quarter of an hour without
Intermission. by the Mercy of God they touched but four,
one Mortally, another had his great Toe shot off, the other

180

two slightly.   I believe they meant by this Piece of cruelty
to atone to their Masters for their being disarmed in the
manner they were.   the next morning the Deputy Commissary came on board to muster the company to see who was
missing.   all that were found wounded were put in Irons
and ordered to lie upon Deck Exposed to the burning Sun:
about 4 o clock P. M. one of the poor fellows died who had
been wounded the night before: they then took him out of
Irons and sent him on shore and buried him.   after this no
usage seemed to them severe enough for us.   we had water
given us to drink that a Dog could scarcely relish, it was
thick and clammy and had a dismal Smell--they withdrew
our allowance of Rum and drove us down every night strictly
at Sunset where we suffered inexpressibly till 7 o clock in
the morning: the gratings being rarely opened before that
Time.   thus did I live with my miserable companions till
the 22d of June when finding myself taken with a fever I
procured my self to be put on the sick List and the same
day was sent with a Number of others to the Hunter Hospital Ship lying in the East River--Here was a new Scene
opened: The Hunter had been very newly put to the use of
a Hospital Ship.   she was miserably dirty and cluttered,
her decks leaked to such a Degree that the sick were de-
luged with every shower of Rain.   between Decks they lay
along struggling in the Agonies of Death, dying with putrid
and bilious Fevers, Lamenting their hard fate to die at such
a fatal Distance from their friends, others totally insensible
and yielding their last breath in the horrors of light headed
Phrenzy: I cannot forbear quoting a few Lines from Milton--

         ---------Immediately a Place
Before his Eyes appeard, sad, noisom, dark
A Lazar house it seemd: wherein were laid
Numbers of all diseasd: all Maladies

Of ghastly Spasms or racking torture, Qualmes
Of heart sick Agony, all fevr'ous kinds
Convulsions, Epilepsies, fierce Catarrhs
Intestine stone and ulcer, colic-Pangs
Demoniac Phrenzy, moping Melancholy
And moon struck madness, pining atrophy.
Marasmus and wide wasting Pestilence
Dropsies and Asthmas & joint racking Rheums
Dire was the tossing, deep the Groans! Despair
Tended the Sick &c--- Lib XI. 480   [Paradise Lost]

Our Allowance in the Hunter to those upon full Diet
was one Pound of Bread And one Pound of fresh Beef. per
Diem. to those upon half Diet one Pound of Bread And one
half Pound of Beef or Mutton per Diem: every other Day
we had a cask of Spruce Beer sent on board. our fresh
Beef was generally heads or shanks and would just answer
to make Soup. a German Doctor attended every morning at
8 o clock and administered such Remedies as were thought
proper. thus things went on, two or three dying every Day
who were carried on shore and buried in the Bank, till
three of our Crew who had got pretty hearty stole the Boat
one night and made their Escape. this occasioned new
Troubles. the Doctor refused to come on board and as he
rowed past us next morning to see somebody in the Jersey,
which lay near us, some of the sick calling to him for Blis-
ters, he told them to put Tar on their Backs which would
serve as well as any thing and so rowed away, However
after two or three Days his wrath was appeased and he
deigned to come on board again. by this time, being about
the 6th. or 7th. of July in spite of all the Remedies I had
taken I found my fever increasing, however it continued to
be of the Remittant kind, had it turned to putrid as it did
with numbers in all probability I must have died as well as
the rest. I had a large Blister put on my back which helped
me amazingly. at length on the 12th of July the Flag came

along side and cleared the Hospital Ship. but the Miseries
we endured in getting to Elizabeth Town were many: those
that were very bad, of which the Proportion was great,
naturally took possession of the hold--No Prisoner was allowed to go in the Cabbin so that I with 20 or 30 others
were obliged to sleep out all the night, which was uncommonly cold for the Season. about 10 next morning we arrived at Elizabeth Town Point were we were kept in the
burning Sun several Hours till the Commissary came to discharge us. I was afflicted with such Pains in my joints I
could scarcely walk and besides was weakened with a raging
fever, nevertheless I walked the two Miles to Elizabeth
Town--here I got a Passage in a waggon to within a Mile of
Crows Ferry, which I walked, got a passage over the Ferry and
walked on as far as Molly Buccleighs where I staid all night--
Next Morning having break fasted on some bread and Millk [sic]
I set homewards; when I came to Obadiah Corner I turned to the
Right and came home round about thro the Woods for fear of ter-
rifying the Neighbours with my Ghastly Looks had I gone thro'
Mount Pleasant--   July 14. 1780.

I forgot to mention that as soon as we came to New
York and things were a little adjusted Mr. Chatham our first
Mate went on board the Aurora and found his chest with
mine and several others broke open and every thing taken
out: so much for English honour and honesty.

N B. wrote a Letter by Hulings to Mr. Gardner but
received no answer. two Days before I was exchanged got
a Letter from Mr. Gardner offering me any thing I wanted
pretending he did not know what Ship I was in. I returned
him a Letter of thanks, letting him know that if he could
get me a Parole it would be the greatest favour he could do
me--The same Day Mr. Robins came along side in a small

boat with fish, offering me what Money I wanted: I begged him to lay the money out in Wine, Oranges and Lemons, and send them to me. He promised to be along side in three hours but I never saw him afterwards. in short I met with nothing but Disappointments among this People, and cannot sufficiently congratulate myself upon having got from among them--[5]

Sir--I take this opportunity to inform you that instead of arriving as I fondly promised myself at the fragrant Groves and delectable Plains of Santa Cruz to enjoy the fruits and flowers of that happy clime, I was unfortunately taken and confined on board a Prison Ship at New York, and afterwards in a Hospital Ship where the damnable Draughts of a German Doctor afforded far different feelings to my Stomach than the juice of the Orange or more nourishing millk [sic] of the Cocoa. [6]

The Pilgrim, No. I[7]

Having taken some pains for a considerable time, in my present retired situation, to obtain a sight of such public papers as are periodically printed on this continent, I could not but observe that there is scarcely one which ever presents the reader with any other essays than such as immediately relate to politics, and the transactions of the times, or local and domestic matters, arising from a variety of circumstances in the constant intercourse of men and business. Morality and refined sentiment are shamefully neglected, and that by a people who have a capacity for tasting and improving literature of every kind to the highest degree of excellence: In some small measure to remedy this defect, and to excite others to turn their thoughts to the noblest of all pursuits, the author of these reflections, observing your publication to be conducted upon very liberal principles, proposes to send you, weekly, a collection of such sentiments as may be worth the notice of men of taste. But considering that every one seems curious to know something of the private character and leading features of an author before they peruse his writings, I shall confine this paper to some account of my life, character and fortunes.

I drew my first breath upon the borders of Switzerland, on the south side and within view of that stupendous ridge of mountains known by the name of mount Jura. Here, in a solitary valley, my ancestors had for many ages taken up their abode, being, as I have been told, plain industrious people, who were acquainted with no other than a pastoral life, perhaps nearly resembling that so much celebrated in the early ages of innocence and simplicity. My father and mother dying, their little estate fell to me, their sole heir, and, for aught I know, might have continued in the family for ages to come, had not some unfortunate events rendered it necessary for the descendent of the famous William Tell (for from him I was derived in the maternal line) to remove from this inchanting scene of rural bliss and experience the vicissitudes of a very different kind of life.

Whether I possess any drops of the anti-monarchial blood of this my renowned ancestor, or be the cause what it may, I have an innate love for republics, and could never be long at ease in the vicinity of kings, emperors, kingdoms or aristocracies, which, in my opinion, are but different words for tyrants and tyranny. What simpletons, said I, are mankind to surrender so many of their just, necessary, and natural rights forever, into the hands of one or more men, which, unless they all prove just, wise, patriotic and benevolent (a miracle not to be expected) commonly renders the people the miserable slaves of ambition, avarice and oppression. -- But I must revert to the history of my misfortunes.

A beautiful grove of ancient oaks had grown and flourished for ages adjoining my progenitor's little estate, which he held in fee simple. His farm house was situated almost under the shade of these oaks; but unfortunately the soil they grew upon belonged to a person who now took it into his head to have the whole forest cut down, and the land cleared for the purposes of agriculture. As from my earliest days I had taken the most exquisite pleasure in rambling among these shades, I had conceived an unspeakable affection for this grove, and heard the sound of the fatal ax with the most lively emotions of grief; had a hamadryad resided in every tree I could not have been more afflicted. My endeavors to dissuade this person from his resolution were vain; he obstinately persisted therein, calling me at the same time a madman for repining at the advantage of an enlarged prospect. This led me to form a design of leaving that country altogether and retiring to some other part of the world: What soon after confirmed me in my purpose was the additional mortifying circumstance of his erecting a building within a stone throw of our old and venerable habitation, which he peopled with a sett of beings whose conversation and humour in every respect was diametrically opposite to my own. Labouring under so many accumulated misfortunes, (which, however, I confess, will appear imaginary to most men) I soon disposed of my inheritance and took my leave of it for ever. The charming solitude and privacy that used to reign through this delightful haunt was now vanished: it was no more impervious to the bleak north wind;

it was laid open to the view of the adjacent country, and to crowds of travellers--a misfortune, indeed! as peace and unobserved retirement were ever the darling objects of my soul: There is something in woods and solitudes congenial to my nature; palaces and towns are my abhorrence; and if any time I have found it necessary to reside in great cities, (as I once did at Moscow in Russia for more than three months) still by intervals I retired to the forests, and conversed with the simple genius of the wilderness, a conversation I infinitely prefer to that of heroes, kings, statesmen, and philosophers themselves.

At the time of the above mentioned unlucky event, I was in the twenty-second year of my age, and having, while a boy, read such books as I could procure, chiefly in the language of the high Germans, they insensibly inspired me with a desire to travel, and to learn something more of mankind than could be gathered from those helps only. I therefore set out upon my travels; but in about six months found my finances at so low an ebb, (as I had been rather too curious to see and learn every thing) that I was obliged to strike out some other scheme for prosecuting my design: A place of some respect soon offered in the train of a Neapolitan nobleman, who was then about to embark on a voyage to the holy land; but this person dying at Tripoli, I was once more reduced to my shifts. After some days' consideration I concluded to set up for a Pilgrim, and, as my thirst for seeing the world was rather increased than abated, determined to gratify my curiosity at the expence of the public of all nations. I quickly provided myself with a girdle, a scrip, a staff, and such other furniture as is indispensably necessary to men of this character, and continued my travels on a new plan. I have now spent upwards of thirty-two years in this way of life, which I can assure you has its hardships, discouragements, and difficulties as well as pleasures. It would be impertinent in this place to particularize my peregrinations; sufficient be it to say that I have more than once shivered with cold under the arctic circle, and seen the waves of the vast southern ocean from the Indian shore; that I have shed a tear upon the tomb of Virgil at Naples, and glowed with heat in the sultry climate of Brazil. It is now more than two years since I arrived on the North American coasts; the fame of these new republics was the chief cause of my coming hither; I had also an ardent desire to see those far-famed heroes who with their swords have established the purest freedom, in direct opposition to the most barefaced tyranny, much of the sad effects of which it has been my lot to behold and experience, in passing through the different countries of the universe. I have now fixed my place of residence in the midst of a very large forest, not many leagues from the city of Philadelphia, where it is likely I may continue for some months, at least 'till I set out again for the east, as I am obligated by a vow to visit the holy sepulchre at Jerusalem once more, if possible, before I go the way of all flesh. I am now in the fifty-sixth year of my age, a time of life at which every man of reflexion ought to have settled all his temporal concerns and prepared for those of eternity: But as long as I reside in this new world, the public may expect to receive, weekly, a piece of writing from my retirement, on political, moral, philosophical, and religious subjects. Were it not that I am engaged in composing a voluminous treatise on an abstruse subject, De Anima Mundi, these lucubrations should appear much oftener: I have been near thirty years in collecting materials for that extraordinary piece, and am the more bent upon finishing it, as I am convinced no person but myself is equal to the task.

The place of my abode, as I hinted before, is in a dismal solitude, exactly co-inciding with the melancholy cast of my mind. From its grotesque appearance and difficulty of access, I much question if this spot has been visited, perhaps for seven years past, by any human being excepting myself. I subsist wholly upon roots and vegetables, being convinced that Pythagoras was right when he forbade the use of animal flesh to his disciples. A kind providence has amply rewarded me for this piece of self-denial, as I have not had an hour's sickness these forty years past, am altogether devoid of ambition, and have never experienced the least inclination to shed the blood of any man, or injure him in the slightest degree. My benevolence is unbounded, and extends even to the meanest of the insect creation. The cavern I possess is formed by simple nature, which has huddled a mass of rocks into a chaos indeed, but inclosing among them a most delightful grotto, perfectly sheltered from the severity of the winter and the violent heats of the summer season, with a small stream of water hard by, that serves for drinking and other uses. I am sometimes, though rarely, seen in the city, where I find considerable amusement in observing the hurry of the great world, their eager concern and anxiety about matters that appear to them to be of the greatest moment, but to me are mere trifles and folly, as I find no relish for any of them. Although I am not at all fond of being known, yet I will so far gratify the curious as to inform them (if that will any way contribute to their satisfaction) that I am in stature considerably above the middle size, of a very swarthy complexion much injured by the weather; am of an atrabilarious habit; walk with a staff of black ebony (which I cut with my own hands on the Balagate mountains, in East India) and constantly wear a pair of temple spectacles, as my eyesight is none of the best. I speak most of the languages of the known world, ancient and modern, with fluency, as having conversed so frequently with the various nations thereof. There are, indeed, a few niceties in the dialect of the Kalmuck Tartars, which I am not so well acquainted with, as also several Chinese characters of less use, that I have been rather neglectful in studying, but I apprehend this to be a pardonable ignorance. If these particulars will at all gratify my readers, they are welcome to make the best of them;--but I hope an unseasonable curiosity will not prompt such persons to fall upon any romantic schemes of discovering my sylvan abode. The search would be fruitless, as chance alone, not industry, conducted me to it. But if, by some miracle, it should be discovered while I am the inhabitant, my vexation will be so great as to hasten me to set out on a pilgrimage to the east, which might otherwise have been deferred a considerable time. From my manner of life, I entitle this paper The Pilgrim; and, after begging the public's and your pardon for speaking so much in the first person, which could not well be avoided in the present number, I remain, sir,

America's Greatness[8]

When Nature first brought forth her infant the American world, to enjoy the blessings and vivifying influence of the new created sun, as if conscious of the injuries this part of her creation was to suffer in future ages, she seemed particularly industrious; she took especial care to place it in such a situation that many centuries, an immense number

of years, must elapse before it could possibly be discovered by the natives of the eastern continent. "Till more than five thousand years have passed away, said she, it shall be inaccessible to all except a few tribes of wandering Tartars, who from time to time will find their way hither by accident, literally the children of nature, wild as the winds and waves, and free as the animals that wander in the woody or watry waste: the magnet alone, continued she, can enable the polished people of the eastern regions to discover and ravage the delectable lands I have formed in the opposite hemisphere; but that fossil, the invaluable loadstone, I will carefully bury deep in the earth, unobserved its wonderful properties 'till destiny and overruling fate, whose decrees no one can obviate, to my grief disclose it to the eye of avarice, ambition and scrutinizing curiosity, and prompt a bold and daring Columbus to go in quest of those shores, which it will not be in my power any longer to conceal."
So spoke nature, the mother of all men and all things. In the mean time ages rolled away; the old world was peopled, unpeopled, and peopled again: Nations grew and flourished; they quarrelled, and fought, and made peace: The four great monarchies succeeded each other and fell again into decay, with their emperors, kings, and heroes, by far less durable than the lifeless marble columns which to this day mark the spot where their proudest capitals stood or their most famous battles were fought. These nations had their ages of politeness and barbarism, ignorance and science, misery and felicity; the follies of one age were acted over by another; and each retired in its turn to the receptacles of silence, solitude and darkness, to make room for succeeding generations.

But still America lay unknown with all her islands,

lakes, mountains, woods, plains, capacious harbours and extended shores. Here the fish sported in the waters undisturbed by hooks or nets, and the beasts of the forest enjoyed a secure repose. The poets of the eastern world were in the mean time amusing their iron-hearted co-temporaries with the fictions of a golden age; their fabulous Arcadias and Saturnian kingdoms, the ideas of which owed their birth to the magic power of fancy alone, as they were wholly ignorant that the happy scenes, the innocent people and pastoral ages they sung of were at that instant existing in another quarter of the globe, as yet unexplored and unknown. But, [sic]

In process of time, as nature had foreseen, this immense continent was at length raised from its long night of obscurity to the view of astonished nations: the inhabitants, like the country, seemed a new race of mortals; they also gazed at the Europeans as a species of men differing in all respects from themselves, and in respect to power and abilities, beings of a superior nature.

As the Europeans had the means, they of course conceived they had the right to extirpate the innocent natives, or drive them from the sea coasts to the interior parts of the country: The most specious pretext for this procedure seems to have been that the aborigines of America did not exert themselves sufficiently to cultivate and improve the lands nature had so liberally bestowed upon them; they were content with the productions of the simple genius of the earth, and therefore were scarcely to be considered, according to these casuists, as lawful proprietors of the immense territories that were now discovered.

Full of this idea the Europeans flocked over and examined the soil and productions of this new found region--

the best lands in North America were observed to lie in a
temperate climate, and the new comers soon found it to
their interest to cultivate a soil that promised so much to
the hand of industry. This roused the jealousy of the natives, who, unwilling to leave their pleasant abodes in the
neighbourhood of the sea, made many attempts (and sometimes not unsuccessfully) to annihilate these intruding
strangers; but as the various divisions of the old world were
at that time over-stocked with inhabitants, who constantly
waged bloody wars with each other, it became absolutely
necessary that many should emigrate. Providence gave permission to the arm of tyranny to drive thousands from their
native lands, and many in hopes of lucre became voluntary
exiles. Among the rest Britain seemed very busy in ban-
ishing and expelling her subjects to this remote region, who
chose the northern coast, as knowing of no other asylum
except the grave, from the scourge of oppression. These,
with a mixture of adventurers from various nations, at
length humbled the savage tribes, and by the force of industry rendered a large proportion of this new country rich and
flourishing. Britain soon cast a greedy eye upon the hard
earned possessions of this exiled race; she claimed them as
subjects, took them under her protection, but said in her
heart, "They shall hereafter be my slaves." The children
of the first emigrants immediately forgot the wrongs of their
fore-fathers and united themselves to her, not as yet aware
of her base designs:--but nature disregarded the connection,
and whispering in the ear of reason, said, "The union cannot be lasting."--Her words have proved true; the people of
the present age have seen the unnatural bonds in a moment
dissolved, the union broken, and the connexion at an end.
Tell me, ye patrons for the dependence of these states upon

Britain, ye who assert that their happiness, their interest, and their glory is bound up in such a dependence, would you not esteem him a madman who should attempt, amidst the rage of contending winds and waves, to bind two husky ships together with a thread of silk, for their mutual safety? Just as reasonable is it to suppose that America and Britain can be happily united under one sovereign.

What a spectacle of derision do the infatuated Britons now exhibit to the world, in seriously attempting to subjugate a country to which nature never gave them a shadow of right, and whose extent alone is a standing obstacle to their success! A little island situated on the extremities of the ocean, incumbered with rugged mountains, barren heaths, and useless, broken lands, a spot whose strength is merely artificial, sending out on impracticable conquests her fleets and armies, the flower of her youth and her ablest commanders, who, the moment they come within the vortex, the sphere of attraction of this huge, unwieldy body, the American world, are immediately swallowed up like straws in a whirlpool, and irrecoverably lost! What a nation of numerous and ingenious mechanics and manufacturers were the English only ten years ago! with the fleeces of their sheep they warmed the inhabitants of either frigid zone; the fine linens of that island were in high estimation in every clime; but to prosecute their mad schemes of reducing to unconditional obedience, or desolating a country naturally invincible, they could have taken the weaver from the loom, and the cobler from his stall; the back of the pedlar is released from its burden; and he who of yore was honestly occupied in fitting garments to the shoulders of his brethren, fancying himself on a sudden a Cortez or an Alexander in search of glory, in quest of never fading laurels, and for the support of his idol, royalty, traverses the wide extended ocean, and leads to imaginary conquests in the trans-Atlantic world![9]

It is not easy to conceive what will be the greatness and importance of North America in a century or two to come, if the present fabric of nature is upheld, and the people retain those bold and manly sentiments of freedom which actuate them at this day. Agriculture, the basis of a nation's greatness, will here probably be raised to its pinnacle of perfection, and its attendant, commerce, will so agreeably and usefully employ mankind that wars will be forgotten; nations, by a free intercourse with this vast and fertile continent, will again become brothers, and no longer treat each other as savages and monsters. The iron generations will verge to decay, and those days of felicity advance, which are so beautifully described by the prophetic sages of ancient times.

My friend the clergyman informs me that after passing a ridge of lofty mountains lying on the western frontiers of these republics, a new region opens, of inexpressible beauty and fertility. The lands are there of a quality far superior to those situated in the neighbourhood of the sea coast; the trees of the forest are stately and tall, the meadows and pastures spacious, supporting vast herds of the native animals of the country, which own no master, nor expect their sustenance from the hands of men. The climate, he says, is moderate and agreeable; there the rivers no longer bend their course eastward to the Atlantic, but inclining to the west and south, and moving with a gentle current through the channels that nature has opened, fall at length into that grand repository of a thousand streams, the far-famed Mississippi, who from a source unknown collecting his remotest

waters, rolls forward through the frozen regions of the
north, and stretching his extended arms to the east and
west, embraces those savage groves as yet uninvestigated
by the traveller, unsung by the poet, or unmeasured by the
chain of the geometrician; till, uniting with the Ohio and
turning due south, receiving afterwards the Missori and a
hundred others, this prince of rivers, in comparison of
whom a Nile is but a Rivulet and the Danube a mere ditch,
hurries with his immense flood of waters to the Mexican
Sea, laving the shores of many fertile countries in his passage, inhabited by savage nations as yet almost unknown,
and without a name.

It is a standing rule in philosophy that nature does
nothing in vain; but if this new world was not to become at
some time or another the receptacle of numerous civilized
nations from one extremity to the other, for what visible
purpose could she have formed those vast lakes in the bosom of her infant empire, which surprize and astonish the
traveller, who, leaving the salt sea behind him to the east,
finds new oceans of a prodigious extent in those tracts
where fancy would have surmised nothing but endless hills,
inhospitable wilds and dreary forests existed. These lakes
uniting with each other, and lastly with the ocean toward the
north east, approaching also very near, by the west, to
several of the navigable branches of the Mississippi, form
an easy communication through a long tract of country, the
intercourse between the various parts of which would in future times, for the purposes of commerce at least, be extremely difficult and laborious, were it not for this continu-
ation of waters that for ages have been waiting to bear the
barque of traffic, urged forward by the sail or the stroke of
the springy oar; as the soil bordering thereon has no less

impatiently expected the operations of the industrious plough.

During a very considerable part of the year the southwest wind constantly blows on this serpentine river, the
Ohio; and even at other times the current of air is more
prevalent in that direction than any other--which, being directly opposed to the course of the stream, moving at the
rate of one mile hourly, is it not evident that providence, or
nature if you please, has so ordered this matter that the
commercial vessels hereafter sailing northward thereon may
have favourable gales to make an answerable progress against
a current that is still contrary and the same, and that those
bound to the south may have the assistance of the ebbing
stream to combat the adverse winds with more advantage?

It would carry me far beyond the bounds of a news
paper essay to point out every particular indicating the future importance of this new country; it is really astonishing,
as I intimated before, that a nation endued with reason, if
they would exercise that gift, should at this day entertain a
serious thought of reducing by force of arms this immense
continent to their absolute sway, a continent lying in another
hemisphere, abounding with a hardy and active race of people,
producing every thing within itself proper for its own maintenance and defence, a continent extending thro' such a number of degrees of latitude and longitude, from the limits of
the torrid zone, the circle of the northern tropic, to those
frozen streams and icy mountains where, chilled with the extreme rigours of perpetual winter, nature seems to have
lost her vegetative powers, and where a few of the human
race, the natives of the polar regions, that are found in
those unjoyous climes, bear so little resemblance in the
features of the mind to what the civilized world calls a man,
that they scarcely deserve the name.

The Absurdities of Fashion[10]

I have found considerable diversion for some time
past in attending to the various opinions of certain curious
idle people in regard to the Pilgrim. My sudden disap-
pearance has given rise to many dismal conjectures con-
cerning my personal safety among that set of readers who
deigned to cast an eye upon my last winter's lucubrations.
Some did not hesitate to assert that I had drowned myself in
the great river that flows by the walls of this city, in a fit
of spleen or melancholy; others, that I had packed up and
gone off to the east in a pet at the squabbling politicians.
One person declared that my evil stars had conducted me
into the bloody clutches of Mr. Simple, who formerly sent
me a challenge, and had now found an opportunity of gratifying his malice by putting me to death. Another concluded
that I had retreated from the noise and vanity of the world
to my rural recess, enjoying once more the society of the
parson, the rustic and my dog.

They were all mistaken--I am neither descended to
the invisible mansions of departed men, nor sailed for the
east, nor retired to my subterranean abode. When I wrote
my last number I perceived a storm gathering on the political horizon, and the atmosphere of the Freeman's Journal
charged with abundance of dark vapours and gross humors
portending something uncommonly terrible. I saw the com-
batants marching out, armed cap-a-pee, to the conflict; but
as I never much esteemed the society of disputants, even in
logic, I slipped from these angry writers, and, as every
prudent man should do in similar circumstances, remained
from that day to this merely a spectator of the fray. As at
the present there is something like a calm, though, not im-

probably, of that delusory kind which are observed in the Indian Ocean to be the prelude of a more violent tempest; still, during the short interval I shall now and then take up the pen, if not for instruction, at least for the amusement of the benevolent few, and the rather as I am embarrassed with epistles sent me from all parts, which would long since, I suppose, have seen the light through some other channel, had they not been moulded in such a manner as only to suit the paper called the PILGRIM. The following was received some weeks ago from an unknown correspondent:

Mr. PILGRIM,

If you have any regard for the feelings of your sex, do pray bear public testimony against the wanton display of female charms. I think it must be wrong for ladies to gratify the avaritious thirst of their vanity at such a painful expence to our feelings. And if the virgins cannot be reclaimed, pray let the married ladies, for their own sakes, (to say nothing of the injury they do their husbands) be dissuaded from the dangerous practice of exposing their naked bosoms to every licentious eye. If your publications should finally fail of effecting a reformation, I beg leave to suggest, as the dernier resort, that it be the universal custom for women of all degrees to disclose the whole bosom, that so those charms, which while partially concealed are so fatal to the eye of sensibility, may, by common view, like the arms and face, become incapable of kindling the fire of love.   MAN OF FEELING.

Leaving my readers to make what reflexions they see fit upon the foregoing letter, I shall go on to observe that the moralists and sentimentalists of all ages have never failed to declaim with an arrogant severity and pedantic acrimony against the reigning modes and fashions of the times they lived in; even those the most perfectly agreeable to reason, and suiting every purpose, useful as well as ornamental: We should therefore be cautious in suffering our judgments, relative to the Beau Monde, to be directed or biassed by the sentiments, representations or invectives of such authors, and only approve or disapprove of the fashions and customs of the day as far as a regard to simplicity and conveniency will justify us.

For my own part, as a friend to mankind, I would rather see the fashions carried to an agreeable extravagance on the female side of the question than that affectation of being too prudishly plain. Young ladies that take no pains to adorn and set off their persons to the best advantage may be aptly compared to spiders that would expect to catch flies without first being at the pains of spinning a web to intercept and hold them in captivity. How vast is that number of females who at this instant would have been experiencing all the inconveniences of the vestal life, had they not in their brighter days called in the aid of the artificial to their natural charms!--and thereby captivated the heart of the simple inamorato, (the rays from whose eyes are generally reflected back convergingly from the first surface) and who had doubtless passed heedless by, and neglected the natural, had it not been for the dazzling splendor of those adventitious ornaments, the plumy head dress, with all its gay streamers, towers and battlements, the rustling silk with its flounces and furbelows, the diminutive foot shrouded in damask, or the neck veiled by the half concealing lawn.

Several of the Pagan tribes in the East Indies, that hold to the opinion of females having no souls, at least not of so dignified a nature as those of men, enjoin their women, nevertheless, under severe penalties, to adorn their persons in the most gorgeous and fantastic attire, and such as in the eye of a European would be thought romantically extravagant; "for, say they, Nature, well knowing that the life of <u>man</u> would be inevitably subjected to care and pain, disappointment, melancholy, poverty and a thousand other evils and misfortunes, took care to provide for the alleviation of those ills in some little degree by bestowing on all her visible works in the firmament and on earth a splendid and agreeable aspect, as well by day as by night.--The earth she clothed in a livery of green, the most pleasing colour of all others to the eye; she also caused an endless variety of plants and flowers to spring from the fertile bosom of the ground, to strike and pleasure out senses with their delectable odours and gaudy appearances;--and it is our own faults if we, as deputies of nature, do not compel our ladies to deck themselves off as agreeably and alluringly as possible, to dissipate and deceive those odious cares and pains that are so intimately connected with the life and lot of man."

But I will by no means allow that a man is as excusable as a woman in bestowing the same attention to dress and ornament--What, shall that sex who were designed by nature for all that is great and noble entertain so mean an opinion of themselves as to imagine they cannot gain the affections of the fair any other way than by those very methods that a lass of eighteen takes to render herself amiable in the eyes of men?--From what I have seen and observed in the different countries of the world through which I have travelled in my time, I have drawn this observation, that there is no class or denomination of men more universally and sincerely despised among women than those called Beaus. The reason lies not deep--Nay, it is obvious--if the Beau endeavours to render his whole external appearance, manner, looks, person and demeanour as much as possible effeminate, how can he expect to conciliate the real regard of any sensible individual of that sex which nature designed should esteem not a woman but a man?

Although I reside in the northern suburbs of this city, where people are in general more remarkable for their active industry, plainness and frugality than those toward the center, yet still my eyes are frequently offended with this hermaphrodite species of mortals, the beaus, several of whom, I know not for what reason, have unfortunately for my peace taken up their residence in this quarter. There is one in particular who is at times very troublesome to me, a little man with long thin legs, which may be aptly compared, when covered by his white silk stockings, to the perforated tubes of the earthen pipes in use among smokers of tobacco. As his residence is not far distant from mine, he some time ago introduced himself to me, in consideration of his understanding the art of logic; and although I am now well convinced he is but a mere pretender, yet I could easily bear with his ignorance, were it not that he is continually in love with one glittering object or another, and teazing me with long narratives of the cruelties of the unrelenting fair, and his unsuccessful suits; in short, I have not been able to clear my hands of him as yet, and begin to think I never shall, unless I remove to the southern extremity of the town, or return to my solitary abode in the wilderness.

This person, if he does not deceive me, is attended twice a day regularly by his barber, who receives fifty pounds a year to keep an eye upon his hair and heard, and see that they are constantly in good order, though, indeed, I believe the friseur will in a short time be excused from

202

bestowing any pains upon the latter, as it is mostly plucked out by the roots with small pincers, so that the whole surface of his physiognamy is at this moment nearly as smooth as the visage of a Brazil Indian.

How variable are the fashions!--What modes and counter modes have mankind been witnesses to since the days of Adam! How should we be surprised could we throw down the partition that six thousand years have raised, and see an antediluvian beau with his beard curled and powdered as modishly as the side locks now a days, or perhaps swaddled in a black bag of a quadrangular form, or cued with a ribband according to art!--There have been fops in all ages, and will be to the last.

Custom prevents the greatest absurdities from appearing ridiculous--The polite European, or the civilized American, loaths and laughs at the Hottentot because he covers his head with a mass composed of hogs' lard and cow dung, and yet the want of this filthy cap would render the African odious in the sight of his mistress!

If custom or constant familiarity does not render all things intirely pleasing to us, it at least makes us indifferent toward them, in our liking or dislike--The people of Cayenne, a country on the main of South America, permit a large species of serpents to infest their houses with impunity; nay, they are so little dreaded as to be suffered to come regularly at meal times, and eat out of a plate, like a cat or any other domestic animal, and sometimes even from the delicate hand of the mistress of the house--and yet the sight of such a guest would throw a Philadelphia lady into a swoon --so great a power has habit over the human mind; and perhaps when we come to examine matters accurately, and see them as they really are, a European or an American fopling is not a much less filthy or ridiculous object with his hair and coat plaistered, sprinkled and bedaubed over with powder and pomatum, than the native of the southern extremity of Africa, with the beforementioned curious head dress, so detested and abhorred by the people of other countries.

A Midnight Soliloquy in the Market House of Philadelphia[11]

How solitary is the place that was but a few hours ago thronged with people!--Great residence of the dead, how empty are thy shambles, to which in the course of the day past flocked an innumerable host of flesh eaters of all sizes, shapes, principles and complexions!--

Have mankind an innate dread of ghosts and apparitions? Cannot they walk over a grave yard in the dusk of the evening, but sticks and stones must be animated into being, and transformed into images from another world; and shall not I at this late hour behold with my mind's eye some few resemblances of the continual succession of dead bodies that have been brought hither daily for so many years and seasons past?--Yes--fancy, potent fancy obtrudes upon my view the ghosts of myriads slain.--Lo! the horned oxen, the tender lamb "that lick'd the hand just rais'd to cut its throat," the sucking calf, the full grown sheep, the winged apparitions of domestic poultry, and lastly the poor mute fishes of several species, many of whom resigned their lives on these flinty pavements, gasping and flouncing in an element not very dissimilar from, but yet by no means perfectly their own.

The clock strikes TWELVE!--the mingled spectres vanish from my view, and I am once more left to my meditations.

Where are those vast, those busy crowds that jostled to and fro' between these frequent columns, and beneath this vaulted roof!--How lonely have they left this paved walk, this receptacle of death, exposed to the unhealthy blasts of autumn--Join those pillars by an intermediate wall, shut up the entrances that front the east and west, and you have a perfect view of the sepulchres of the ancient Egyptian kings, faintly illumined by the glimmering beams of an untrimmed lamp--such too is the interior of the grand pyramid, where even the bones of the mighty monarch that raised it, (such is the caprice of fortune) were not suffered to repose.

But with all thy horrors, O repository of ruin, thou art the only visible cause of our activity. Deprived of thy diurnal supplies, all flesh would languish and return to native dust--deprived of these, the courage of the soldier drops, the voice of the orator fails, beauty withers, industry dies--and wit, immortal wit is constrained to mingle with the fumes of dullness, the mother of repose!

Alas! what deep silence pervades this noted rendezvous of busy mortals! No sound assails my ears but that of the lonely watchman, travelling his weary round, and preaching to a sleepy, unheeding, inattentive world, that the hour is past, which can never return--no--not a moment of it to be re-purchased by the mines of Mexico, the diamonds of Brazil, or all the wealth that might be collected from the prolific bowels of a hundred Indies!

Hark!--what step is that advancing toward me!--It is a man, or the resemblance of one--he groans--he is sick--he reclines his head, as it were in anguish, upon one of the stalls--he vomits up a mass of mingled liquors and half digested viands--He is just returning from a midnight debauch

205

--his senses are stupefied--his reason has forsaken him--
he talks nonsense and utters wild incoherent sentences--Ah,
like a swine wounded by a butcher's knife, down he falls into the midst of the loathsome fluid disgorged from his filthy
stomach--he makes a feeble effort to rise, but finds it im-
possible--his face and nose are battered and bloody--and,
trust me, a truer beast was never conveyed hither in a
cart, nor cut into quarters, and impaled upon those iron
hooks that were designed to support the weight.

The market house, like the grave, is a place of perfect equality. None think themselves too mighty to be seen
here--nor are there any so mean as to be excluded. Here
you may see (at the proper hour) the whig and the tory--the
Churchman and the Quaker--the Methodist and the Presby-
terian--the moderate man and the violent--the timorous and
the brave--the modest and impudent--the chaste and the
lewd--the philosopher and the simpleton--the blooming lass
of fifteen and the withered matron of sixty--the man worth
two pence and he of a hundred thousand pounds--the huxter
with a paper of pins and the merchant who deals in the produce of both the Indies--the silly politician who has schemed
and written himself blind for the service of his country and
the author who wears a fine coat, and is paid to profusion
for writing nothing at all!   W. H.

A Discourse on Esquires[12]

There is nothing which in my opinion renders a man
more truly little and contemptible, or manifests more limited understanding than a habit of peevish churlishness and
moroseness of disposition, which, however it may be disgust-
ful or injurious to others, in its effects generally renders
the unhappy possessor of such a temper, whether natural or

acquired, a plague and a torment to himself.

Among the lower orders of mankind, a person cursed with this hateful disposition is constantly avoided and execrated even by those of a congenial soul. Hence, if he is of such a profession or trade as renders him dependent upon the good will and opinion of others, he is obliged out of a principle of policy to turn hypocrite and conceal the venom that rankles in his heart, or vent it upon such objects as are incapable of revenging an insult, or retorting an affront. I once knew a mechanic who, not thinking it proper for his own interest to let his unhappy and malevolent disposition be universally known, used to give vent to it by locking up his wife or his dog, and kicking them unmercifully whenever he received an affront abroad, either real or imaginary, from a person whom he dared not to insult or treat with abuse or scurrility.

One might, however, pardon a great deal in these poor people, were their case rightly considered--these lower orders of mankind commonly labour under real necessities and are harassed with great difficulties in rubbing through the world, and we must allow that all men cannot be supposed to have leisure, or resolution, or philosophy to conquer natural bad temper and ill habits.

But of all insolence, that of men in high office is most intolerable; these for the most part seem to entertain a conceit that a high station, or an office of public employ places them beyond the obligations of common civility to a humble, a deserving or perhaps an injured applicant who at the same time asks for nothing but what is his own. The grandeur and the necessary consequence of these men gives them an imaginary patent to be surly and morose: It is certain that a multiplicity of business, especially when difficult and intricate, has a tendency to sour the temper, and this might serve as an excuse for an ordinary fellow who had been raised to something great from a low condition, but for a man of genius and ability, or even a man of real business to be eternally flustered and fretful at every interruption shews a little contracted mind indeed. The abilities of some men are so very narrow that it is impossible for them to turn their attention to more than one thing in the course of a day or week, but these men are not fit for posts of consequence. I know a cobler who cannot make but a shoe, a clergyman who can write nothing but sermons, and a lawyer who can speak on no other subjects but such as are handled in courts of justice.

For my own part I have no connexions with great men, and have seen enough of the world to be convinced that it is best for all whose situation will permit, to stand off at a proper and a cautious distance from them, especially from those who may be called the imaginary great, who of all others are the most detestable. I have not to complain of mortifications or affronts received from them, but I have seen some whose fortune in life has compelled them to dangle after these irritable geniuses, who have been obliged to pocket affronts that would wound a man of sentiment and feeling to the inmost recesses of the heart.

This surliness of disposition, strange as it may seem, is more or less constantly attached to people in office, however insignificant that office may be. When I walk the streets of this city, where bye the bye I am a mere stranger, I can tell who are people in authority, merely by the assumed significant superiority of countenance, visible as the nose on their faces--in these often, too often, I plainly discern the soul of a mendicant begging me for some token of respect, which sometimes out of pity to their frailty I condescend to bestow.

Some time since, in travelling through a distant part of the country, I was a good deal diverted with a character answering to the above description, one who had lately been created a justice of the peace, and being very ignorant of the world had no less ideas of his own importance and power than Caesar, Alexander or Xerxes had in their day of theirs.

Through mere neglect I had set out from home without the proper permit for travelling any considerable distance, and of consequence had not proceeded more than sixty or seventy miles on my journey when I found myself stopped by some country men, who informed me I must go to the squire along with them and give an account of myself--In these people's faces I immediately discerned a consciousness of authority. The law of the state had put them into power for a moment, they were all officers and great men, had my person in their power, and thus all I had to do was to go quietly and slowly along with them to the aforesaid justice.

By way of digression I would observe that this consciousness of superiority from accidental superior circumstances is not restrained to the human species. A stately coach horse, high fed, duly currycombed, adorned from head to tail with his spangled furniture, his head full of instructions of the groom, and perhaps taken more care of than his master's children, carries himself with a prouder air, looks fiercer, and kicks at you with much more virulence than the humble, patient, hard faring animal that travels with his squalid attire in a drayman's cart through the dirt and mire of the ill cleaned streets of this city.

But to return (if I may use a pulpit phrase.)

As I travelled on with the before mentioned people under whose guidance I now was, I was entertained by them with terrifying accounts of the severity and crabbedness of justice Goslin, (that was his name) before whom and at whose judgment seat I, a miserable culprit, in their opinion, was shortly to appear. By their accounts, the sternness of squire Goslin's visage was such, and such the terrifying keenness of his eye, that many people had been scared into compunction and a confession of their guilt and had suffered accordingly, who otherwise might have defied the world, the devil and all his angels to make any thing appear against them.

At last after many hours' riding, the fatal dome appeared, in which I was to be called to account before this redoubtable personage: it was a wooden building with a white washed chimney top running out of the roof, and of such a form that it is possible the architect might have been inwardly composing soliloquies on the bowl of a tobacco pipe at the time he was constructing it. When we came to the door (which my conductors called the outer court) madam Goslin, the old squire's lady, as I afterwards found her to be, first made her appearance, and instantly retreated, calling out there was a prisoner in the yard. This personage was an old woman apparently about sixty years of age, and the moment I saw her, I saw she had something official in her phiz. --This is an officer in petticoats, said I, but where is the officer in breeches?--It seems he was too great a man to appear at the door in person, and therefore kept within till he was properly accoutred for receiving me. The guard had now ordered me into the kitchen, and while there I heard a hoarse and angry voice call for his law book, staff, spectacles and elbow chair. There were several servants in this apartment, all of whom peeped at me with a look of commiseration, but at the same time there was something in the cast of their eyes that betokened them to be slaves of a man in power; but what do I talk?-- in the face of the very house dog there were some lineaments of magistracy.

The same voice which had called out so magisterially for the law book, staff, spectacles and elbow chair now bawled out a second time, "Let the prisoner be brought before me!" A narrow door, which discovered the entrance of a dark passage, was then thrown open, and I advanced through it with composure and respect toward the great man in the chair--Having approached within two yards of him, "Sirrah, said he, come not too near my person, but stand off at a proper distance that thou mayst be fairly adjudged and convicted for thy various and manifold crimes."

My God! thought I, does the man accuse me of crimes before he has heard a word of my case, and when he knows as little of me as he does of the Age of the Janizaries at Constantinople!--But I will describe this man of consequence. He was a little squat, smoky figure in a long banyan and buckskin jacket, and according to my conceptions answered nearly to the description of the wooden household gods, spoken so much of in the Roman poets. His wig, instead of being grey, had become of a dull yellow with extreme age; his breeches were of black dyed leather, and might have once belonged to a more respectable animal. His hose--but I could not see the hose, because his legs were covered by a pair of large boots, which it is by no means impossible might have served the whole purpose of the hose.

211

After he had examined and cross examined me, although I gave as good an account of myself as it was possible for one in similar circumstances to do, I was ordered in a tone of decisive authority to proceed on to the county jail with the escort, as at least a person of doubtful character. Finding it needless to say any thing more in my own defence, to a person who was determined at any rate to make me feel the effects of his superiority, I mounted my horse and rode off, accompanied by the guard, to one of whom the squire delivered a paper he called a mittymus. When we came to the village in which the jail was situated, I had the good fortune to fall in with a gentleman of my acquaintance, a resident in that part of the country, who became security for me, and I was suffered to proceed on my journey.

On my return, some weeks after, in the midst of a thick wood, I met the good justice Goslin travelling on foot. I immediately perceived a strange alteration in his whole countenance--the consequential grimace was done away--he looked altogether like a man out of office; but amidst his confusion he made a shift to tell me that he had been robbed a little before, by some highwaymen, of the horse he rode on and what money he had in his pocket, and concluded with beseeching me, as he was no less than seven miles from home, to suffer him to get up behind me. If you will condescend to ride on the crupper, said I, you are welcome; but I am sure a man of your importance cannot submit to that. He felt the force of the reply, and slunk away silent and ashamed into the wood.

Let no man affront another wantonly, for he knows not how soon he may stand in need of the assistance of the injured; and remember that the various inequalities that chance

212

has made amongst men ought not to make us forget that we are brothers. G.

The Editor to the Reader[13]

Courteous Reader,

The following poem was found amongst the papers of my lately departed and very valuable friend, Robert Slender. Some short time previous to his last illness he one day called me to his bed-side, and among other serious and edifying discourse, observed to me that he had ever been so entirely convinced of the vanity and folly of authorship, that he had hitherto published little or nothing of his numerous writings himself, but begged that if any of his intimate friends should discover any thing amongst them after his decease, which should be, in their opinion, at all worthy of the public notice, they would not fail to communicate it in due time and season.

I answered that I, for my own part, should be ever ready on all occasions to do every thing that lay in my power to oblige an old friend, and do honour to his memory, but at the same time wished to know why the fate of his works was so particularly impressed on his imagination at this time?

He then sighed heavily, and soon after intimated to me that he was well aware of the malice of critics, the ignorance of the generality of readers, and the small degree of attention the world pays to any production whatever that is not at least two thousand years old, and imported upwards of one thousand leagues: "This, however, (continued he) ought to be matter of small concern to men in my situation, be they weavers or authors; I find the lamp of life is burning low within me, the flame will soon be in the socket, and

213

then farewell to you, Robert Slender!"

Being at a loss how to account for, or in what sense to understand this odd speech, I only took occasion to observe by way of reply, that, provided he had lived well, and attended faithfully to the duties of his loom, it was a matter of little, very little consequence whether he departed this life at the age of forty or at eighty-five, and that the world would never think the worse of him for having lived to be only "once a man, and not twice a child."--[14]

"That I am well convinced of (replied he), but there is one weakness, or rather a delicacy of mind, of which I fear I shall not be able wholly to divest myself in this transitory life, and that is too great an anxiety for the future fate of that bundle of writings which are at present locked up in my strong box: I am inclined to hope they will be looked upon in after times not as the rags of a beggar, but rather as the remnants of a prince: as to death, I consider it to be as natural to mankind as sleep; man is no more than a shadow of the great world of nature, which like him must, after the accomplishment of very many ages, be also buried in a lasting state of unconscious repose."

A few days after, he became delirious, and I saw him no more till he had departed hence to mingle with the celebrated weavers of antiquity. He had been several times heard to say that the perfecting of the following little piece cost him full eight months severe labour; and though he could not be persuaded to print it himself, several manuscript copies were nevertheless handed about among his friends during his life time, which, it was said, afforded them considerable entertainment as well as edification. But, unhappily, this indulgence was not without its evil consequences, inasmuch as a number of various readings occur in the several manuscripts, occasioned, no doubt, by the ignorance of copyists; but the reader will, in this edition, find these carefully corrected throughout, from a copy preserved in the author's journals on the left hand page, compared with several other earlier manuscripts of the same work in the hands of his friends.

It may well be supposed that the comparing of the various copies (some of them no better than execrable scrawls) has proved a painful and laborious task; but when I considered the delectable amusement a printed account of this interesting Journey would be likely to afford to all good humoured travellers, I was encouraged to persevere, and have at length been enabled (thro' mercy) to accomplish that which has been in long and anxious expectation.--Vale, et fruere nostris laboribus;

Thine, in all good fellowship,
ADAM BUCKSKIN.[15]

Advice to Authors[16]

There are few writers of books in this new world, and amongst these, very few that deal in works of imagination, and, I am sorry to say, fewer still that have any success attending their lucubrations. Perhaps, however, the world thinks justly on this subject. The productions of the most brilliant imagination are at best but mere beautiful flowers, that may amuse us in a walk through a garden in a fine afternoon, but can by no means be expected to engage much of that time which God and nature designed to be spent in very different employments. In a country which two hundred years ago was peopled only by savages, and where the government has ever, in effect, since the first establishment of the white men in these parts, been no other than repub-

lican, it is really wonderful there should be any polite original authors at all in any line, especially when it is considered that, according to the common course of things, any
particular nation or people must have arrived to, or rather
passed, their meridian of opulence and refinement before
they consider the professors of the fine arts in any other
light than a nuisance to the community. This is evidently
the case at present in our age and country; all you have to
do then, my good friends, is to graft your authorship upon
some other calling, or support drooping genius by the assistance of some mechanical employment, in the same manner as the helpless ivy takes hold of the vigorous oak and
cleaves to it for support--I mean to say, in plain language,
that you may make something by weaving garters or mend-
ing sails when an Epic poem would be your utter destruction.

     But I see no reason that, because we are all striving
to live by the same idle trade, we should suffer ourselves
to be imbittered against each other, like a fraternity of
rival mechanics in the same street. Authors (such I mean
as are not possessed of fortunes) are at present considered
as the dregs of the community: their situation and prospects are truly humiliating, and any other sett of men in a
similar state of calamitous adversity would unite together for
their mutual defence, instead of worrying and lampooning
each other for the amusement of the illiberal vulgar. --And
I cannot do otherwise than freely declare that where the
whole profits of a company amount to little or nothing at all,
there ought not, in the nature of things, to be any quarrel-
ling about shares and dividends.

     As to those authors who have lately exported them-
selves from Britain and Ireland, and boast that they have in-

troduced the Muses among us since the conclusion of the late war, I really believe them to be a very good natured sett of gentlemen, notwithstanding they, in the course of the last winter, called me poetaster and scribbler, and some other names still more unsavoury. [17] They are, however, excuseable in treating the American authors as inferiors, a political and a literary independence of their nation being two very different things--the first was accomplished in about seven years; the latter will not be completely effected, perhaps, in as many centuries. It is my opinion, nevertheless, that a duty ought to be laid upon all imported authors, the nett proceeds of which should be appropriated to the benefit of real American writers, when they become old and helpless, and no longer able to wield the pen to advantage.

If a coach or a chariot constructed in Britain pays an impost of twenty pounds at the custom-house, why should not at least twice that sum be laid upon all imported authors, who are able to do twice as much mischief with their rumbling pindaric odes, and gorgeous apparatus of strophes, antistrophes and recitavos?--I, for my own part, am clearly of the opinion that these gentlemen should be taxed, not that I would wish to nip their buds of beauty with the untimely frost of excise, but merely to teach them that our own natural manufactures ought to be primarily attended to and encouraged.

I will now, gentlemen, with your leave, lay down a few simple rules to which, in my opinion, every genuine author will make no difficulty to conform.

1. When you write a book for the public, have nothing to do with Epistles dedicatory. They were first invented by slaves, and have been continued by fools and sycophants. I would not give a farthing more for a book on account of its

being patronized by all the noblemen or crowned heads in Christendom. If it does not possess intrinsic merit enough to protect itself and force its way through the world, their supposed protection will be of no avail: besides, by this ridiculous practice you degrade the dignity authorial, the honour of authorship, which ought evermore to be uppermost in your thoughts. The silly unthinking author addresses a great man in the stile of a servile dependent, whereas a real author and a man of true genius has upon all occasions a bold, disinterested and daring confidence in himself, and considers the common cant of adulation to the sons of fortune as the basest and most abominable of all prostitution.

2. Be particularly careful to avoid all connexion with doctors of law and divinity, masters of arts, professors of colleges, and in general all those that wear square black caps. A mere scholar and an original author are two animals as different from each other as a fresh and salt water sailor. There has been an old rooted enmity between them from the earliest ages, and which it is likely will forever continue. The scholar is not unlike that piddling orator who, cold and inanimate, not roused into action by the impelling flame of inspiration, can only pronounce the oration he has learned by rote; the real author, on the contrary, is the nervous Demosthenes, who, stored with an immensity of ideas awakened within him he knows not how, has them at command upon every occasion, and must therefore be disregarded as a madman or an enthusiast by the narrow and limited capacity, as well as the natural self-sufficiency of the other.

3. It is risquing a great deal to propose a subscription for an original work. The world will be ready enough to anticipate your best endeavours; and that which has been

long and anxiously expected rarely or never comes up to their expectations at last.

4. If you are so poor that you are compelled to live in some miserable garret or cottage, do not repine, but give thanks to heaven that you are not forced to pass your life in a tub, as was the fate of Diogenes of old. Few authors in any country are rich, because a man must first be reduced to a state of penury before he will commence author. Being poor therefore in externals, take care, gentlemen, that you say or do nothing that may argue a poverty of spirit. Riches, we have often heard, are by no means the standard of the value of a man. This maxim the world allows to be true, and yet contradicts it every hour and minute in the year. Fortune most commonly bestows wealth and abundance upon fools and idiots; and men of the dullest natural parts are, notwithstanding, generally best calculated to acquire large estates, and hoard up immense sums from small beginnings.

5. Never borrow money of any man, for if you should once be mean enough to fall into such a habit, you will find yourselves unwelcome guests every where. If upon actual trial you are at length convinced you possess no abilities that will command the esteem, veneration or gratitude of mankind, apply yourselves without loss of time to some of the lower arts, since it is far more honourable to be a good bricklayer or a skilful weaver than an indifferent poet. --If you cannot at all exist without now and then gratifying your itch for scribbling, follow my example, who can both weave stockings and write poems. --But, if you really possess that sprightliness of fancy and elevation of soul which alone constitute an author, do not on that account be troublesome to your friends. A little reflection will point out other means

to extract money from the hands and pockets of your fellow citizens than by poorly borrowing what, perhaps, you will never be able to repay.

6. Never engage in any business as an inferior or understrapper. I cannot endure to see an author debase his profession so far as to submit to be second or third in any office or employment whatever. If fortune or the ill taste of the public compels you even to turn shallopman on the Delaware, let it be your first care to have the command of the boat. Beggary itself, with all its hideous apparatus of rags and misery, becomes at once respectable whenever it exhibits the least token of independence of spirit and a single spark of laudable ambition.

7. If you are in low circumstances, do not forget that there is such a thing in the world as a decent pride. They are only cowards and miscreants that poverty can render servile in their behaviour. Your haughtiness should always rise in proportion to the wretchedness and desperation of your circumstances. If you have only a single guinea in the world, be complaisant and obliging to every one: if you are absolutely destitute of a shilling, immediately assume the air of a despot, pull off your hat to no one, let your discourse, in every company, turn upon the vanity of riches, the insignificancy of the great men of the earth, the revolution of empires, and the final consummation of all things. -- By such means you will at least conceal a secret of some importance to yourself--that you have not a shilling in the world to pay for your last night's lodging.

8. Should you ever be prevailed upon to dedicate your book to any great man or woman, consider first whether the tenor and subject of it be such as may in some measure coincide with the age, temper, education, business and general

conversation of the person whose patronage is requested. A friend of mine once committed a great error on this score. He wrote a bawdy poem and dedicated it to the principal in the department of finance.

9.   Never make a present of your works to great men. If they do not think them worth purchasing, trust me, they will never think them worth reading.

10.   If fortune seems absolutely determined to starve you, and you can by no means whatever make your works sell, to keep up as much as in you lies the expiring dignity of authorship, do not take to drinking, gambling or bridge-building as some have done, thereby bringing the trade of authorship into disrepute; but retire to some uninhabited island or desert, and there, at your leisure, end your life with decency.

The Sailor's Relief[18]

Alexander Dismal, Inn-holder, to the Printer of the Weekly Gazette.

Right Worthy!

Since all are for the public good distrest,
And each proposes what he thinks is best--
Why may I not propose, among the rest?--

I am one of the numerous tribe who, under the smiles of heaven, endeavour to make an honest livelihood by keeping a house of decent entertainment for such as chuse to favour me with their custom:--but I beg leave to observe (I hope without offence) that there is no class of people by which our fraternity, adjacent to the river, so much suffer at times as by sea-faring men, though none expend their money with a more liberal hand and heart, as long as they have a single sixpence in their funds to draw upon.--Sunday last, the twenty-third of January, 1785, was a time of woeful humiliation to us poor publicans. The river opened on a sudden, the sailors went off in triumph, and, for the most part, considerably indebted to those who had for several weeks preceding found them in victuals and lodging. As I am a sincere and hearty friend to all sea-faring men, having myself been formerly master of a small coasting packet, and notwithstanding I have frequently been a considerable sufferer by the roguery of some individuals, I would nevertheless beg leave to remark that in a country like this, so remarkable for its public and private charity toward our unfortunate fellow men, it would well become us to provide some resources, either by a general tax, or certain tolls to be paid by every vessel passing and repassing Gloucester Point, to assist, comfort, cherish and support such sea-faring men, in needy circumstances, as happen to be detained here during the winter season by the temporary interruption of our navigation, particularly those who are unable, through mere mischance, mishap, old age, or other incapacity, immediately to help themselves.

In pursuance of this plan I would humbly propose that a three decked ship, of about four hundred tons burthen, should be forthwith built and finished off in a plain manner at the public expence, with commodious and comfortable apartments throughout for poor and distressed seamen, regard being always had, in the distribution of the various apartments, to the known rank and station of the party relieved. I do not mean, however, that this vessel should be launched into the water. Every purpose of accommodation would be much better answered by letting her remain upon dry land, and many disagreeable accidents thereby prevented. It would nevertheless be necessary that her station should be as near as possible to the river, as no true Jack-tar can endure to be long out of sight of navigable water. The most applicable name I can at present think of for this humane foundation is THE SAILOR'S RELIEF.

It is obvious, at first glance, that such a ship as this would not cost so much to the public as one designed for real sea service. She would not require more than one half of the crooked timber commonly made use of in vessels of the proposed burthen, nor need her planks be more than three fourths of an inch thick, or at most one inch. Sailors are never truly and fully contented except when on shipboard; consequently they would be no where better pleased than in such a situation as this, where they would enjoy all the merriment and good humour of a sea-faring life, without having those bitter gales and mountainous waves to encounter which, for a great part of the year, are so fatal and terrible to the marine fraternity on these coasts. --I would further propose that the ship should be kept constantly victualled by contract, or otherwise, with common sea provisions, faithfully laid in, and a cook to be provided by the public who had not been previously less than seven years at sea in that capacity. --Rigged she should be completely, to the end that the older sailors might be constantly practicing their various manoeuvres according to the state of the winds and weather, and the younger ones taught to be ready and dextrous in the art of working a ship when in actual service. Over and above the standing rigging, she should be furnished with a complete sett of running geer, including every article from the topgallant sheets to the jeer falls and clue-garnets: Not a brace, bowline, top-rope, sheet, halyard, bunt line, clew line or reef tackle should be wanting; and the masts, yards, sails, stays, shrouds and tops should be as punctually supplied, and as exactly arranged in their proper

places, as if they were really to travel the high seas. --
Some distressed or disabled old sea-commander, of good
character and sober conversation, might preside here, in the
two capacities of master and chaplain, with the proper officers under him, during the hard season, for keeping the
crew in order; but whenever the river is clear of ice, I
would have all hands discharged (excepting such as should be
found absolutely helpless, and a few others) and the skuttles
barred down till the navigation should be again obstructed,
and these useful men once more seen wandering about the
streets to look out a shelter from the unpitying storm.

I leave it to others to point out a proper spot of ground
whereon to erect this pile of benevolence, only taking care
that the horizon should be as little obstructed as possible,
that they might every day have an opportunity of determin-
ing the latitude and longitude of the ship with the precision
in such cases necessary. As to the manual labour on
board, I am of opinion it would not be excessive, especially
as the helm, the anchor, and the pump would require little
or no attendance, --yet an allowance of weak grog would be
absolutely necessary to keep up the spirits of the crew, and
it would be a standing rule among them to take in all sail
at sun-set, for fear of being incommoded with squalls in the
night.

A certain sailor sent off clandestinely a few days ago,
no less than fourteen pounds three shillings and fourpence
in my debt, leaving an old sea chest in my possession for
security, which, upon the word of a Christian man, con-
tained nothing more than two pair of old frocks and trowsers,
a small brown wig (three fourths gnawed away by the rats)
a sea cap which by its appearance may, for aught I know,
have circumnavigated the globe half a dozen times, and a

book called the Seaman's Assistant, which I will adventure
to say would not fetch ninepence, even if it were to be set
up at Bell's auction room to be disposed of to the highest
bidder, and recommended by all the persuasive oratory of
that truly original humourist. --There is also, among his
other trumpery, a sort of strange diary or journal of his
proceedings, which seems to have been penned while he
lodged in my house. Three of four paragraphs of this elegant performance I shall transcribe for the amusement of
yourself and your readers, and therewith conclude this paper.
The bad spelling your compositor will be pleased to correct,
for I really have not skill enough in language to do it myself.

DECEM. 20, 1784. This day I came in from sea in
the brig Ragged Fortune-- settled with the captain--the bal-
ance in my favour being four dollars and two thirds. --N. B.
The captain, I suspect, cheated me damnably, but upon my
taking a cud of tobacco into my mouth, and telling him as
much, he gave me a glass of your right stiff grog, true old
stingo, which squared accounts, and set all to rights again.
I then signed a receipt in full.

DECEM. 22. Had high fun last night at Moll Clinker's,
but upon my feeling in my pockets for money to pay the
reckoning when I was leaving the house, found not a farthing
to bless myself with. --Mem. No getting through life without now and then falling in with breakers, and thumping on
the shoal grounds--left my new silver buckles in pawn.

JANUARY 3, 1785. Find myself woefully in debt al-
ready--dream every night of old Carlisle and other picka-
roon constables. --Mem. to keep a good look out from my
tops, and if possible steer clear of those cutter built sons
of whores till the river opens. --Jan. 5. At 12 last night,

fell in with a watchman, the new building then bearing due
west, and Christ church steeple nearly south east. As bad
luck would have it he carried no lanthorns, so that he suddenly boarded me in the dark, and at the first shock carried away all the breast hooks of my new blue jacket, the
starboard lifts of my half worn castor hat, and nearly two
thirds of the after leech of my old great coat. Note, he
battered my hull severely, but I suspect his main top was
somewhat the worse of the judicious and masterly dis-
charges I made upon it with my short oaken cudgel.--After
engaging, as near as I could judge, about half a glass, he
thought fit to sheer off, with his cutwater in a shattered
condition and his dead lights beaten in, and so left me to
pursue my course without further molestation.

JANUARY 10. This morning, about eight o'clock, being then in the latitude of Swede's church, (the weather cold,
with strong gales from the northwest) saw a very ugly fellow with his jib-boom unrigg'd, steering after me, directly
in my wake.--As I judged him to be in chace, I instantly
put about and stood to the northward. He pursued me at a
great rate, and for a while neared me every minute hand
over hand; but my manoeuvres were so uncommonly excellent and well timed that I fairly lost sight of him by half
past twelve, P.M. the Methodist meeting house then bearing
S.S.E. distant one hundred and fifty yards by dead reckoning.--Nothing remarkable this afternoon, except that the
wind changed to southwest.

JANUARY 15. My landlord begins to look sour at me,
and talks of nothing else but scarcity of money and the
hardness of the times.--Possibly he means to carry me into dock--I want new sheathing, it's true; but I'll be d----d
if they shall lay me ashore at spring tides, however--one

has no certainty when they'll float again. --I once lay three long weeks fast aground on my beam ends in Baltimore jail, and, by the diamonds on our <u>bosen's</u> nose, did not get off at last till I had thrown overboard the very watch from my pocket, and--ah poor Sue!--thine own ring from my finger, to lighten me!

JANUARY 19. Still beating to windward upon a very short allowance--my grog all out, my rigging daily becoming worse and worse, and something every hour giving way. --Yesterday morning at three quarters past four, the wind blowing fresh at east-south-east, half east, with rain and sleet, I carried away the lee strap of my larboard boot hose, back stays and all, in making the best of my way to avoid one of the most active, privateer-built devils of constables that ever cruised in these seas. He rather outwalked me, going large, but by keeping well to windward, that is, by skulking through the narrow allies and by-streets, I had evidently the advantage till sunrise, when I very fortunately got clear of him by favour of a thick fog and heavy rain.

JANUARY 21. At 25 minutes past eight, had the misfortune to run foul of a large black double decked transport belonging to the <u>holy see,</u> with a grey goose in tow. In less than two minutes I cut away his main spritsail yard, bob-stay, topping lifts, quarter cloths, foretopsail bowlines, and the weather lanyards of his main shrouds. In the conflict, which was very dreadful, they threw overboard a volume of <u>Ernulphus's</u> curses and other contraband Romish commodities, together with a large bundle of certificates, which I picked up and made off with, intending to restore them (at least the certificates) to the right owners, the poor devils of soldiers, upon their paying me <u>two and sixpence</u> in

227

the pound. [19]

It would be presuming too much upon the patience of your readers, Mr. Printer, to transcribe any more of this strange animal's remarks. He has writ me a letter from the Delaware capes, however, in which he promises to pay me honourably when he returns, even if he should be forced to go to the very centre of the north pole, or to a certain outlandish people he calls the Hantipods, to earn the money.

The Academy of Death[20]

There are a thousand things which an author may propose to himself as the objects of his serious study and attention during his waking hours, which he nevertheless, upon trial, finds himself unable to make any thing of, at least, so as to satisfy himself and his readers. --Of this nature have been several subjects which I have from time to time undertaken to write upon, and as often thrown aside from a conviction that I did not possess capacity equal to, or materials sufficient for investigating them thoroughly. The reality of the apparitions of the departed, the nature of the spiritual world, the seemingly self-produced operation and organization of matter, the harmony of discord, and the ultimate design of the material creation have been some of those that puzzled me the most. --But instead of perplexing you, my dear Momus, with these matters as much as I have puzzled and perplexed myself, and that to no purpose, I will, if you are in your usual good humour, relate an imaginary excursion which I lately made in a dream, during a long stormy night in the month of January, when the whole face of nature being under the temporary impressions of death, a visit to the domains of that monarch was by no means unseasonable.

I imagined I was setting out on a long journey, the term of which was not fixed in my own mind. Upon looking forward, in idea, it appeared to me like casting the eye along an avenue of many miles in length, which terminated in darkness, closed in, seemingly, upon both sides and prevented any farther prospect. --I had scarcely entered this avenue when I discovered it to be no other than the common passage of mankind into another state of existence.

The passage was dark enough, to be sure, but was by no means so frightful as I had imagined. "The gods (said Seneca) conceal from men the happiness of death, that they may endure to live!" Be that as it may, if I was not perfectly happy, the very worst circumstance attending me was the want of company. I was consequently left entirely to my own reflections and ideas, which, you very well know, are not at all times the most eligible companions.

After several hours travelling, this narrow passage opened into a pleasant country, variegated with streams, forests, plains, hills, and vallies. --Being now fully sensible that I had made a passage from one state of existence to another, I observed to a man whom I overtook, heavy laden with books of theology, that "this region greatly resembled the world from which I had lately departed."--The man replied that there "was certainly a resemblance; but be not deceived, (continued he) the world you have come from is no more than a shadow of this in which you now are. That was only reflection; this is reality itself; and the great body of light you see in our firmament is not a sun such as formerly warmed you, awakened the winds, and caused the plants to grow; it is the luminary of TRUTH, which pervades all things here, and without the real or the reflected influence of which, all things in the universe would be no better to created beings than phantasms and delusions."

I now wandered at full liberty in a very pleasing country till I arrived at a building of immense size, and which seemed to contain many hundreds of apartments. Over the principal door in the front was written in large letters, THIS IS THE ACADEMY OF DEATH.

As the door of the building stood wide open to all comers, I made no hesitation to enter. The first thing that particularly attracted my notice was the cirumstance of the name of the inhabitant being inscribed over the door of every apartment. At the first glance I distinguished Aristotle, Archimedes, and the names of a number of other celebrated men with whose characters I, although a simple weaver, had been formerly acquainted while upon earth. From what I saw, it was natural to conclude that the persons themselves resided in the apartments thus allotted them--and if they have brought their ideas with them, thought I, they cannot be any other than good company.

A loud noise now interrupted my observations for a moment. A poet and a mathematician, both just arrived, struck up a hasty agreement to take up their abode together in the kitchen garret of the academy. Finding every other apartment pre-occupied, they preferred that humble situation to any other in a different part of the country, as they would here be neighbours to the ancients, and from their shreds might probably receive frequent assistance. They had conceived a strange notion too that they might mutually throw light upon each other's studies by living together in the same room.--"As you shined in the walks of Fancy, said the mathematician, and I was celebrated for the investigation of strict truth, we shall be of good use to each other. Your fine fancies will contribute to enliven my speculations, and

my invariable attachment to truth and certainty will give
your ideas a colouring of rationality."

They quarrelled, however, before the one had resolved a single problem or the other written five lines of a
new poem. The governor of the academy was then called,
who immediately enjoined SILENCE, and upon hearing the
cause of their dispute, ordered a partition wall of solid
adamant to be instantly run up between them, in order to
prevent future misunderstandings. There may be a great
deal of truth (said he) in the works of fancy, but I never
yet knew any occasion for fancy in the works of truth.

Finding now that the governor of the academy was
leaving us without assigning me even the least apartment in
the building, I began to conclude that no other than men of
acknowledged fame and merit upon earth were to be accommodated in this edifice after death. Struck with a consciousness, too, that I had not attained to any post or employment in the other world above that of a simple weaver, I
was preparing, with some reluctance, to travel farther on
to seek the habitations of the spirits that had moved in my
own humble sphere of life, when the governor of the academy again made his appearance, who, as I should have mentioned before, was no other than Death himself.

"You have been loitering here some time (said he) Mr.
Slender. A moment's reflection might teach you that these
apartments were not designed for men of your level. Cast
your eyes to the door of every chamber in this academy,
and you will find no other names written thereon than those
of the sages, and heroes, and geniuses of antiquity. You
cannot make any pretensions to be equal to the most insignificant among them: retire therefore, without delay, and
advance farther on towards the hovels belonging to the men

of the loom in yonder forest."

Great monarch of these silent abodes (replied I) not an individual amongst the dead can be more deeply conscious of his meanness and incapacity than him that now has the honor to address you. All the favour I have to ask before I depart hence to mingle with the weavers of antiquity is that some few of these doors may be opened, and that I may have a transient view of those ancient sages, of whom I heard so much talk among the men of sentiment in the other world.--"Almost all the better sort that come hither, answered the superintendant of the academy, have made the same request. And I would willingly gratify the curiosity of all, were it not that the far greater part of these men, especially the philosophers, are of a bashful and solitary turn: and more than that, they are (as in the other world) almost continually at their studies, hate company, and, above all things, cannot endure to be stared at.--However, as I do not recollect that any weaver, excepting yourself, has ever made a similar request, I will, in some measure, gratify your wish. You shall not only have a sight of them, but some few among them shall speak, for your entire and more complete satisfaction."

He then stamped with his foot, and immediately the door opposite to him flew open, over which was written the name of

LUCIAN, the Rhetorician of Samosata.

As I had in my life time read a translation of this celebrated humourist of antiquity, I had expected to see a merry old fellow, abounding in jokes and laughable conceits.-- Judge then what must have been my disappointment when I saw a little, crabbed looking old man, sitting by a table and writing something with a steel pen on a tablet of wax.--He

232

is doubtless, thought I, notwithstanding his serious face, contriving some humourous dialogue. He cannot, however, be employed in ridiculing the popular religion of his country, for the time of his probation has been long expired: he must now be acquainted with the truth, if ever; and it is not likely that a probationary religion can have any toleration in this country, where the condition of the dead is absolutely fixed and unalterable. I then made free to advance further into his apartment, with a view of having some conversation, if possible, with a man that had been so remarkable for his wit, when he instantly caught up his walking stick and gave me a smart rap over the shoulders, at the same time ordering me to leave the room, as he wished me to know that a man is never more seriously inclined than at the moment he is contriving a story that will make the world laugh heartily; and that although those ludicrous fables may, in an instant, impart pleasurable ideas to the gay fellows that read them, yet nothing is more certain than that every thing valuable of this nature is produced amid silence, solitude, and melancholy. --I must confess I felt somewhat hurt by a manner of treatment so different from what I had expected, and that too from one of the first wits of antiquity. --"But I would have you to know, Mr. Slender (said he, laying down his stick) that although I might have been regent of Alexandria, yet I was not torn in pieces by dogs, as some have asserted. It is the nature of the busy world on earth to lay a great man in the dust by the most infamous means possible; and I am sorry this idle report has met with so much credit among them as it has. If I ridiculed the gods and philosophy of my age and country, whose systems TIME has at length, also, proved to be false, no one amongst all the dead or living can say that I denied

233

the existence of the PROVIDENCE that superintends all things."

As I still felt the effects of the rap he had given me over the shoulders, I forebore to make him any reply, and turned my face another way.

The next apartment that was opened to me was that of PLATO, the Philosopher of Athens. I cast my eye full upon this fanciful sophist of antiquity. He was sitting on a bench and looking horizontally, as if meditating on something future, at the same time holding imaginary dialogues with his master Socrates, who was not present.--"You may think what you will of it, Socrates, said he (musing) but I will honestly confess that I was an enemy to the poets, and ordered them to be banished from my visionary commonwealth, only because I failed in my early endeavours to make poems equal to those of Homer, the poet of Chios. I found also that the rhapsodists had been before hand with me in involving the mysteries of religion in poetical fables; finding that I could not rival them in this line, all the part that was left me was to substitute philosophical fables in the stead of their poetical ones.--And pardon me, Socrates, if I made you argue so long a time in behalf of the immortality of the soul, against the sects that, during my abode upon earth, were retainers to a contrary opinion.--You may remember we talked so long on the subject that we fairly lost ourselves, and only proved at last what you had previously asserted, that in the other world we knew nothing."--So much candour as the Athenian philosopher discovered in this short soliloquy could not possibly do otherwise than afford me some degree of satisfaction.--He was, no doubt, a lover of truth, thought I; but he took some strange methods to come at it. He reasoned in a circle instead of a right line. Every step we took in his writings, we imagined ourselves just within the grasp of the desired object. When we attempted to lay hold of it, we were utterly deceived, and found we had been only entertained with a pleasing flow of fine and flowery language.

I was preparing to depart, finding the philosopher to be in a very pensive and melancholy mood, when he again cast his eyes towards something which he imagined to be Socrates, and began a discourse upon LOVE.

"Love, (said he) my dear Socrates, was the daughter of Jupiter and the fine ether of the firmament, whereas the other inferior gods of the celestial nature were only produced from Jupiter and the air, which you know is a substance of much grosser quality than the other, and was represented in the Grecian theology by the goddess Juno. -- LOVE, after passing some time in the courts of Olympus, at length descended to the earth to receive the homage of men, and by the charms of her person and behaviour so gained upon the affections of mankind that, from a state of savage ferocity, they soon became a civilized and social race of beings. --After a certain time, Jupiter himself also descended upon the earth, and of course several natural children were the consequence of his amours among the daughters of the forests.

"One of these, a female, very much resembled the child LOVE, that was formerly born to him by the fine ether of the firmament, and for that reason he called her by the name of DESIRE, which is of a somewhat similar import. No sooner had this counterfeit beauty grown up to a full age than she was almost universally preferred to the other by the sons of men, although her features were neither so delicate, her countenance so innocent, her ideas so exalted, or her person throughout possessed of half the elegance and charming simplicity of the other.

"The sky-bred damsel took umbrage at this perversion of taste, and finding that her shrines were deserted, and that mankind in general paid their whole adoration to her sister Desire, she resented the neglect, passed most of her time in solitude, and soon after retired to the deserts of the wilderness. --Love was afterwards addressed by very few, and when addressed, it was only by those who had nothing but deformity to recommend them.

"Now, my dear Socrates, as wise a man as you were, you seem not to have made a proper discrimination in your notions of these two deities, or you never would have paid your addresses to Xantippe, who, at best, had nothing more to recommend her than a good person and a fresh complexion. Love came from heaven, and is therefore of a celestial nature and origin; Desire is from the earth and, as such, can boast of nothing more than what is earthly. --And what did you see in marriage that could tempt the heart of a wise man? Had you not penetration sufficient to discover that human felicity is always prodigiously abated, oftentimes wholly annihilated, by the possession of the desired object? You must have been sensible, from your deep knowledge of human nature, that the hours of courtship, and the minutes while the maid is yet coy, are the pleasantest of a man's whole life; and yet you foolishly abridged the term, and thus all your fine ideas terminated in disgust. Had you continued single, you would have been in love as long as you lived, nor would those charming colours have vanished so speedily which I fear were, for the most part, obliterated within a month or two after your nuptials. Had it not been for this one false step, I say, you would have been always in love, nor would Xantippe, by means of so unequal a connexion, have been known to posterity as nothing better than a vixen and tormentor. "--Here he ended his speech.

He still retains his old notions of sentimental love, said the superintendant, but his own example did by no means correspond with his doctrines. He chose to live single, it is true, but the virtue of chastity in him was nothing more than mere appearance. Though he was fond upon all occasions to consider LOVE as a passion in a high degree sentimental, yet his feelings were no other than those of a man. At the very time when he set up his Academy at Athens, and disciples flocked in to him from all parts, I have incontestible proofs that two ladies, Lasthenia, the Mantinian, and Axiothia, the Philasian, attended his lectures in the habits of men, and passed several hours every night with this very Plato, conversing on subjects very different from those of philosophy, rhetoric, or the moral perfections of the Deity.

The next door that flew open, in obedience to the signal of the governor, discovered

ALEXANDER, the Hero of Macedon.

His countenance was fierce, daring and disdainful; and I could not avoid noticing, on this and other occasions, that the countenances of the personages in this world of the departed, for the most part, accorded exactly with the characters that the best historians had given us of their minds in the terrestrial world to which they formerly belonged.

Alexander was engaged in conversation with an odd looking ghost whom I recollected, from the accounts given of him in history, to be no other than Diogenes. --"Tell me now, Sawny, said the Cynic, (with a malicious grin) were you sincere when you said you would wish to be Diogenes in preference to all other men, had you not happened to be Alexander ?"

I was so far sincere, replied the conqueror, that, had it not been my lot to be born a king, to rule over and enslave the persons of mankind, I should have wished to have been born a philosopher, that I might, in like manner, play the tyrant with their minds.

"But, as matters stood, (continued Diogenes) you were far from being a wise man. Your boldness and daring exploits have so fascinated the judgments of mankind that your faults are forgotten in the splendor of the single and, I had almost said, brutal virtue called courage."

I do not recollect that I ever acted like a fool, said the hero.

"Your history, however, will afford numberless instances of folly, returned the cynic. --I will not at present mortify you with the mention of more than one. When you had proceeded so far into the burning climates and sands of India that your army, being in want of almost every thing, had determined to proceed no farther, you foolishly advanced in front of them and declared that if they did not persevere, you yourself would march on alone to meet the host of the enemy, and encounter them all with your single spear. --Had your soldiers taken you at your word and suffered you to march forward, how ridiculous yourself and your conduct would have appeared!--But Fortune favoured you, and your soldiers were fools enough to be charmed with your desperation. --They followed you and conquered.

"The Roman in yonder pavilion acted with much more caution and prudence in such a dilemma. His army was inclined to desert him on a similar occasion. --Stay behind, then, in the name of all the gods, said Cesar--I will take

238

the tenth legion, and with them march on to death or victory. --Here was the policy which you wanted--a spirit of emulation and jealousy was kindled in a moment among the soldiery; and for fear the tenth legion should gain the victory alone, the whole host at once became heroes and volunteers of honour."

The door of Alexander's apartment now closed of itself by some invisible direction, and I was, in return, presented with a view of

ARISTOTLE, the Despot in Philosophy.
I was disgusted with this spirit the first moment I beheld him. He had a malignant vivacity in his eyes that plainly proved he was choleric and impatient of contradiction. He seemed to be engaged in the instruction of a number of pupils in the mysteries of the invisible nature, but it was easy to perceive that his ancient dogmatical spirit still remained. He dealt altogether in positives, confessed himself ignorant of nothing, advanced numerous opinions without thought or reflection, and had afterwards the impudence to defend them simply because he had so advanced them. --I turned from him with disgust, and was in the next place presented with a view of

HOMER, the Poet of Chios.
He did by no means resemble the first of the human species in shape and features. On the contrary, his appearance was rather vulgar and far from engaging; and I was even inclined to doubt whether this could really be the man that had composed the Iliad and the Odyssey, till the governor of the Academy, perceiving my surprise, desired me not to distrust the reality of the representation. This is the genuine poet of Chios, said he: you see him now just as he appeared when he had completed his two grand performances,

and was sixty-five years of age.--"In my opinion, said I, Mr. Governor, this poet has attracted so much notice in the world rather by the beauty of his expression than by the solidity and depth of his knowledge. Yet his works have produced legislators and philosophers, saints and heroes, and his various pictures of life are faithfully copied. His religion is to this day the religion of the human heart. We secretly love his theology upon earth from a principle inseparable from human nature, because his gods are like ourselves, and similitude always begets affection." I then turned round to accost the poet and, contrary to my expectation, found him affable and talkative.

If an everlasting remembrance amongst the nations of mankind can at all gratify the souls in this state, said I, you, illustrious bard, cannot be otherwise than completely happy. Who would set a life of poverty and hardship in competition with a tomb over which was written--Here lies the man for the honour of whose birth seven capital cities of Greece contended!

"You are mistaken, stranger, said the poet, if you imagine that what is called fame among men has any influence upon the condition of the dead. It is true, the recollection of those charming ideas that passed through my mind when I wrote the Iliad and Odyssey still afford me something like pleasure, but the fame that has accrued is nothing. How dearly, too, did I pay, while upon earth, for what in itself was no solid satisfaction. I was born in a rude and barbarous country, where men were yet so much inclined to the savage nature that prisoners of war were always either sacrificed to the gods or reduced to a state of slavery. I spent the bright days of my youth in acquiring the knowledge of arts, sciences and languages among the philosophers of

Egypt; I afterwards applied myself to travelling, and passed many years in wandering from place to place, to observe what I could of men and manners, the variegated face of nature, and the progress of the arts in different nations.

"But still this was nothing but infelicity, and while I was endeavouring to acquire the knowledge and ideas of a God, I lost that share of content and satisfaction which is usually allotted to a man. When I found myself arrived to a maturity of judgment and observation to set about my two great poems, my best days were gone, the sun had passed the meridian, and I found myself verging rapidly towards old age and misery. Thus cruelly did Nature deal with me upon earth. After infusing into my veins a portion of the warm blood of Apollo, she left me to sink into the dust with as little regard as she had previously shewn to Irus and Thersites. --Old age and poverty, with the superadded calamity of blindness, overtook me at last, and it was with the greatest difficulty I subsisted at all by singing fragments of my poems through the several cities of Greece. It has been reported upon earth that I had a conference with Lycurgus, the legislator of Sparta, upon the subject of legislation. It was no such thing. That severe lawgiver was too deeply intoxicated with his own opinions to pay much regard to the fancies and fictions of a retailer of Rhapsodies: -- Nay, I was not even his cotemporary. Possibly, however, I justly merited all the mischiefs I suffered. I disguised many matters in my poems with the real truth of which the world had a right to be acquainted in after times. Amongst these it may be worth while to mention that Ulysses might have returned home in less than the tenth part of ten years, had Penelope been really the model of conjugal virtue I have pictured her. Alas, poor man, that was not his case!--She was, in fact, one of the most noted termagants and jilts of her age, and the poor wanderer remained abroad ten years after the destruction of Troy, for no other reasons than that he might be out of the hearing of her tongue, and not be mortified with repeated instances of her infidelity."

There was something so pleasing in the ideas and language of this man of Chios that I thought I could have remained a century in his apartment without weariness, provided he would continue talking.--He then seemed to recollect himself, and thus went on--

"There was Helena, too, the wife of Menelaus. The critics have found great fault with the Grecian States for having involved themselves in a long and desperate war on account of an idle woman, whom they had much better have left in possession of the Trojans. Possibly their notions may be just; but if I am rightly informed, many wars have been declared since my time upon equally trifling provocations.--You will admire, [21] perhaps, at the conduct of this princess. What (you will say) could have induced her to leave her husband and her friends, a crown, a palace, and whatever was most flattering to the human heart, to follow a stranger into the small territory of Priam, over which his numerous tribe of elder brothers made it extremely improbable he should ever have any the least dominion? As I have not given the true reason in my poems, I will now candidly acknowledge what was the real cause of the preference she gave the Trojan. Menelaus, her husband, was considerably advanced in years, and wore blue garments. Paris, on the contrary, was a young fellow, and never appeared habited in any other than superfine scarlet. That circumstance was sufficient to turn the scale of female affection in his favour."

242

Here the governor stamped with his foot, and the door instantly closed. You must have no further conversation with Homer,[22] said he; what he has been telling you are secrets that ought not to be divulged for the honor of antiquity, as well as of his own poems.--the next ghost I saw was

ARCHIMEDES, the Geometrician of Sicily.

"They may deny it, if they please, said he; but Syracuse would have submitted much sooner to the Romans than it did, had it not been for my machines. As to the burning glasses, I did really contrive something of that sort too, but the historian told a lie when he informed posterity that I set the Roman galleys on fire therewith. I remember it was with some difficulty that I only singed off one of the eyebrows of an inhabitant of Agrigentum, for which he would have taken my life, had I not instantly slipped out of his way. "

If this man lived at lodgings in Syracuse, said I, they could certainly afford to entertain him at a cheap rate. I remember to have heard that his mind was generally so absorbed in deep study that he would frequently forget to eat his victuals for days together; and when the city was at last taken, he was so intent upon resolving a geometrical figure in his Museum, that he knew nothing of the matter, and chose rather to be cut to pieces by a soldier than leave his favorite study. Such conduct would be ridiculed in a common fabricator of almanacs in modern times; yet in Archimedes, the ancient, it is reckoned praise worthy. But I am of opinion the investigation of truth is scarcely worth a man's pains when it so occupies the mind as to suspend all regard for self-preservation----

The Folly of Desiring Fame[23]

Upon my return homeward, I halted, several miles short of the out skirts of the forest I inhabit, at a solitary cottage a very small distance from the high way, where a painted board, suspended from the branch of a tree, projecting horizontally, advertised me that hospitality was to be sold in that place for money. Upon my entering the inn, I found every thing in uproar and confusion. It seems a wedding was to be held there the same evening for a young couple of the neighbourhood, and this event, which is by far the most important of their whole lives among the bulk of mankind, in respect to themselves, had occasioned these preparations for the festivity of the approaching night.--I should have passed on without delay from this fantastic scene of momentary mirth, had not the importunities of a certain blind musician (who was hired to regulate the music, according to an ancient custom still kept up on such occasions) in a manner compelled me to sit down on a bench at the door and tell him the news of the day. After gratifying him as well as my scanty knowledge of the affairs of the great world would at that moment allow, he further requested me to inform him what might be the opinions of the people in the capital in regard to his own late performances on the violin?--Upon my honour, friend, replied I, to the best of my knowledge the people in the capital, at least those with whom I have happened to be conversant, are not as yet sufficiently acquainted with your merits to have made your performances the subject of public conversation: possibly, however, I may be mistaken; I am but very slightly known in the city, and those few with whom I associate are, for the most part, wholly disconnected with, as well as en-

244

tirely ignorant of music in all its branches and modes of expression.--"Not acquainted with my merits," replied the musician--"Is it possible there are any people in Philadelphia that have not heard of David Quiverstring, the famous blind fiddler, who can at any time play more than three hundred of the newest and most fashionable tunes without the assistance of the book of Notes!--I would wish you to understand, Mr. Traveller, (continued he, somewhat angrily) that I am not only known but well respected throughout this continent, and even in Europe I have good reason to think my merits are not altogether disregarded or unnoticed!"

When he had uttered these words, he swaggered back to the company, and began to strike up some miserable airs as a specimen of his transcendent abilities. Being now at liberty, I pursued my journey homewards, not without reflecting by the way on this unaccountable fondness in mankind for fame and extensive reputation. To acquire the esteem and good-will of valuable men is certainly an innocent as well as a laudable endeavour, but to pass sleepless nights and anxious days, to toil in the walks of science or to exhaust the spirits on the rack of invention, and our principal aim in all this being nothing more than merely to become popular, is certainly absurd in itself, at least so far as regards the peace and happiness of an individual, but is without doubt a principle implanted in us by nature for the general advantage of the human species, when formed into societies and civil connexions.

When I had returned to my cavern, after refreshing myself with a mess of roots and a draught of pure water from the adjacent rivulet, I at length fell unexpectedly into a gentle slumber, when the blind fiddler once more intruded himself upon me in a dream, and I now imagined he had arrived to such an insufferable degree of conceit and impertinence as to request me to recommend him as one qualified for the place of first musician to the <u>royal family of France</u>.

Vexed at his forward and arrogant behaviour, I instantly turned him out of my cave, at the same time desiring him to recollect that merit and modesty have ever been inseparable companions, and that he who is employed in trumpeting forth his own praises has already anticipated that return, be his merits what they may, which he might have had pretensions to expect from the world.

After the dismission of this visionary personage, I conceived myself to be suddenly transported to a large plain, which was called <u>the Walk of human life</u>. I found myself, I cannot tell how, placed in the midst of this plain, which extended east and west, and was sufficiently enlightened; but what most surprised me was that it began and ended in darkness. I was now apparently carried westward by a propensity of self-actuating motion, which I could neither resist nor account for, and, in my way, saw at a distance a large black building, over the marble gate of which was written in capital letters, THIS IS THE TEMPLE OF OBLIVION. The spirit that superintended the affairs of this melancholy edifice appeared soon after at the middle gate, and fixing his eyes full upon me, beckoned to me to advance towards him. A strange horror immediately took possession of my soul, notwithstanding which I obeyed his intimation, advancing towards him with a trembling step. He then made an attempt to take me by the hand, as if to welcome me to the environs of his dreary abode, when I shrunk back from his grasp, alarmed at the idea of any of my limbs coming into contact with the cold substance of an inhabitant of the world of spirits. He smiled at my fears, bidding me at the same time to attend to what he should say, and he would teach me wisdom. "This plain (said he) is the passage of all mankind into the ocean of forgetfulness, and through this temple, which is dedicated to oblivion, every individual without exception is once doomed to pass. That other spacious building which you see at a distance, and situated some miles off to the right, is called the Palace of Fame. Cast your eyes eastward, and observe what millions of the human race are travelling this way! They are, to a man, conscious that the palace of oblivion may finally receive them all: and yet, strange to behold, there is not a single individual among them that does not make use of his utmost endeavours to take the Temple of Fame in his way, notwithstanding the distance is much more considerable, and the road full of sharp rocks and other dangerous obstacles, with which the direct path to the Palace of Oblivion is not in the least encumbered. Let us go towards them and observe their designs and motions."--After a long walk we at last came to the place where the two roads separated, one leading directly west, and following the course of the sun to the Palace of Oblivion, the other, by a circuitous and difficult rout, to the Temple of Fame. The road to the latter appeared to be very little worn, being almost overrun with briar and thorn bushes; and I could not help taking notice of a number of sour looking spirits in the several shapes of owls, asses, monkeys and wolf-dogs, inhabiting the confines of this region, whose whole employment seemed to be the driving back, and otherwise ill treating, such as attempted to pass this way. In consequence of their malicious activity, most of those who had entered the road, and had even made some progress towards the Temple of Fame, were soon discouraged by so much ill usage, re-measured their steps to the spot where the two roads separated, and then passed quietly on with the innumerable multitude that were irresistibly hurrying away to the Palace of Oblivion. -- There were some few, however, who, either by a daring and animated perseverance, undaunted fortitude, a native pride and dignity of soul, or by some fortunate circumstance, evaded the activity of these morose spirits and with immense difficulty reached the Palace of Fame.

"Let us walk thither, said the superintending spirit, and we shall soon discover whether their entertainment in the airy Temple of Fame is at all worth the trouble, anxiety and vexation they experienced and underwent in attaining to it." He had no sooner uttered these words than we were at the place he mentioned.

I was surprised on our first approach when I observed that this spacious building consisted of scarce any thing else than doors and windows. No refreshment of any kind was offered, and the only person we could hold any conversation with was the Genius of the Temple, who was almost constantly employed in blowing upon a trumpet, and looked so miserably meagre and gaunt that I would have sworn that, from all appearance, a meal of solid food had not entered his stomach in half a century.

The rooms within were all arched and circular, and the least whisper was re-echoed a thousand times from wall to wall and from chamber to chamber. Here and there, labels of paper were suspended, inscribed with the names and titles of former visitants; and I saw a very few persons loitering about in different parts of the palace whose countenance bespoke hearts full of disappointment and chagrin. -- "These are some of the few, said the superintending spirit, who with so much difficulty and vexation surmounted all obstacles and discouragements, and foolishly imagined they should be completely happy if they could but by any means attain to these abodes: Alas, they are as discontented as ever! here is nothing that can sufficiently reward them for their nights of labour and days of anguish, for their pains, and solicitudes, and loss of pleasures which might have been better seized while opportunity permitted. First image and reflection of the Deity, O Virtue, such shall be the lot of all who do not make thee, simply, the end and basis of all their actions. --How happy would they have been had they passed contentedly with the herd of mankind in the short and easy road to the dark valley of oblivion! But the spirit of deception had been busy among them, and not a few were persuaded that their final and most felicitous abode would be in this place. --That was delusion indeed! I shall permit them to remain here but a small number of hours; they shall have time given them to inscribe their names upon a few bits of paper and suspend them from the wall--this is in reward for their perseverance and heroism--they shall then pass through the back part of the Palace of Fame, and disappear with the rest of mankind in the dark cloud that verges on the Palace of Oblivion."--The superintending spirit had scarcely uttered these words when a violent wind began to blow thro' the temple, and tore away a great number of the paper labels that had been tacked to the walls, ceilings, doorposts, and other parts of the building, inscribed with the names of celebrated men of different ages. --"It is thus, continued the spirit, that even the memory of these candidates for everlasting fame is dissipated and lost forever: Those vain labels of paper are mostly blown away with their owners into yonder dark and impenetrable cloud, and those

249

that remain will, by some future commotion of the elements, be treated precisely in the same manner."

Thus it is then, said I, that mankind are the sport of endless deceptions! Tell me, kind spirit, for what wise purpose could man have been designed, and why is he continued in his present state of existence merely to be actuated by desires which were never meant to be gratified, and tormented with expectations which, in the end, are answered only by delusions?

"The miseries of your species, replied the spirit, are principally owing to the suggestions of the spirit of pride. What is the race of man, that they should be panting for habitations beyond the stars! You imagine yourselves the most curious work of the Deity because you possess five distinct senses--Believe me, there are beings in the universe that possess as many thousands. The qualifications that Nature designed for man in his present state are ever in his power. It is by seeking for things that are beyond him, and incompatible with his abilities for enjoyment, that he becomes miserable. While the horse is satisfied with the herbage of the plain and the wholesome spring or rivulet of clear water, he is happy because he has the full enjoyment of all that Nature intended for him; but should he once loath his natural food, and be only anxious to attain the fruits that hang on the boughs of lofty trees, or strong spirits produced by the arts of distillation, he would instantly become wretched because he would desire what his station and condition did by no means entitle him to. At the same time, I could wish you to understand and remember that this discontent with himself and his situation, so peculiar to man, ought to be an undoubted evidence with you that there is something within him different from mere material mechanism, totally distinct from the elementary principles, and which shall live again in after ages in the bright regions you see beyond the skies. --Yet to himself, continued the spirit, man is an absolute mystery: he emerged from yonder cloud of darkness in the east, and in a similar state of obscurity he must be again involved. The wisest among you have never yet been able to unravel the designs and views of the great original Spirit in permitting existence to man: I will, however, be so candid as to acknowledge that some few have been born possessed of souls of so much sagacity as to be able to look thro' yonder dark cloud that bounds the visible existence of man, so far at least as to have some faint glimmerings of the real intentions of the Deity in this matter: but whenever I discover any such, I am obligated by a most sacred oath to kill them in their infancy, lest the secrets of the Creator should be unseasonably revealed.

"You must know that this plain lay, for a prodigious succession of ages, a mere lifeless mass of matter. There was not a tree nor a bush to be seen, not a blade of grass, nor an animal, nor running streams, nor vegetables, much less the majestic race of man. At last Volatilio, the spirit of activity, came to spend some ages in these remote parts of the universe, after having passed twelve thousand <u>years of the first order</u> in traversing the immensity of space, and in erecting a prodigious variety of mundane systems in the course of his travels. One day, in looking around him, he cast his eyes upon this plain, but it did not please him. The perpetual solitude that reigned here did not agree with his active and sprightly imagination; and he soon after applied to the first principle of animation for leave to people it with several ranks of beings compounded of the soil of the plain and the water of the ponds, the whole end of whose existence should be his own amusement, in the same manner as the characters on a theatrical stage are employed to entertain their evening audience. It is but just, said he, that I should have something to divert my fancy after so many ages of fatigue and wandering through the cold and comfortless regions of inanity.

"The spirit of animation had never been averse to gratify every reasonable request of the spirit of activity, who was exceedingly dear to him, but could not on this occasion reconcile himself to the notion that creatures compounded of two such mean principles as dust and water should be admitted to a knowledge of the harmony and beauty of the universe, and to a view of those operations of Nature which he suspected would afford them too clear an idea of the DEITY for beings of their wretched and despicable origin. At last, however, upon repeated solicitations, he complied with the request of Volatilio, on condition that the faculties of the principal creature should be extremely limited and narrow, that they should have a glimpse of the wonders around them only thro' a medium of thick air, and that, after displaying a little while on the stage of human life, they should, as the law of their nature, individually revert into the identical substances of which they were originally composed, after passing thro' the Temple of Oblivion, where the perceptive faculties, according to their present organization, should forever be destroyed, and that the principle of REASON alone remain.

"Volatilio accordingly formed numberless animated substances of various shapes and qualities; but man he contrived with a particular view to his own amusement, a compound of contradictions and absurdities, virtues and vices, sorrows

252

and joys, wisdom and folly. All their disputes in philosophy, their ideas of the operations of the superior nature, their systems of astronomy, their legislation, their commerce, their wars, their massacres, their bloody devastations, their religions--all were to him matter of laughter and merriment. He saw nothing in the affairs of mankind that ever cost him a sigh or a tear, or one uneasy sensation; as some compensation, however, for the amusement they afforded him, he gave them every enjoyment that could in any way be deemed suitable or necessary to their natures; and if they still chose to perplex themselves with aiming at more than he intended for them, it only added to his pleasure, or at most excited his pity. --But I will be so candid also as to acknowledge, they were not designed to be completely happy. This gave the spirit of animation a momentary idea of sorrow, nor could it be otherwise, since he is benevolence itself. He therefore, as some alleviation of their misery, bestowed upon them the divine present of sleep, by the influence of which one third at least of their sufferings is annihilated before the final and unalterable sleep is brought upon them. Moved also with compassion at the view of those evils which, in some sense, are unavoidable, as being casual and incidental to the nature of man, he has deigned to relieve them further by different means. Cast your eyes over the plain, and you will see two personages designed for consolation. "

In compliance with his request I looked among the crowd, and saw two females of the most enchanting beauty playing upon harps and lutes, and other musical instruments, and reciting songs and airs, which every now and then seemed to brighten up the countenances of those that paid their attention to them.

"These, said the superintending spirit, are the heavenly arts of <u>Music</u> and <u>Poetry</u>. Without them, how dull and tedious would be this journey of human life! The spirit of animation has not given the heavenly Muse invain except to those who, incapable of tasting the consolation she affords, are amusing themselves with the grunting of swine and the croakings of ravens."

But was it not cruel, replied I, in the spirit of <u>Activity</u> to tantalize the human race with a view of those wonderful realities of Nature they are so capable of admiring, and which they must nevertheless forever part with after gazing at and admiring them but a moment?--"You wrong the spirit of animation, said my attendant, in calling it <u>cruelty.</u> What honour could there be in remaining in the torpid state of the clods of the valley? Who would not prefer a momentary illumination into life and perception to an eternity of unconscious sleep? This sun, this moon, these stars, this beautiful fabric of land and water, this whole system of animation, are they not well worth the trouble of beholding, though it be but for a moment?--What are all the miseries and perplexities of life when put in competition with a single glance of these stupendous wonders that are continually passing before you on the great ocean of matter? But what am I saying! Are not the pleasures that always attend upon virtuous actions a full recompence for the shortness, the wretchedness, and the uncertainty of life? The Deity is pleased with the exercise of virtue because that is the essence of his nature; and the reward of virtue is constantly found in the composure and felicity that is, or ought to be, enjoyed by every virtuous mind.

"I must now return to the Palace of Oblivion, continued the superintending spirit, to give those their eternal dismission into the abyss of darkness who have been collecting and loitering at the portal since I have been talking with you. Your time of dismission is not yet come, so that I must once more leave you in the region of human life, where I would, however, wish you to be as happy as you possibly can: Give me your hand, then, and I will conduct you into that charming part of the country that is dedicated to silence and solitude, abodes where the men of sentiment and virtue were ever inclined to dwell, and where I, as the superintending spirit of this fantastical region, would wish to leave you."

Having spoke these words, he offered to take me by the hand, but I shuddered at the idea. --I had ever (said I) a secret dread of the inhabitants of the spiritual world: your hand must be so cold! Kind spirit, you are of so strange an aspect I tremble to touch you. Grant me at least one of my own species to direct me to the charming solitudes you mention, and there I will remain till I am destined to behold you once more in the palace of forgetfulness.

"Be not afraid," said the spirit, with a good natured smile; "all the inhabitants of the world of spirits are, without exception, friendly to mankind: you are your own enemies in affixing ideas of mischief and malevolence to a class of beings that would cease to exist the moment they ceased to be virtuous."

Having said this, he seized me by the left hand to conduct me to the habitations of virtuous men, when the fright, occasioned by the sudden grasp of so formidable a spirit, awakened me just as the dawning of the day began to glimmer through the apertures of my cavern.[24]

255

A Speech on a New Subject[25]

There is a character, gentlemen, in common life, which I feel myself most earnestly inclined to copy, were it only for my own amusement, and I can assure you without having any particular person in view to hold up as the butt of my observations, a part which I have ever held to be both unfriendly, unjust and ungenerous.

The character that I would wish to copy from the aggregate of real life is no other than that of an old sea Captain, become feeble with age and hardship, and now resolved in earnest to pass the remainder of his days on shore.

We will suppose that he has hitherto had no house nor home except that which has so long floated with him on the bosom of the ocean. Having, then, quitted his vessel and bid adieu to her forever with tears in his eyes, when he first finds himself seriously and in good earnest a man of the shore, he looks about him with as much wildness and anxious concern as a landsman would that is left swimming for his life in the middle of the Atlantic.

After sauntering about awhile in the city, taking especial care never to lose sight of the river, he at length agrees to board by the month at some boarding house as near as possible to the wharfs, that he may have a full view of the shipping and an uninterrupted prospect, as well as the odoriferous smell, of the docks and salt water.

His continuance here, however, is commonly of short duration. He has been so long accustomed to command that he cannot endure to be controuled by the Landlady, who already begins to take airs upon her, and treat him in the same manner as he used to treat his second or third mate.

After shifting about from place to place, and having pestered every tavern and eating house in the city to supply him with lobscouse, sea pies, and pease porridge, he at length takes it into his head to look out for himself a wife. If you hear him describe the woman he would wish to make love to, it is in such a style and language as the following: -- I would choose to have her full bowed and lean abast-- built with a handsome sheer, but not moonsided. Breadth of beam is what I ever admired, as this gives her good bearings; her water ways ought to be well caulked, as small leaks here might do great damages, &c. &c. --After some time he marries some old seaman's widow, who, from former conversation, can understand his discourse, and from a similar cause can endure the smell of pitch, tar, rosin, and turpentine, one or more of which substances he always has in moderate quantities sticking to his coat, breeches, waistcoat, or hair.

He now begins to think of building a house. In this view he purchases a lot as close as possible to the river side, and where the yard arms of the shipping may extend entirely over his roof. If the high tides come into his cellar, so much the better; this he calls dead water, and it pleases him much, as it sets all hands to work at the pumps, and gives them all the labour and trouble of a leaky ship in a gale of wind without danger of going to the bottom. --As to his carpenters and joiners, they soon conclude him to be half crazy, as he is perpetually talking to them of dead lights instead of window shutters, bulk heads instead of partitions, and spar decks instead of roofs and upper floors. -- Instead of lapping or grooving his weatherboards, he insists upon square joints which he obliges them to caulk with two or three threads of oakum, and pay over with hot pitch. If

257

there are any butts, he has them secured with strong spikes or butt-bolts with a key and forelock, altho' a common twelve penny nail or two might answer the purpose effectually. --If he keeps a shop it is sure to be in the ship chandlery way, as he abominates the scent of all other merchandize; and indeed either the ship chandlery business or a tavern, with boarding and lodging for sea faring men, commonly finishes the career of his existence. --Should he by any accident be obliged to remove into the country, he is unhappy if not settled on the side of a river, where he may row out, and now and then take the latitude by observing the sun's altitude with a Hadley's quadrant. If he travels in a passage boat, he obstinately refuses to turn in during the heaviest rain, altho' the hands belonging to the vessel be amply sufficient for every purpose upon deck. --In a journey by land he always lays by if the wind blows hard the contrary way--Egg-nog is his favourite liquor in the morning--grog at eleven o'clock, and such wine as he can afford after dinner, which generally consists of salt port and pease, with sea biscuit instead of bread. When he finds himself near his end, the idea that he is going to make a voyage upon discoveries constantly recurs to his imagination, and he makes his epitaph accordingly.

Such, gentlemen, are the strange vagaries of this extraordinary character--I have only however stretched out some of those principal traits which may give you some idea of the surprising influence of habit upon the human mind--much more might have been said, which, nevertheless, for good reasons I have thought best to leave to the exercise of your own imaginations.

A Discourse Upon Horse Shoes[26]

When I first arrived in this town, the residence of the Beloved Chief and the Great Council of the Thirteen Fires, my attention was very much attracted by those huge floating machines in which the white men pass over the immense waters from country to country, and even (they tell me) to those remote limits where the great star of the day rises over the regions of the east. My imagination was busied in contemplating the wisdom and sagacity not only of those who have with so much art constructed these machines, but also of those men who are entrusted with the management and direction of them on the face of such a dangerous and vastly extended element as my understanding tells me the ocean must be. How, said I, is it possible for them when once they have left the main shores, to direct the prow with so much art and precision to some small spot of earth, placed like a hill in the midst of the unfathomable waters! Doubtless they must be possessed of sagacity superior to the rest of mankind.

Such were my reasonings at that time. But I have since discovered that the men of the present age possess the accumulated knowledge of the thousands that have elapsed. Every past century has been gaining little by little, and at length the weight of all their knowledge has fallen upon the heads of the men of the time in which we now live.

On a certain day my curiosity led me (in company with my interpreter) to go on board one of these big canoes.[27] I was surprised to find it furnished like a house, accommodated with every necessary for passing many months with comfort on the great ocean which rolls over the immeasurable spaces towards the east. My various enquiries were amply gratified by the commander through the

259

mouth of my interpreter. He seemed particularly complaisant to me, as being a stranger, and endeavoured to make me comprehend particularly the use of every part of the furniture that was subservient to the navigating and manoeuvring of his vessel.

Indeed my own simple reason and observation could, in some degree, account for the end and design of the greater part of the objects that I saw. At last, directing my observation to the lower extremity of one of the masts, I could not avoid asking myself what could be the purpose of nailing a thin plate of iron of a form approaching to circular and pierced with several small holes, thereupon. After forming a thousand conjectures, but not one that in the least cleared up my doubts, I directed the interpreter to enquire of the master what could be the use of this flat piece of semi-circular metal?

He immediately replied that the iron which had so much attracted my attention was no other than a common HORSE SHOE, which he himself had nailed in that spot previous to his embarking on his first voyage.

True! replied I, upon recollection, it is indeed a horse shoe, and such have I frequently seen heretofore in my own country. But of what possible use or advantage can this be to the great canoe that travels only upon the face of the watry element!

The commander seemed somewhat confused at my question. But instantly recollecting himself, he desired me to retire with him and sit down in his wigwam; and then, pouring out a bowl of red wine which he desired me to drink off, he addressed me in the following manner:

"You must know that there is a certain wonderful connexion and sympathy between the things above and the things below, the invisible parts of the animated creation and those parts which on this earth are the objects of our sight and other senses. Among the invisible intelligences there are not a few orders that take a supreme delight in injuring and throwing miseries and misfortunes in the way of mankind. It is these that wing the hurricane, scatter the seeds of pestilence through the air, and blast the fruits of the earth at a time when our hopes and desires are fixed upon their prosperity. Against these, therefore, it is our duty to be upon our guard, and, by every method we can devise, repel if possible the shafts of their vindictive malice.

"Time has been when men wandered over the ocean without the least knowledge of the virtues of the horse-shoe! Those times, however, thank Heaven, are past and gone. With this inestimable jewel for a companion we can now traverse the seas in safety, and not be in constant dread of the destructive influences of every vagabond atom of mischievous volition that rambles through our atmosphere, and by some unknown means harasses us even from the orbits of the superior planets.

But, you will ask me, by what strange means does the horse-shoe ensure safety to the ship, her crew, and her cargo?

"I answer that it is only in particular circumstances and positions that it ensures any safety at all. For instance, a horse shoe new from the blacksmith's anvil would be of no avail against the malevolent powers. The shoe must have travelled many hundreds of miles attached to the foot of the animal, and even be worn to a certain degree of roundness on the outer edge before it will answer our purpose. It is our custom also, evermore to place the open part downward, as by this means the shoe represents an arch (which is the token of strength) as well as the rotundity of the heavens over our heads, which are fixed, durable, and to last forever.

"It is by effects only that we can hope to arrive to any knowledge of a cause. If, therefore, I can honestly assure you that I have sailed there five & forty years upon the deep seas, and never experienced any dangerous accident in such ships or barques as had this particular piece of iron attached to them, but constantly the reverse in those vessels wherein I neglected it, be assured there must be some reality in the matter, and that horse-shoes, when thus applied, have the undoubted power of keeping mischief at a distance. "

The mystery being thus, in some sort, explained, I bade farewell to the master of the great canoe, not without amazement when I considered the almost universal influence of folly and superstition over the most intelligent minds. This man, said I, has subjected the winds and tempests to his controul; he has so cunningly contrived things that the rays of the sun, instead of only serving to afford him light and warmth, are, by the intervention of some curious instruments, compelled to be his guides and directors; and yet, with all his knowledge, and a great deal more, he is weak enough to make his secret dependence for safety upon certain imaginary effects proceeding from a worthless scrap of crooked iron! What a number of barques and canoes have I since visited, and not one of them all but has its horse-shoe!

Such is the wisdom of the white men. They laugh at us for our credulity in maintaining some scores of paw-was to avert, by their howlings and lacerations, the vengeance of the great evil Being. They despise us for believing in our good and bad <u>Moneetas</u>, and paying a superstitious reverence to certain animals in the forest; they call us rude, savage and unenlightened at the very instant when they themselves are putting their trust in HORSE SHOES!

On Epic Poetry[28]

In order to mount at once to the very principle of poetical fame, let your first attempt in this way be an Epic poem. It is the grandest work, says a French critic, that the human mind is capable of conceiving or executing. For my own part, however, I see no such wonderful difficulty in the matter, and I think, brother Eliakim, I can put you at once into the way of writing a very good Epic poem, and at the same time run no risque of crazing your brain by deep study, or losing your eye sight by gazing with too steady an attention upon the bright side of Nature's workmanship.

In the first place, borrow or purchase Pope's Homer's Iliad, the Odyssey, Pitt's or Dryden's translation of Virgil, and if you please, (by way of learning how to avoid the <u>bathos</u>) one of Blackmore's Epics, either Prince or King Arthur, it matters not much which. Read these over by night and by day (and do not forget to put them under your pillow at night) till you have got the complete sing-song-Heroic in your head--This I can assure you is one great step towards writing Epic poetry.

In the next place, look out diligently for a <u>Fable</u>. You might as well make pumpkin pye without pumpkins, or turtle soup from a calf's head, or lastly build a house without first laying a foundation, as make an Epic poem without a fable. If you cannot find one readily in ancient or modern history, apply to your old school-sachel and peradventure you will find somewhat there that may answer the purpose tolerably well.

If nothing else seems to be proper for this purpose, turn to the ancient Jewish history (as compiled by Josephus and others); you will there find matter plenty for your purpose--There can be no true Epic poem without plenty of butchering work; and here it is displayed to perfection in the annals of the Hebrew butchers, there being authentic accounts of now and then of eighteen or twenty thousand young children having been cut to pieces of a morning by order of the supreme Being (alias the Priests.)

No epic poem can be a good one wherein the dreams and nonsense of antiquity have not a preference given to them over modern rationality. --You must (as of old) consider this world as comprizing within itself the universe-- the supreme being must be (blasphemously) represented as taking one side in the miserable quarrels and savage contentions of the inhabitants of this earth; wretches, who crawl into existence they know not how, waste their little life in murdering and destroying each other while here, and then retire in an agony of pain they know not where.

Nonsense is a considerable ingredient in every true epic--and is frequently found to have a wonderful effect in making a poem popular: for instance, in describing a battle over-head, you may say--"In fields of air unreal hosts contend;" that is to say, there is a battle in the air fought by no body. If this be not some of your right epic stuff, I am sure I know not what is.

If at any time you are (comparatively or otherwise) describing a storm at sea, and a ship caught therein, be sure to lose sight entirely of the improvements of modern navigation--you may, for instance, describe the operations on ship board, at such a time, in the manner following:

"Dissolv'd in terror, sailors eye the wave,
Lift ardent prayers, and wait the gaping grave."

However, as a modern, I pronounce that captain a mere old woman who, in our day, suffers his seamen to act in this manner. I appeal to any man that has ever been to sea, if sailors are not rather at such times employed in sending down yards and top gallant-masts, bringing the ship to wind, or scudding before it under bare poles, with other manoeuvres usual in similar cases.

These few rules will be sufficient to give you some idea how to set out in your epic career; after these are well studied I may perhaps give you some additional instructions in the same way.

The Rights of the Indian[29]

(All our curious dock-walkers must have taken notice of the fine Indian Head of the ship Delaware, belonging to this port. Whether it was from a late attentive survey of that figure (which is a model of perfection in its kind) or from what other cause I know not, but upon my retiring to rest a few nights ago, I no sooner fell asleep than I imagined myself standing upon one of the wharves, with the carved Indian figure full in my front, when it instantly assumed the mien and attitude of an orator, and with a menacing frown uttered the following speech to a crowd that had collected upon this extraordinary occasion.)

"I have every reason to believe, gentlemen, that I was placed here as the emblem of valour, activity, perseverance, industry and cunning. So far, therefore, have your countrymen testified in favor of an opinion, almost universally exploded, that the inhabitants of the western forests have some affinity with the human species. I wish they had gone a little farther, and in their general conduct towards our tribes in peace and war treated us as beings possessed of reason, and practicing some few of the inferior virtues. Alas, it is too evident from their actions that they place us upon a footing with the beasts of the wilderness, and consider an Indian and a Buffaloe as alike entitled by nature to property or possession.

"My heart bleeds within me when I reflect upon the wrongs of my countrymen, the insignificant rank they appear to hold in the scale of animated being, and their probable extirpation from the continent of America.

"Nature is cruel in all her works. She successively destroys not only the individuals of a species, but at certain periods a whole class of a species; nay, even the species itself sometimes totally disappears. This cruel mother is nevertheless so merciful as, for the most part, to bring about such events imperceptibly and gradually. Why then would you anticipate her designs, and by every means in your power hurry us in a moment from this earth before nature has said, There is an end to the children of the forest?

"Our habitations were once on the borders of the rivers of the ocean, and in the pleasant vicinity of its shores. The sails of Columbus, and Cabot, and Raleigh appeared. With grief we saw your superior skill, your surprising pre-eminence in art, your machines of death before which our arrows and darts were no more than the toys of children-- In dread of your superior power, we retreated from the shore to the Allegany, from the Allegany to the Ohio; we have bid an everlasting adieu to the pleasant land of Kentucky; you have at length followed us over the Ohio--you meditate to drive us beyond the Mississippi--to the lake of the woods, to the frozen desarts of the north, and to the regions of darkness and desolation. But how unreasonable, how cruel are your designs. Compelling us to remove farther into the forests is the same to us as death and ruin. We must there fight for the possession of the soil before we can hunt in safety, as independent possessors; and as we retreat before you, remember that foes of our own colour and kindred increase upon us, like swarms from the hollow tree: Nations extremely tenacious of their hunting grounds, less enervated with your baneful liquors than ourselves, and consequently more warlike, more robust, and even gods, in comparison to the feeble tribes who yet exist between you and them.

"You detest us for having the feelings of men; you despise, in us, the virtue of patriotism, so natural to all mankind and so extolled by yourselves. But what were your feelings when, only a few years ago, the great king on the other side of the water intruded upon your rights? You filled the world with your clamors--heaven and earth were called to witness that you were determined to defend those rights which had been bestowed upon you by the Great Man above, and for the preservation of which you prayed him to smile upon your warfare. He heard your prayers and you were successful; the enemy retired with shame, and your warfare was crowned with an honorable peace.

"You yourselves are now, in your turn, become the oppressors. Do not blame us then for possessing the same feelings with yourselves on the same occasion. Your desperation carried all before it, and why would not ours do the same, when we are obliged to act against you from the same motives?

"Say not that you have purchased our territory. Was a keg of whiskey, some bundles of laced coats, or a few packages of blankets an equivalent for the extent of a kingdom? or was a bargain with some drunken chiefs of one or two nations an obligation upon an hundred tribes?

"How much do ye stand in your own light, ye free white men of America--How are you duped by the deep and designing!--Not a single soldier need be sent to act offensively in the Indian country. Our commercial intercourse with you would effectually destroy us as fast as you could advance your frontier by cultivation and natural population. Your neighborhood is death to us. We cannot exist among you--but suffer us, we beseech you, to disappear gradually from this miserable stage of human existence, and not like a taper, by a sudden blast, be extinguished in a moment!

"You have, at different times, been at much expence in sending among us religious missionaries to effect our conversion to your faith. I wish those gentlemen had been as assiduous in inculcating the practice of the moral and social virtues as they were busy in pestering us with mysteries.--They have, however, said enough upon the virtue of temperance to persuade us not to destroy ourselves with rum, brandy, or New-England Whiskey during the remainder of the present century.--These good men have now quit us entirely, and given us up to the god of nature--you send armies in their room, not to convert, but to destroy us, to burn our towns and turn us out naked to the mercy of the elements, to shoot us down wherever they can see us, and propagate a principle as disgraceful to your pretended age of philosophy as it is repugnant to truth and reason, that the rights of an Indian are not the rights of a man!---"[30]

Being suddenly awaked by the yelpings of a spaniel,

268

that constantly sleeps at the foot of my bed, I lost the remainder of this extraordinary speech.

Sentiments of a Republican[31]

A certain prince once asked one of his ministers how
he should counteract the ideas of liberty which he had observed to prevail among his subjects in certain parts of his
dominions. "Force them, (said the minister) to rebel, and
thus punish them by confiscating the very means they will
have of supporting a struggle for liberty." The advice was
followed, and with the wished for success. Lewis XIVth
asked Cardinal Richelieu how he should annihilate the remains of liberty which still existed in the kingdom of
France. "Fill your kingdom (said the Cardinal) with places
of public amusement, and by these means divert the people
from thinking or talking upon the affairs of government."
The efficacy of this measure in completing the despotism of
the late French government is too well known to be mentioned.

From the present signs of the declining state of liberty in our country, it would seem as if some demon, un-
friendly to human happiness, had whispered in the ears of
the first Congress that assembled under the present government, that the most speedy and effectual method of destroying the liberties of the United States was to establish and
perpetuate among them a national debt.

Innumerable have been the evils introduced by the
funded debt of the United States. But the most alarming
one is, it has produced so much inequality in point of property among our citizens as to endanger the safety of our
government. The most barefaced efforts have been made
to substitute, in the room of our equal republic, a baneful

monarchy in our country; and it is too evident these efforts originate with those states and with those individuals who are most interested in the funding system. Examine the newspapers and the journals of Congress, and you will find that the propositions for titles, for an equestrian statue, for keeping birth days, and for emitting royal coin all come from those two quarters. The propositions are as degrading to the President of the United States as they are dangerous and insulting to the people, for they are calculated to reduce him to a level with the titled and royal banditti of Europe, who govern their subjects by fraud or violence.

If our wealthy speculators, in and out of Congress, cannot enjoy their immense estates without creating among us a power that shall hereafter ennoble them, let them transport themselves across the ocean and back in the splendor of courts, birthday assemblies, and royal pictures and statues in some old and corrupted country. Let the United States disgorge such beasts of plunder and prey; and let them do more, let them immediately devise ways and means for the payment of every farthing of the national debt. It is a millstone about the neck of our country. It is even worse than a calamity that induces suffocation and death. It is a monster from whose foetid bowels proceed monarchy, aristocracy, and slavery.

Rules for Changing a Limited Republican Government
into an Unlimited Hereditary One[32]

I. It being necessary, in order to effect the change, to get rid of constitutional shackles and popular prejudices, all possible means and occasions are to be used for both these purposes.

II. Nothing being more likely to prepare the vulgar

mind for aristocratical ranks and hereditary powers than TITLES, endeavor in the offset of the government to confer those on its most dignified officers. If the principal magistrate should happen to be particularly venerable in the eyes of the people, take advantage of that fortunate circumstance in setting the example.

III. Should the attempt fail, thro' his republican aversion to it, or from the danger of alarming the people, do not abandon the enterprize altogether, but lay up the proposition in record. Time may gain it respect, and it will be there always ready cut and dried for any favourable conjuncture that may offer.

IV. In drawing all bills, resolutions, and reports, keep constantly in view that the limitations in the constitution are ultimately to be explained away. Precedents and phrases may thus be shuffled in, without being adverted to by candid or weak people, of which good use may afterwards be made.

V. As the novelty and bustle of inaugurating the government will for some time keep the public mind in a heedless and unsettled state, let the Press during this period be busy in propagating the doctrines of monarchy and aristocracy. For this purpose it will be particularly useful to confound a mobbish democracy with a representative republic, that by exhibiting all the turbulent examples and enormities of the former, an odium may be thrown on the character of the latter. Review all the civil contests, convulsions, factions, broils, squabbles, bickerings, black eyes and bloody noses of ancient, middle and modern ages, caricature them into the most frightful forms and colours that can be imagined, and unfold one scene of the horrible tragedy after another 'till the people be made, if possible, to tremble at their own shadows.--Let the discourses on--then contrast with these pictures of terror the quiet of hereditary succession, the reverence claimed by birth and nobility, and the fascinating influence of stars, ribbands, and garters, cautiously suppressing all the bloody tragedies and unceasing oppressions which form the history of this species of government. No pains should be spared in this part of the undertaking, for the greatest will be wanted, it being extremely difficult, especially when a people have been taught to reason and feel their rights, to convince them that a king who is always an enemy to the people, and a nobility who are perhaps still more so, will take better care of the people than the people will take care of themselves.

VI. But the grand nostrum will be a PUBLIC DEBT, provided enough of it can be got, and it be medicated with the proper ingredients. If by good fortune a debt be ready at hand, the most is to be made of it. Stretch it and swell it to the utmost the items will bear. Allow as many extra claims as decency will permit. Assume all the debts of your neighbours: In a word, get as much debt as can be raked and scraped together, and when you have got all you can, "advertize" for more, and have the debt made as big as possible. This object being accomplished, the next will be to make it as perpetual as possible, and the next to that, to get it into as few hands as possible. The more effectually to bring this about, modify the debt, complicate it, divide it, subdivide it, subtract it, postpone it, let there be one third of two thirds, and two thirds of one third, and two thirds of two thirds: let there be three per cents, and four per cents, and six per cents, and present six per cents, and future six per cents. To be brief, let the whole be such a mystery that a few only can understand it; and let

272

all possible opportunities and informations fall in the way of these few, to clinch their advantage over the many.

VII.   It must not be forgotten that the members of the legislative body are to have a deep stake in the game.   This is an essential point, and happily is attended with no difficulty.   A sufficient number, properly disposed, can alternately legislate and speculate, and speculate and legislate, and buy and sell, and sell and buy, until a due portion of the property of their constituents has passed into their hands to give them an interest against their constituents, and to ensure the part they are to act.   All this however   must be carried on under cover of the closest secrecy; and it is particularly lucky that dealings in paper admit of more secrecy than any other.   Should a discovery take place, the whole plan may be blown up.

VIII.   The ways in which a great debt, so constituted and applied, will contribute to the ultimate end in view are both numerous and obvious.   1.   The favourite few, thus possessed of it, whether within or without the government, will feel the staunchest fealty to it, and will go through thick and thin to support it in all its oppressions and usurpations.   2. Their money will give them consequence and influence, even among those who have been tricked out of it. 3.   They will be the readiest materials that can be found for an hereditary aristocratic order, and whenever matters are ripe for one.   4.   A great debt will require great taxes, great taxes many taxgatherers & other officers: & all officers are auxiliaries of power.   5. Heavy taxes may produce discontents; these may threaten resistance; and in proportion to this danger will be the pretence of a standing army to repel it.   6. A standing army in its turn will increase the moral force of the government by means of its appointments,

273

and give it physical force by means of the sword, thus doubly forwarding the main object.

IX.　The management of a great funded debt and an extensive system of taxes will afford a plea not to be neglected, for establishing a great incorporated bank. The use of such a machine is well understood. If the constitution, according to its fair meaning, should not authorize it, so much the better. Push it through by a forced meaning, and you will get in the bargain an admirable precedent for future misconstructions. In fashioning the bank remember that it is to be made particularly instrumental in enriching and aggrandizing the elect few, who are to be called in due season to the honors and felicities of the kingdom preparing for them, and who are the pillars that must support it. It will be easy to throw the benefit entirely into their hands, and to make it a solid addition of 50, or 60, or 70 per cent. to their former capitals of 800 per cent. or 900 per cent. without costing them a shilling, whilst it will be so difficult to explain to the people that this gain of the few is at the cost of the many, that the contrary may be boldly and safely pretended. The bank will be pregnant with other important advantages. It will admit the same men to be, at the same time, members of the bank and members of the government. The two institutions will thus be soldered together, and each made the stronger. Money will be put under the direction of the government, and the government under the direction of money. To crown the whole, the bank will have a proper interest in swelling and perpetuating the public debt and public taxes, with all the blessings of both, because its agency and its profits will be extended in exact proportion.

X.　"Divide and govern" is a maxim consecrated by the

experience of ages, and should be as familiar in its use to every politician as the knife he carries in his pocket. In the work here to be executed the best effects may be produced by this maxim, and with peculiar facility. An extensive republic made up of lesser republics necessarily contains various sorts of people, distinguished by local and other interests and prejudices. Let the whole group be well examined in all its parts and relations, geographical and political, metaphysical and metaphorical; let there be first a northern and a southern section by a line running east and west, and then an eastern and western section by a line running north and south. By a suitable nomenclature, the landholders cultivating different articles can be discriminated from one another, all from the class of merchants, and both from that of manufacturers. One of the subordinate republics may be represented as a commercial state, another as a navigation state, another as a manufacturing state, others as agricultural states; and although the great body of the people in each be really agricultural, and the other characters be more or less common to all, still it will be politic to take advantage of such an arrangement. Should the members of the great republic be of different sizes, and subject to little jealousies on that account, another important division will be ready formed to your hand. Add again the divisions that may be carved out of personal interests, political opinions, and local parties. --With so convenient an assortment of votes, especially with the help of the marked ones, a majority may be packed for any question with as much ease as the odd trick by an adroit gamester, and any measure whatever be carried or defeated, as the great revolution to be brought about may require. It is only necessary therefore to recommend that full use be

275

made of the resource: and to remark that, besides the direct benefit to be drawn from these artificial divisions, they will tend to smother the true and natural one, existing in all societies between the few who are always impatient of political equality, and the many who can never rise above it; between those who are to mount to the prerogatives, and those who are to be saddled with the burthens of the hereditary government to be introduced; in one word, between the general mass of the people, attached to their republican government and republican interests, and the chosen band devoted to monarchy and mammon.

XI. As soon as sufficient progress in the intended change shall have been made, and the public mind duly prepared according to the rules already laid down, it will be proper to venture on another and a bolder step towards a removal of the constitutional land-marks. Here the aid of former encroachments, and all the other precedents and way-paving manoeuvres, will be called in of course. But, in order to render success the more certain, it will be of special moment to give the most plausible and popular name that can be found to the power that is to be usurped. It may be called, for example, a power for the common safety or the public good, or "the general welfare." If the people should not be too much enlightened, the name will have a most imposing effect. It will escape attention that it means, in fact, the same thing with a power to do any thing the government pleases "in all cases whatsoever." To oppose the power may consequently seem to the ignorant, and be called by the artful, opposing the "general welfare," and may be cried down under that deception. As the people, however, may not run so readily into the snare as might be wished, it will be prudent to bait it well with some specious popular interest, such as the encouragement of manufactures, or even of agriculture, taking care not even to mention any unpopular object to which the power is equally applicable, such as religion, &c. &c. &c. By this contrivance, particular classes of people may possibly be taken in who will be a valuable reinforcement. With respect to the patronage of agriculture, there is not indeed much to be expected from it. It will be too quickly seen through by the owners and tillers of the soil, that to tax them with one hand, and pay back a part only with the other, is a losing game on their side. From the power over manufactures more is to be hoped. It will not be so easily perceived that the premium bestowed may not be equal to the circuitous tax on consumption, which pays it. There are particular reasons, too, for pushing the experiment on this class of citizens. 1. As they live in towns and can act together, it is of vast consequence to gain them over to the interest of monarchy. 2. If the power over them be once established, the government can grant favours or monopolies as it pleases; can raise or depress this or that place, as it pleases; can gratify this or that individual, as it pleases; in a word, by creating a dependence in so numerous and important a class of citizens, it will increase its own independence of every class, and be more free to pursue the grand object in contemplation. 3. The expence of this operation will not in the end cost the government a shilling, for the moment any branch of manufacture has been brought to a state of tolerable maturity, the exciseman will be ready with his constable and his search-warrant to demand a reimbursement and as much more as can be squeezed out of the article. All this, it is to be remembered, supposes that the manufacturers will be weak enough to be cheated, in some respects, out of their

277

interests, and wicked enough, in others, to betray those of
their fellow citizens, a supposition that, if known, would
totally mar the experiment.   Great care, therefore, must be
taken to prevent it from leaking out.

XII.   The expediency of seizing every occasion of external danger for augmenting and perpetuating the standing
military force is too obvious to escape.   So important is
this matter that for any loss or disaster whatever attending
the national arms, there will be ample consolation and compensation in the opportunity for enlarging the establishment.
A military defeat will become a political victory, and the
loss of a little vulgar blood contributes to ennoble that
which flows in the veins of our future dukes and marquisses.

XIII. The same prudence will improve the opportunity
afforded by an increase of the military expenditures, for perpetuating the taxes required for them.   If the inconsistency
and absurdity of establishing a perpetual tax for a temporary service should produce any difficulty in the business,
Rule 10 must be resorted to.   Throw in as many extrane-
ous motives as will make up a majority, and the thing is
effected in an instant.   What was before evil will become
good as easily as black could be made white by the same
magical operation.

XIV.   Throughout this great undertaking it will be wise
to have some particular model constantly in view.   The work
can then be carried on more systematically, and every
measure be fortified, in the progress, by apt illustrations
and authorities.   Should there exist a particular monarchy
against which there are fewer prejudices than against any
other: should it contain a mixture of the representative
principle so as to present on one side the semblance of a
republican aspect; should it moreover have a great, funded,

complicated, irredeemable debt, with all the apparatus and
appurtenances of excises, banks, &c. &c. &c. upon that a
steady eye is to be kept.   In all cases it will assist, and in
most its statute-book will furnish a precise pattern by which
there may be cut out any monied or monarchical project
that may be wanted.

XV.   As it is not to be expected that the change of a
republic into a monarchy, with the rapidity desired, can be
carried through without occasional suspicions and alarms, it
will be necessary to be prepared for such events.   The best
general rule on the subject is to be taken from the example
of crying "Stop thief" first. --Neither lungs nor pens must
be spared in charging every man who whispers, or even
thinks, that the revolution on foot is meditated, with being
himself an enemy to the established government and meaning to overturn it.   Let the charge be reiterated and rever-
berated, till at last such confusion and uncertainty be produced that the people, being not able to find out where the
truth lies, withdraw their attention from the contest. [33]

Many other rules of great wisdom and efficacy ought
to be added: but it is conceived that the above will be
abundantly enough for the purpose.   This will certainly be
the case if the people can be either kept asleep so as not
to discover, or be thrown into artificial divisions, so as
not to resist what is silently going forward. --Should it be
found impossible, however, to prevent the people from
awaking and uniting; should all artificial distinctions give way
to the natural division between the lordly minded few and the
well-disposed many; should all who have common interest
make a common cause and shew an inflexible attachment to
republicanism in opposition to a government of monarchy
and of money, why then ****--

Power Belongs to the People[34]

Every friend of man and the rational rights of man cannot but rejoice at the disappointment of the combined royalists in their late campaign against France.--Despotism never, in any age, avowed his principle more directly and openly than in the daring attempt of these powers to deprive a nation, by violence, of the natural and inherent right of making laws to suit itself, and to establish such a mode of government over themselves as they should see fit. In this attempt is completely developed the accursed, overbearing nature of despotic or absolute power, which has hitherto existed by ignorance, imposture, bloodshed, and devastation.   Like the devil, it has been a murderer from the beginning; and whoever reads the history of Europe only will find from thence that in all ages the people have been led to the field of slaughter either to gratify the imaginary wrongs of individuals, to glut the thirst of personal ambition, and in fact for almost every purpose except that of ensuring peace, liberty, property, and happiness to themselves.   From the melancholy example of past ages may the world learn that power only belongs to the people, and that every individual to whom it is delegated ought to be held immediately and continually responsible to them, the fountain of all authority, for the exercise thereof, a neglect of which precaution has given birth to myriads of crowned and titled monsters, the disgrace of human nature in every century that has passed and the bane of nineteen twentieths of the habitable globe at the present hour.

How to Relieve Congress from Thinking[35]

In public bodies where the members are honest and

independent, a difference of opinions is the natural consequence. It is the tax which liberty pays for its defence against internal danger. There are some, however, who undervalue the object so much as to be unwilling to hold it under this incumbrance. The admirers of the present British system consider as a less evil that ministerial corruption which unites and secures a ready majority on all questions. In the United States such a remedy for the disease would be premature. It is necessary that some further evacuations of republican bile should be premised. In the mean time a good hint may be taken from a paragraph in the last Gazette of the United States, in the chapter of COMMUNICATIONS, which ascribes the happy union of the majorities in the House of Representatives on subjects of finance to the management of the business by one person, and contrasts therewith the discordant opinions of the opposers of the system, who presume to think for themselves. It would be curious to examine into the mode by which the opinions of the majority are thus rescued from the disagreement under which the minority labours. But it is of more importance to improve on the example as stated, by extending the advantage to all other cases as well as that of finance. For this purpose it is humbly proposed that the business of legislation be divided into the several distinct classes of subjects which compose it, and that the management of each class be put on a like footing, and so as to have the like effect with that ascribed to the provision already made. The legislative body, or a majority at least, might then free themselves altogether from the trouble of thinking, the public business would go on more systematically, expeditiously, and oeconomically; the different plans conceived by the individuals of the minority would gradually

281

disgrace them, opposition would cease within doors and the calm there would lead to that delicious serenity and sweet repose throughout the community which distinguish the governments where the natural right of thinking is extinguished as a necessary sacrifice to the objects for which man enters into civil society.

The Monarchy Lovers[36]

All efforts towards monarchy and aristocracy being rendered abortive by various circumstances, we now find the former advocates of titular distinctions declaring that they only heretofore recommended such things in jest, and never once entertained a serious thought that distinctions of this kind could be countenanced by any constitution in the United States while the people remain what they are. It is also denied by the secret advocates for American monarchy "that any king-making party exists of the United States."--This is probably true: the current of popular opinion is become so strong against every idea, intimation, and attempt of that nature that the advocates and planners of such schemes no longer dare venture abroad with their propositions for giving the government a twist towards royalty, the eager though somewhat concealed object of a well known faction for at least four years by-past, if not from the very hour of the conclusion of the war. They now lie in petto, have hawled in their horns, and are completely astounded at the ungracious prospect before them, and are even assuming a tone of language directly opposite to what they formerly held;-- they may therefore be considered as extinct, and their venom almost as harmless as that of the old tories of 1776.

Materials are now collecting, and there will, at a day not very far distant, be published a curious history of the efforts that were made three or four years ago to introduce Titles and Hereditary Orders into the United States. It was presumed that the popular enthusiasm, roused as it was on a certain memorable occasion, would unsuspectedly establish the much wish'd for power and dignities, civil and ecclesiastical. --At this period mitres and maces were first imported; and laughable, indeed, it is to recollect when the births of the well-born were regularly published in a certain gazette (the editor of which, it is said, had the promise of being made Equerry of the stables in case the titular system had succeeded) and the people in a fair way of being taught to look up to the offspring of their public servants as to a set of superior beings, young masters and mistresses to whom they were hereafter to pay court, cap-in-hand, and bow the knee of servile obedience.

Altho' the good sense of the people soon saw thro' and despised these stupid attempts at aping the nonsense and villainy of European courts, yet the wiley abetters of those tinsel dignities and distinctions were not easily discouraged. No endeavor has been omitted, ever since the period above mentioned, to poison and infatuate the minds of the people, and to prejudice them against that honest simplicity in the administration of government which ought never to predominate in an American republic. The scene of affairs, however, in France, has operated as a perpetual discouragement to such high-minded innovators amongst us; and the total downfall of royalty and nobility in that country (as has been expressed on another occasion) will, like an early frost, utterly blast and annihilate the germ of this poisonous weed in America.

It is curious to observe how the ideas of your American monarchy-mongers have flowed altogether in corrupted

European channels. For instance--In order to fix a precedent "for him that is to come after," the birth-day of a
popular or meritorious character cannot pass without his being pestered with long splay-foot odes on that occasion. Incense is offered that is disdained to be snuffed--and which
is yet offered, and even attempted to be puffed up the nos-
trils, in spite of the most marked contempt. To prevent
expressions of disgust in future, poet-laureats are now
talked of for this purpose, who, as being supposed men of
ability, would be able to cook up the incense in such a manner as to make it at least tolerable to the olfactory nerves.
But who ever heard of a poet-laureat in a plain, frugal republic?--It is an office altogether monarchical, and when established, ought (if right took place) to be rejected with the
other paraphernalia, trappings, and tinsel of exploded royalty. If, however, it should be thought necessary in future to
continue regularly in this country the practice of birth-day-
ode-making, a proper character ought in due time to be
pitched on for the purpose. --That he should be a sycophant
and a toad-eater would be the first great requisite. In other respects, he should be one who has turned off an epic or
two, and who, if required, can write as many as the renowned Blackmore[37] without fainting--and such, to our hon-
or be it said, we can find in abundance by turning our views
a little eastward. [38] If he happens to have a good deal of
the courtier in his composition, so much the better, for
however the mere poet in any country may have reason to
reflect upon the world for not having searched out or properly rewarded poetical merit, there is no doubt but the
court-sycophant, under any government, will always find
himself amply rewarded for the servile adulation he pays to
men of weak minds and ambitious expectations.

For a Republican Theatre[39]

A theatre is now erected in Charleston, S. C. in consequence of a repeal of a former prohibitory law of the legislature of that state, and we hear strenuous exertions are shortly to be made in Boston for a like repeal of the law in force against stage exhibitions in that state. Under judicious management, there is no doubt but a theatre might be rendered morally instructive and innocently entertaining even in a democratic government; at the same time it is too true that many plays, now in high vogue, ought to undergo a sentence of expulsion as illy adapted to inculcate that virtuous simplicity, humility of demeanor and love of equal liberty which ought alike to actuate governors and governed in a pure and virtuous republic. If, on the American stage, we are to be entertained with dramatic productions exhibiting the theatrical foppery of fretful, passionate kings, pouting queens, rakish princes and flirting princesses, knavish ministers and peevish secretaries, lamenting misfortunes in which the bulk of mankind are no way concerned, daggering, poisoning, or hanging themselves for grievances that are purely imaginary--better that we were without them. --Regal conquests and the struggles of regal ambition, the base plots of aristocracy and the splendid feats of military butchers are by no means proper subjects for an American stage, except only when held up as objects of public abhorrence and detestation. But even in such case, scenes of this kind are dangerous, as the false glare of valorous achievement and the deceptive colourings of poetic art too frequently lead the unsuspecting auditor to a sort of tacit approbation, a tear of condolence, or a sigh of sympathy with the royal, the noble, or the heroic sufferer. Few stage exhibitions can, indeed, be useful in any degree, except such as inculcate an observance of the moral and social duties, or in some shape tend to better the heart without vitiating the understanding by an overstrained address to the fancy. It has ever been the policy of ministers of state, in all monarchical governments, or governments verging towards monarchy, to create and countenance alluring amusements, in order to prevent the people from thinking. A few years ago, when parties ran high in England, Garrick was employed by the government to give a jubilee in honour of Shakespeare, at Stratford upon Avon. The scheme succeeded beyond expectation. Wilkes and Liberty were neglected, and for a long time nobody meddled with politics. To the same purpose the celebrated dancer, Vestris, was afterwards imported, I forget whether from France or Italy, and for some years danced away every political idea of the English nation. The old despotic French government, when it found itself going, made an effort to divert the people with balloons, and for some time the project seemed to take, but finally failed of success; and both French and Americans have since shewed the world that they know how to enjoy rational amusement without surrendering up the faculty of thinking to certain gentlemen, who from time to time have kindly (tho' rather officiously) offered to take the trouble off their hands.

War is Unnatural to Man[40]

Mr. Fox[41] intimates in one of his late speeches that War is the natural passion of men, and (he feared) would always continue to be so. --It may well be questioned, however, whether this propensity is not rather artificial than natural, and introduced thro' the vice of governments rather than instilled into the human constitution thro' the immediate design of the creator. Man is naturally unprovided with dangerous offensive weapons. The <u>hand</u> was evidently designed for the works of peace, the efforts of industry for the support of life, the operations of beneficence, and not for the destruction of the species. "God has made man upright, but he has sought out a variety of inventions." We may observe in several species of the brute creation that native propensity which some philosophers suppose inherent in man. A young bull or a goat, for instance, will perform their mode of military exercise with the head before there is the least appearance of those offensive weapons, the horns; and a whelp-lion will go through all the formality of roaring, tearing, and rending before the claw has firmness or sharpness enough to inflict the least possible injury. But in the young of the human species, we observe in their general temper innocence of heart, smiles, gratitude, benevolence, and affection, which continue till such times as they become corrupted by false principles of education, and false motives of action, which pave the way for their turning monsters to each other in riper years, under the discipline and example of the great school of royal government.

The very virtues of monarchy have all a cruel and sanguinary tendency, and excite the human mind to perpetrations of mischief and horror. An extravagant over-partial love of country is first inculcated; ambition, emulation, and super-eminence are made the incitements to action; a savage revenge of injuries, artfully provoked by court-magicians, against one or the other country, is encouraged and rewarded by the crowned sovereign. Monarchy originated in murder, violence and robbery; what wonder then, if in all ages its violent adherents have been and still are in effect

murderers and robbers, and that kingly government, from
the nature of its prerogatives, sooner or later, winds up in
a scene of horror and tumult.   Monarchy, or the monarchical principle foisted onto republics, is the fuel that supports
the flame of discord in this world, that sets man against
man to their mutual destruction, and operates that seeming
degeneracy in human nature which is by some supposed to
have originated from a particular event in a remote period
of the history of man.   Upon the whole, we may safely conclude that man is naturally good, but that his species has
been vitiated and debased by preposterous modes of government, which have well nigh effected a second nature, through
so long a succession of ages.   Whether a system of pure
democracy universally diffused (after the heads of all kings
are lopped off) will work the desired reformation is an experiment yet to be tried; but if there is virtue enough among
mankind to give it fair play, it will most probably succeed.

American Affection for France[42]

The genuine display of affection for the cause of
France by the citizens, on the arrival of the minister, has
once more abashed aristocracy and hailed equality triumphant.   The bosoms of many hundred freemen beat high with
affectionate transport, their souls caught the celestial fire
of struggling liberty, and in the enthusiasm of emotion they
communicated their feelings to the worthy and amiable representative of the French nation.   What a delicious repast
for a mind interested in the cause of humanity!   There is
something ennobling even in the contemplation of liberty; but
the energy of philanthropy, which its presence imparts to
the soul, exalts and purifies human nature.   Incommunicable
and incomprehensible as this is to the well-born of the

earth, it is not less difficult than the assimilation of virtue and vice. We have an amphibious kind of character, which is neither possessed of qualities to give it distinction, nor modesty enough to make it content with the humble vale of equality, that sickens at every exhibition of the sovereignty of the people; these, like the animal plant, shrink from their approach into the cleft of insignificance. --May they ever hide their diminished heads!

The contrast, which the conduct of the citizens, friends to the cause of freedom, formed with that of the merchants, who, stimulated by the sordid considerations of self-interest alone, had the modesty in their own names and with their own sense, to speak the SENSE OF PENNSYLVANIA, must give a charm to the characters of the one, while it reflects dishonor upon the others. The milk and water production of sycophancy, which was carried in procession, was as destitute of energy, as devoid of dignified and manly expression as the motives which produced it were devoid of the genuine spirit of liberty. It was a climax of weakness and of servility. Pennsylvania has not yet depreciated so far from the character which she sustained during the late revolution, as to suffer the noble feelings of gratitude to be entombed in British influence and British corruption, and to prostrate the republican character at the shrine of Plutus. Let the mercenary band, who bask in the sun-shine of court-favour, and who, in the accumulation of wealth, forget the dignity of man and the savage character of the people around whom they entwine themselves, and the barbarous means they used to bend our necks to the iron yoke of Britain, let them declare themselves neutral, neutral to every feeling but that excited by money; let them declare themselves opposed to countenancing the French Republic; but let them remember that in so doing, a sentiment so ungrateful, so unworthy, reaches not beyond the limits of mercantile apathy or of British influence. --Proclamations unsanctioned by preceding laws and processions of merchants are equally indifferent to freemen, when opposed to the rational dictates of the head and the warm impulse of the heart. --Thanks to our God, the sovereignty still resides with THE PEOPLE, and that neither proclamations nor royal demeanor and state can prevent them from exercising it. Of this the independent freemen of this metropolis gave a striking example in their reception of Mr. Genet. Tho' neutrality was enjoined by proclamation, or in other words indifference to the French cause, or if you please, an equal affection for all the belligerent powers (Great-Britain amongst the number!) they were not to be the slavish receivers of proclamatory principles, nor to be deterred by them from acting as became the dignity of freemen and citizens under the dominion of a virtuous sensibility. --FELLOWS, as some of the would be noblesse termed the respectable citizens who walked in the procession to congratulate the minister, supported the tottering fabric of liberty against the machinations of such wretches, who fancy themselves of a gender too perfect to herd with the people, and at this moment sustain the virtue and independence of the American character. --Are there any fellows in a free government but those who transgress the laws, or those who apply the degrading epithet to the people? The man who conspires against his neighbour's rights and the man who attempts my life or plunders me of my property are fellows alike; they are both murderers and robbers. Let such fellows beware; worth only "makes the man, & want of it the fellow"[43] in a land of equality; and an insulted people may give them a serious lesson, that their worth is of a different cast from that which ignorance or vanity may have taught them to believe.

The noble simplicity which the minister of the French Nation displayed on his journey and entry into this city carried the face of genuine republicanism. Tho' he is the representative of the most puissant Republic upon earth, he had no princely equipage to scatter brilliance around him and excite the admiration of the gaping multitude; he had no cavalcade of servants to display his superiority, but his splendour and dignity consisted in a virtuous simplicity.

When the human mind was immerged in ignorance, forms and ceremonies were thought essential to religion, and superstition usurped the empire of reason; but those shackles have been broken by truth, and the purity of the gospel has received additional strength from its present simplicity; in like manner, ostentation, splendor, and parade were thought necessary to impress the "swinish multitude" with ideas of superiority and sovereignty; but as the lawful sovereignty is now established and the people know the importance of their rights and the dignity of their character, every royal folly of this sort must be considered by them as an insult upon their understandings and an usurpation of their prerogative. Simplicity is a gem of republicanism; it gives a native, unsophisticated brilliance incomparably superior to the glimmering of royal baubles. --May the dignity of an American consist in virtue, and not in the externals of folly!

It must not be imagined from what I have said that my voice is for war. Could we render France any essential assistance, war would be our duty, it would be our security; but the assistance which we can give her may be better accomplished in peace. Tho' actual hostility is not my wish,

291

it is a disgrace to America to place France upon the same footing with the powers with whom she is at war; for, according to the laws of nations, we can fulfil any defensive engagements with her without trespassing upon the laws of neutrality. --If it is the interest of Great-Britain to go to war with us, a pretext will not be wanting; for she has pretexts at command, and she has hitherto consulted her interest at the expense of every honorable principle. Shall we, for fear of giving offence to Great-Britain, behave with a disgraceful apathy to the minister of France, as the big men of our country wish us? Is it a trespass upon neutrality to give the minister of France the reception of gratitude? Pity that gratitude should only glow in the bosoms of the people! Should the expressions of interest for the cause of France and the manifestations of joy for her success be declaratory of hostility, let the trumpet of war sound thro' our country; for rather let America join in the combat with France than forfeit her honor and her virtue.

A Guide to the Heavens[44]

To Mr. B-----,

"On the wings of mighty wind,"[45] republican-like "he rode!"

SIR,

As I understand you are making preparations for your 46th aerial flight to the celestial regions, and having an irresistible desire to contribute to the utmost in my power towards the success of your laudable and (to us) novel expedition, I send you inclosed a letter which I beg you will deliver with your own hand, --it may be of use to you.

As I have been an astronomer, an astrologer, and an almanac-maker for these forty years past, my correspondence with and knowledge of the world above are consequently very great, as hath often been acknowledged by most of the brightest luminaries on earth, and in a more particular manner by that prince of astronomers, Mr. R----e himself.

I will therefore take the liberty of giving you a few simple directions: At the beginning of your diurnal evolution, after you have passed the perigeum, and proceeding through the different windings of the zodiac-circle, be cautious of approaching too near Scorpio.

By all means avoid the Sun's disk, as its heat will be too vehement, and may scorch your silken tabernacle.

Take great care of the Dragon's tail; fiery and poisonous effluvia issue from it. Tell Mars, our good and potent ally, to display his flag and hurl his thunder bolts on the heads of the combined despots; tell him there's almost an universal combination of the sons of gun-powder in this terraqueous globe against France and liberty: tell him that in spite of them, France will still hold up her head and be triumphant! and tell him the tremendous and undoubtable hero! the BRUNSWICKEAN QUIXOTE, is discomfited and sunk like a fallen star, to rise no more!

Avoid Venus; she is a coaxing slut and exceeding fond of silk petticoats. Greet the Planets, salute the Moon in your passage, and enquire of her, what mean those spots on her disk?

Whether they be beauty spots, silver mines, water, earth, vulcanos, or the broken fragments of an old solitary, decayed world?

Whether she be a maid? (if so, she must be a very old one indeed, and I'd have nothing to do with her) if not,

Whether the Man in the Moon, (as is vulgarly expressed) be her husband? if not,

293

Whether she be a widow? if so, and she hath any inclination to enter into a conjugal state, I'm her man; and
the next trip you take, I will accompany you, and no doubt
when she beholds my ephemeristic phiz, we shall instantly
agree upon a match, to ours and the world's mutual advantage; for, as I am at least 5376 years younger than she, I
have the vanity to think I can add lustre to her charms, and
double the number of stars in the firmament.

If you see Enoch, Elias, Moses, Lazarus, Mahomet,
Descartes, Galileo, John Clare, Tom Jacobs, Tom Godfrey,
or Sir Isaac Newton, (for they were all balloon men) pray
present my compliments to them, and if they have any thing
to communicate in the almanac-way, I shall be infinitely o-
bliged.

Again, when you have ascended as high as Cassiopoea,
and mounted the Bear's tail, endeavour to find the opening
of the Galaxy, (the entrance into the third heaven) through
which they say St. Paul passed, for, as that Milky-way is
composed of an innumerable number of half-born stars, (like
shad-ries in embryo) that touch each other, there will be no
possibility of pushing through unless through that aperture.
You need not ascend so high as the Georgium Sidus; that being a royal emigrant star, and you a French citizen and republican, perhaps you may quarrel and one or both of you
be decapitated, or a-la-lanterned.

Neither soar so high as Saturn, as he will receive you
but coolly, (if at all); he'll not so much as offer you a drink
of whiskey; he's a dull, leaden headed, melancholy, phleg-
matic old flubberdegullion and a rank aristocrat.

Beware, above all, of running foul of the star Worm-
wood, as mentioned in the book of Revelations; 'tis a bitter
star, and you may rue it.

Should you be constrained to take up your lodgings and abide a night or so, and Venus and you can't agree on moderate terms, (as she will expect, doubtless, an extravagant price for her favours)--shun her and try to find out jolly old Bacchus's quarters, who, I'll warrant, will receive you with joy and hospitality, send you one of his most favourite nymphs, carouze with you the whole night, and swim in nectar and ambrosia.

Should you find your balloon likely to be exhausted of dephlogisticated air, apply to Boreas, who will supply you at first cost at his wind shop and original ware-house, at the sign of the Bellows, somewhere about the north, or north-west corner.

Now, as I am full as well acquainted with St. Peter as I am with St. Patrick, the former, on the receipt of the above-mentioned letter, will no doubt furnish you (should there be occasion) with his old net, as he hath long since left off catching fish, to wrap round your balloon to secure it from accidents, and should a storm arise, he will also open wide the gate for you.

But should you fail in this, as his net is probably, by this time, worn out or lost, Jacob will lend you his ladder, if it be not broken, and should that be the case, you must then cry aloud for father Abraham, who will take you in his benevolent bosom, balloon and all,[46] and waft you safe to Jove's splendid palace.

Wishing you an agreeable ascent, and anxiously waiting your safe return, I am, Sir, your most obedient and unknown friend and humble servant,

An old ALMANAC-MAKER.

P.S. Pray enquire of Sir Isaac what has become of the Comet we so long expected, and whose appearance, as we

calculated from his tables and logarithms, would be in the
year 1789?

We astronomers have been shockingly out in our chro-
nology, and are laughed at and called loggerheads by every
one. I am terribly afraid it will hurt the sale of my next
year's almanacs--do let me know how it is.

Whether there has not been some unaccountable revolution or wars in the planetary system.

Whether Comets ever sleep, or get tired? or,

Whether he has not in his rapid course left the beaten
track and perambulated through unknown worlds and dreary
regions, (hitherto unexplored, nor even contemplated by
Jupiter himself) lost himself, or been stopped in his career
by some strange, unknown, uncouth, unmethodized, uncre-
ated monstrous body far mightier than himself, and in a
dreadful conflict have been transmutated, swallowed up, or
crushed to invisibility!

A. O. A. M.

Dialogue between a Citizen of Philadelphia
and a Jersey Farmer (ten miles from town)[47]

Farmer. Ho!--who are you, you yellow-fever-looking-fellow;
and what business have you out of your city?
Citizen. Sir, I do assure you, upon my word of honour,
that there is not a sounder man in New-Jersey than myself.
I eat my three meals a day, have not even had a finger ache
these six months, and can take an oath upon the holy evan-
gelists that the doctors have not had a nine-pence from me
these seven years. Feel my pulse, and convince yourself.
Farmer. Feel your pulse, Sir!--may I die by the grip of
an anodyne necklace if I would come within ten yards of you

for ten pounds. Why, sir, your breath is pestilence--your face is the very image of destruction--your eyes are death's poop-lanthorns--you are a moving mass of putridity, corruption, plague, poison, and putrefaction.--Your pulse!--not I, faith--nor do I believe you have any more pulse than a man that was laid in his grave thirty years ago. (The citizen advances towards him.) Avast! avast, sir! advance not, I beseech you, if you have any regard to your soul's health--keep to leeward, or by the prongs of my dung fork, I will make ghost's meat of you!--I will instantly finish what the yellow fever has begun!

Citizen. The sun draws low! a night's lodging in your barn, or even in your horse stable, would claim my eternal gratitude. I feel weary with my long walk, a nap of sleep would be refreshing, and by peep of day I will be jogging.

Farmer. Your weariness, or rather weakness, arises simply from the raging fever that now burns like a fiery furnace within you.--Sleep in my barn!--very pretty indeed!--why, my very horses would catch the yellow fever from you. In such a horrid state of contagion are you that in one night the pestilential vapours, and blue fogs arising from your carcase, would infect forty tons of hay. I pray you to walk on, and leave me and mine. You are upon the verge of another world, and we wish no connexion with you. Retire, I say.

Citizen. Walking through ten miles of heavy land has, I assure you, given me considerable of an appetite. Could I have a bit of victuals for my money? The taverns are every where shut against me--a luncheon of cold beef, a slice of ham, a bit of bacon, or a chunk of bread--you might surely venture to reach one or more of these articles to me on the point of a pitchfork.

Farmer. Beef for a man in your situation!--You are, beyond all doubt, raving mad and light-headed. If you were in
your right senses you would rather ask for tartar-emetic,
jalaps, purges, collery morbus, hippecacahna, doses of
Spanish flies, and cartloads of drugs, physics, and medi-
cines of every denomination and description. For God's
sake leave me; talking with you is like talking to a ghost--
hoist your black flag and away to potter's field!
Citizen. I want no physic. I shall now depart from your
borders and return home, but not without first observing to
you that the common duties of humanity between man and
man should have as much weight with a rational creature as
the great duty of self-preservation itself, and be equally observed. Cowards shrink from danger: the brave, when necessary, meet it with fortitude: and trust me, you will find,
in at least ninety instances out of a hundred, that cowards
perish through the very effects of their fears, while the firm
escape and enjoy a comfortable length of existence.--Adieu.[48]

A Free Press and Freedom[49]

Whoever takes a view of these States at the present
period must be convinced that a great political reformation
has within these three or four years past been gradually taking place. Aristocratical innovations are on the decline, and
their authors and abettors grown out of all consequence with
the people. In a great degree, this happy change may be
imputed to the exertions of free and patriotic presses, oper-
ating upon the good sense of the great body of citizens of
the United States, who in general are too enlightened to be
long misled without detecting the imposition and resenting
the insult. Go on, then, in this, your useful line of duty,
all honest and benevolent writers, printers, and editors!

Though your labours may not always meet with their just
and deserved reward, tho' yourselves may be calumniated,
your views misrepresented, and your principles decried by
the selfish votaries of interest or the secret or avowed enemies of the rights of man, yet by a prudent perseverance,
despising their resentment and regardless of their abilities,
you will ultimately have the satisfaction to see tory machin-
ation and malice, aristocratical seclusion, court ambition,
court mystery, court intrigue, and every other poisonous excrescence of imported royalty withering into an eternal non-
existence before that fatal scythe, which tyranny and tyrants
never could withstand---

A FREE PRESS.

On Law[50]

Such is the corruption of the age in which we live,
that LAW and JUSTICE are absolutely different things.--
The present system of law in America, as derived from the
British mode, in confounding the reason of man abridges his
natural freedom.   The lawyer has his forms and his positive institutions, and adheres to them with a veneration altogether religious.   The worst cause cannot be so prejudicial to the litigant as his advocate's, or attorney's, ignorance or neglect of these forms.   A law-suit is like an ill
managed dispute in which the first object is soon out of
sight, and the parties end upon matter wholly foreign to
that on which they began.--In a law suit the question is,
Who has a right to a certain house or farm?--And this question is daily determined, not upon the evidences of the right,
but upon the observance or neglect of some forms of words
in use with the gentlemen of the law, about which there is
even among themselves such a disagreement that the most

experienced veterans in the profession can never be positively assured they are not mistaken. Ye who are initiated into the mysteries of the law, inform me, have I a right to eat the bread I have earned by the hazard of my life or the sweat of my brow? One grave law doctor answers me in the affirmative: another of them replies in the negative: the learned barrister reasons upon one side and upon the other, and concludes nothing. What shall I do? An antagonist starts up and presses me hard. I enter the field and retain these three persons to defend my cause. My cause, which two farmers from the plough could have decided in half an hour, takes the court twenty years. I am, however, at the end of my labour, and have, in reward for all my toil and vexation, a judgment in my favour. But hold--a keen scented lawyer, who was retained against me, has found a flaw in the proceedings. I have used or instead of and, or some mistake small in appearance, but dreadful in its consequences, and I have the whole of my successes quashed in a writ of error. I remove my suit; I shift from court to court; I fly from equity to law, and from law to equity: equal uncertainty attends me every where; and a mistake in which I had no share decides at once upon my liberty and property, sending me from the court to the prison and adjudging my family to famine and beggary.--We may say, in respect to human laws, that where mystery begins justice ends. Lawyers have erected another reason besides natural reason, and the result has been another justice besides natural justice. They have so bewildered the world and themselves in unmeaning forms and ceremonies, and so perplexed the plainest matters with metaphysical jargon, that it carries the highest danger to a man out of that profession to make the least step without their advice and assistance.

Thus, by confining to themselves the knowledge of the foundation of all men's lives and properties, they have reduced all mankind into the most abject and servile dependence. We are tenants at the will of these gentlemen for every thing; and a metaphysical quibble is to decide whether the greatest villain breathing shall meet his deserts or escape with impunity, or whether the best man in the society shall not be reduced to the lowest and most despicable condition it affords.

The President's Prejudice against France[51]
To PRESIDENT WASHINGTON

SIR,

In your Speech at the opening of the present Congress, you said--"many of the nations of Europe, with their American dependencies, have been involved in a contest unusually bloody, exhausting and calamitous, in which the evils of foreign war have been aggravated by domestic convulsions & insurrections, in which many of the arts most useful to society have been exposed to discouragement and decay, in which scarcity of subsistence has embittered other sufferings, while even the anticipations of a return of the blessings of peace and repose are alloyed by the sense of heavy and accumulating burthens, which press upon all departments of industry, and threaten to clog the future springs of government."

There is little doubt, sir, that you meant these observations should apply to France. The world is able to judge whether they be true or not. The fact is that they are materially false if applied to her--and it is observed by many of your best friends that, had you gratitude or generosity, you would rather have passed in silence her unhappy situation, supposing what you said to be true--than to have thus uncharitably exposed the miseries of a revolution as important in its effects, as glorious in its principles.

But, sir, since you have exposed evils which affect not this country, and which consequently concern us not,--why did you not tell the Congress and the world the benefits these states have lately received from France, and are about receiving from her; I mean the Treaty with Algiers, which I am told was owing principally to the interposition and good will of the French--and that which you announce so far advanced with Spain, to the same cause; for you know that Mr. Pinckney,[52] in communicating to you the good prospect he has of finishing an advantageous treaty with the Court of Madrid, observes at the same time that it is owing to the good offices of the French minister.

If these facts be not founded, let them be contradicted --if they be founded, I leave the world to judge whether you have acted with candour towards France and this country. You will pardon these observations from an old comrade who feels unhappy at the least reflection against that nation which insured to us our liberty, and fought our battles--and you may be assured that although you have said on another occasion that the friends of the French in this country are participants to war and confusion, it is false as respects war.

England and France[53]

The treaty negociated by Mr. Jay, Envoy extraordinary, from the United States of America to Great Britain, is arrived, but has not yet made its appearance in public. Among other articles in this treaty, it is said, one provides for delivering up the north western posts on the 1st of June, 1796, and another allowing American bottoms a free trade with the British Islands in the West-Indies. --The public are still in the dark whether the restitution of American property captured by British cruisers during 1794 and 1795 makes an article in the treaty or not.

It is perpetually asserted and re-asserted in the British newspapers, and in their Parliament, that the French nation is in a state of anarchy. But what species of anarchy is it by which such fleets, such armies are equipped, directed and supported? What anarchy, by which the old and orderly governments of Europe, as they would be called, are prostrated or humbled? Will it be said that the changes in the convention denote anarchy? Far from it. We see, indeed, party succeed party, but still not in confusion, but as the regular succession of the most interesting drama: first Fayette, then Brissot, then Danton, then Robespierre, then Tallien, but all in their own order, all with views well adapted to the moment, the last party and most moderate because at the door of peace.

But if there hath been really a system of annihilation in Europe, hath not Britain all the credit of it to herself? Was it not her intention to have annihilated both America and France? In the one place she claimed a right to tax us in all cases whatever; in the other she ordered a famine; in Holland she directed inundations. But can a power thus boasting of wealth, accumulated at the expence of injured nations, always play this game? Will not, in the order of Providence, justice be done? Have not nations like individuals a place where the wicked cease from troubling and the weary are at rest? Yes! America is that country; the ball of empire is rolling westward, & her enlightened citizens, by the accumulated force of time, of population, and of commerce, in conjunction with their brave allies, yet suppress the power of despots, and secure and ascertain[54] the liberty of all seas and of the world.

The depredations on the commerce of the United States since the TREATY with Great Britain has been signed are not confined to the piracies of the British pickaroons in the West-Indies. The ships of war of his Britannic majesty, now on our coasts, follow up the trade briskly, few of our vessels escape insult, and many suffer material injury: the Bermudians capture, libel, and condemn every American vessel they meet with coming from French ports in the West-Indies, and bound to the United States.

The French Republic having now got complete possession of the Dutch Provinces, or rather by their driving out the English and their allies, having thrown the weight of that country into her own scale, an invasion of England seems every day to become an object more and more practicable. The wealth, maritime skill, and commercial industry of Holland formed the only rival England had to dread, and whose friendship secured to them the dominion of the seas. Their sea-ports are geographically calculated to be vitally fatal to England, since she has no opposite ports into which her great ships can enter; consequently, the Dutch flat bottomed ships, by their construction, may annoy the English in their own bays and rivers, where the fleet cannot protect them. The Dutch sailors fully rival the English in seamanship, and have in common with all their countrymen a rooted enmity to England--the arsenals of Holland, too, are filled with naval stores of all kinds, and so situated as to procure these stores at all seasons, without its being in the power of an enemy to prevent the supply.[55]

Observations on the Treaty with Great Britain[56]

1. Before the astonishing successes of the French, it is a fact that reiterated overtures for a Treaty were made by this country to Great Britain, but she treated them with little less than contempt. Ever since our Independence she has manifested the most inveterate hatred to these States, and contemplated their misery and subjugation. For this end armaments have been actually made; and the triumphs of France, only, saved us from her malice and the horrors of British warfare.

2. It may be asked, why then has she condescended to treat with us now?--It may be answered, Necessity, expectations of getting much by us, or a prospect of effecting something prejudicial to France have alone conquered the British repugnancy to treat with us.

3. Is, or is not our commerce necessary to Great Britain?--Her eulogists in Congress have endeavoured to persuade us that Nova Scotia and Canada would supply the wants of her colonists: but their own subjects have falsified the opinion, and demonstrated that the British West-India colonies were actually dependent upon the United States. --If then they are obliged to look up to us for subsistence, had we it not in our power to dictate our own terms to Britain if we did treat, and compel her by commercial restrictions to make full restitution for her robberies and piracies?

4. In the Treaty sent over to us by Mr. Jay from Great Britain, commercial advantages, it seems, are to be deemed a compensation for national injury, injustice, and dishonour. The object of his mission was understood to be a demand of full satisfaction for the shameful spoilations

305

upon our commerce, the invasion of our territory, and the detention of the western posts--Have these complaints been adjusted? Is the reference for indemnity for British piracies to British courts of justice an adjustment of our complaints--Is the reference of a national right, which has relation to a state of war, to commissioners one or two years hence an adjustment of our complaints,--Is a similar paper obligation with that made at the peace, to surrender the western posts two years hence, an adjustment of our complaints?

5. It is far from being impossible that the object of Britain in Mr. Jay's much talked of treaty is to excite the jealousy of France against us, and produce misunderstandings between the two republics. Could this be effected, it might be deemed an adequate amend for the loss of the United States, and for granting even favorable terms to us; and that this is in contemplation is strongly to be suspected.

A Treaty will give Great Britain a footing among us which she had not before, and by means of her intrigues and corruption, she may produce worse consequences than the negociation was designed to avert. Scarcely a country in Europe but has been a prey to her intrigues. Scarcely a nation that has not been convulsed by her corruptions, and shall the United States of America give her an opportunity to practice her seductions upon them? Shall we invite the serpent to our bosom, that when cherished by our vital heat, she may sting us to death! Forbid it Heaven!--

Citizens, Freemen of a favoured and happy land, arouse from your slumbers! Storms and tempests menace your peaceful dwellings; prepare to avert them! Your inveterate and implacable enemy is seeking to obtain a footing among you; chace the conspirator away! Remember that where despotism and corruption obtain an establishment, there liberty is insecure; and let it never be effaced from your minds that Great Britain sought to enslave you, that she is the enemy of freedom, that she is at this moment waging a cruel warfare against it, and that no effort of hers will remain untried to exterminate it from the Earth.

Reflections on my First Entering the Great City of the White Man[57]

Here, then, am I arrived with my brethren of the woods after a long travelling of more than sixty days![58] Over how many rivers have we passed, thro' how many pathless woods have we strayed since we departed from our wigwams, directed in the night by the star of the North, which remaineth forever immoveable, and in the day-time by the splendid luminary of the universe which enlighteneth all things.

But what is all this I behold!--how changed is the country of my fathers! Instead of the green forests that once shaded the plains, here are wigwams innumerable, of immense height and size, and in comparison of which our council-house itself, and the grand wigwams of the chiefs of our nation, are but the wretched habitations of the ant, the mole, the reptiles of the earth, the most contemptible insects and animals of the ground.

These huge structures may be very pretty, but the first view of them disgusts me. Fond of the vales and declivities of life, fond of the fire on my own hearth, why have my countrymen sent me to solicit trifles they might well do without, or necessities for which they have substitutes in abundance,--to make treaties that will end in our destruction by bringing us into a more intimate connexion with the white men, who have ever proved proud, cruel, base, and treacherous, enemies to what they call the uncivilized life, promoters of wars and blood-shed, and the industrious distributors of those pernicious liquors, the effect of which has already devoted to death more of the original nations of this huge continent than have perished by the swords of a thousand invaders.

What is this I walk upon?--not even the surface of the earth, as created by the great spirit,[59] is permitted to the sole of my foot. --I dislike these pebbled ways, these little lazy channels of putrifying water, this cracking of whips, the anxious, discontented countenances of all I meet, proving alas! too clearly that all are the slaves of care--care that clouds their best days because they have turned aside from the walks of Nature.[60]

A company of fighting men, led by a big-captain, advances to meet us: they conduct us to the town-house: I hear the sound of the drum: we are welcomed to their great village by the head men, and made to drink of their strong waters in token of welcome--now I am conducted to the house of a Publican, a man whose business it is to entertain travellers for their money. --I hate this inhospitality --it is not so with us. The man is cold, unconversable, and disobliging--I perceive already he is no friend to our nation--but the woman of the house is a handsome squaw, and has already obliged me with a pipe of tobacco. They have shewed me an apartment where I may deposit my blanket, my bow, my arrows, and my hatchet--and where I may shut my eyes in safety through the dark hours of the night. --This is all good; and I foresee that in this place, during my abode in the great village, I am to pen down some notes for the information of my countrymen towards the south and

308

the west.

The White Way and the Indian Way of Life[61]

As I travel through the streets and bye-ways of this
village, I never fail hearing the condition of my brethren
and myself commiserated by the men and women of the
place, on account of what they call our savage way of life
when at home.

We, in our turn, no less pity them for living cooped
up in dark cages and narrow boxes where they have scarcely room to turn or breathe, where the cheerful rays of the
sun never yet penetrated but are concealed from the wretched
inhabitant by walls of stupendous height and thickness.

The most unrelenting storm, the darkest mourning
cloth of clouds that ever over shadowed the face of the
Heavens is sooner or later scattered & dissipated before the
light of the great luminary: but in these deep alleys and narrow path-ways reigns a perpetual gloom, the source of pining discontent and peevish melancholy.

There sits the artist[62] on his bench, pale as the grass
beneath the thick spreading oak; actuated, like a machine,
by the will of another, he moves not from place to place,
but is restrained by an artificial necessity to his gloomy
habitation.

But in our country, and with us, a tree, on occasion,
will serve us for a house. Our largest wigwams are erected and finished in a day, and admit the light and air in
abundance. In summer, we allow the winds to blow freely
through the sides, made of cane and wattles: in the winter,
the fire is placed in the middle, and all enjoy an equal
share. Our woods supply us with plenty of fuel, and for
nothing, while here it is brought to the inhabitant in little

niggardly parcels, and at the cost of much money. In many of their habitations here we are not allowed to see the cheerful blaze--it is confined in a thick dark case of iron, and throws out a deadly smothering heat that never fails to deject & afflict my spirit.--In others, the fire place is in the side of the wall--the master of the wigwam only enjoyeth the heat, and looketh with a stern eye on those who approach to partake of his little sneaking fire of two sticks.

But before the night is advanced too far, and the taper that yet burns brightly before me shall grow dim in the socket, I will put down some few particulars of the manner of what is called the savage life by the white men.

I feel a glow of re-animation at the recollection of the charming vision, and would instantly return to enjoy it, were I not restrained by the frowns of the big men of the council, who have strictly enjoined my brethren and myself not to return without at least the looking-glasses, blankets, and brandy.

In the morning early we rise from the bed of skins to hail the first dawn of the sun. We seize our bows and arrows--we fly hastily through the dews of the forests--we attack the deer, the stag, or the buffaloe, and return with abundance of food for the whole family. Wherever we run it is amidst the luxuriant vegetation of Nature, the delectable regale of flowers and blossoms, and beneath trees bending with plump and joyous fruits.

By this time the stomach receives its food with a pleasure unknown to the puny sons of this huge village. Our drink is the milk of the goat, mingled with the clear water of the stream flowing over the white sand or yellow pebbles --It is that which every wise Indian prefers, because it is the drink prepared by the hand of NATURE.

310

Every desire of the heart is considered as a blessing of this, our common mother. These desires are few and simple, and are almost always within our power to gratify. We can vary them at pleasure, and thus they are always new.

We are strangers to the cruel passion of jealousy, and consider that man as under the dominion of the foolish spirit who is distrustful of his wife. Our young women live constantly under the golden star of Love; nor do we think the less of them if, before they are married, they indulge in that amiable passion.

In the forests, we acknowledge no distinction of property. The woods are as free as the waters; and the odious land-mark was never seen to arrest the foot of the hunter.

We are carried along upon the great wheel of things. We trouble ourselves not about the uncertainties, or the seeming irregulations of its motions. When the comet extends its long glittering tail over our thick forests, or when the moon puts on her black mantle of mourning, we apprehend no cause of alarm. It is the work of the great spirit of the universe, who sleepeth not, but day and night guides his wonderful machine in the way that is best.

However numerous may be our wives or our children around us, we afflict not our souls with trouble to know what will become of them when we are no more. Whether they shall be doomed to carry wood, as slaves, on the borders of the white men, or to bring the heavy load of waters from the springs of Owya menah, it is the same thing. We leave them to the care of that good Being who is the protector of the destitute.

We hear not the voice of the tax-gatherer at our doors, to take away our bed of skins to support the luxuries of the proud and governments that riot on the spoils of the poor. We despise all tributes, and abhor those burthens which are imposed on the white men to tame and degrade the spirit.

Surrounded by forests that have no lines of boundary, we fear no storms--they blow far above us, and are spent in the regions over the tops of the trees. We are in dread of no droughts, for nature has so overshadowed the soil that the sun-beams cannot scorch it. It is therefore always moist and favourable to the little gardens that give us the vegetables we want. The most impetuous torrents are arrested by the woods and thickets, and cannot sweep away our harvests before them.

Our manner of life renders us alert, cheerful and courageous. We live in the midst of content, and when the time comes that we must depart to the silent mansions of our fathers, we depart without regret, because we are sure that our sleep, though in reality it may be long, can be, to us, but a moment. When that interrupting pause of life is once made, a total oblivion of the past ensues; but we suppose we shall soon revive, young, vigorous, and beautiful, to enjoy once more the chace of the forest and the pleasures of the wigwam. This seems to be the oeconomy of Nature, at least with regard to the men of the woods.

To Opay-Meeko [63]

Health be to him that dwells by the waters of the forest!--I have retired from the great village to pass away two days by the side of the deep river, at a distance from men, the noise of their chariots, and the sound of their bells.

As I lie down in their solitary meadows, I perceive a motion in the waters for which I can give no reason, and to account for it would weary my understanding. You, that have passed more than eight hundred moons under the shade of the cypresses that grow by the side of the lake of Kitchi-tevah, have never seen such a thing. Those beautiful waters forever remain at the same mark upon the shore. As they do not waste, they stand in no need of being replenished. That lake is always full, always perfect, nor in any thing resembles the rivers of these white nations.

How often when wearied with war and hunting have I laid myself down in your wigwam and drunk with delight of that clear and delicious fluid! You mixed it with the milk of the wild cow, and I was satisfied: but here I taste the ooze of the bottom, and the troubled stream yields me nothing like pleasure.

Too many moons have passed over your head that you should ever think of travelling on your own feet to be a witness of this swell and decay of these waters. I will therefore describe to you as nearly as I can the strange travellings of this river, its retreat and its advance, its waste and its recruit of strength. When the Moneeto, whether good or bad, created this water, he said, let it have no rest; let it be forever in motion, sometimes in flight, as from an enemy, now pausing a moment, and then returning with the strength of a warrior to a renewal of the attack.

Impetuous waters! when the great lamp of the night shines with a round face they rush in from the deep and distant world of fluids with redoubled violence; they lift themselves up to the doors of the white men, and threaten destruction to all their works. A little while they remain without motion, like an Indian huntsman tired of climbing to the top of Ora-zeeba, who rests there a short time after the violence of hunting. So do these waters repose after the weary race that has been allotted to them.

313

One of the big white council men has told me that these waves, which follow each other into the streams of the woods, come from the main salt ocean: I asked him why they brought none of its salt with them? He could tell me nothing that I understood. He indeed made some signs, as if he would say that the salt waters do their best to enter here, like an enemy coming from afar, but were twice every day and night driven back by the strong waters from the hills.

But I must go on to tell you how the river behaves when it is grown to its full power of strength. It is without motion for about a time that one of our hunters could take three thousand steps. It then rushes away, like a torrent from the hills, and discovers a great part of its bed. It carries with it the big and little canoes--sticks and straws and bulrushes are wafted to its secret abode of rest.

There its running is again arrested. The river lies low in the valley, and for a little while you would suppose it was to return no more in its flow of youth and power. But this is no more than a transitory death. It is at first, in its return, as weak as an infant--then it acquires the nerves of a boy--of a young huntsman--of a warrior, and at last glories in the strength of a wild buffaloe, and brings on its bosom the big white sail from the ocean.

When we first came to this village, I employed myself every day and night in watching the motions of these streams. I have done so ever since during our tedious abode in this place among men of different manners and of customs odious to me. When the moon is round and shines in her full beauty, these waters are proud, rapid, and lofty: they seem to rejoice in her brightness and swell to embrace her. As she becomes small, they are feeble also--but I cannot tell you why it is, old man of the lake, that when she is wholly darkened, these waters resume their pride, and are again of the strength of a giant, when I should have supposed they would have been like a sick man, weak and of no motion.

But this is only one of the many great wonders I have to tell you of, when I see you again. Will that time ever come--These blankets--this brandy--these tomahawks and arms of thunder!--how slow are the white men in putting in-to our hands what the big council has demanded as the price of peace.--If long we are to remain here, our number will dwindle into nothing. To-ro-wo-sahti, one of the brothers of our embassy, has fallen in love with a white squaw of these wigwams, whose trade is to sell fish in the market house--he speaks well, and could have persuaded the men of this village to have listened sooner to our errand. He is now careless, and has thrown aside his blanket for a red coat.--Match-a-wali is become dull & melancholy with vexa-tion at long absence from our forests, and I fear will soon be governed, like the river, by the planet of the night.---Tun-gi-como spends almost the whole of his days & eve-nings with a tamed Indian, who lives in the woods about one day's journey from this village. As to the rest of our com-pany, what are they!--They were born only for the bow and arrow, and to be followed from path to path by the boys of the wigwam--to riot at the feast of new moons, or to quaff the midnight cup of jollity and know not when to be satis-fied.

I am anxious to be sent away with the waggons that are to be drawn by tamed buffaloes (oxen). What the white men have promised us to be put in these may refresh the big men and warriors of our nation for at least seven moons. I am dying to revisit the cypress trees of the south, and to

315

talk once more with the simple people of the forest: for here are little else than men of two tongues and double faces, with appetites as greedy as death, with design in everything and sincerity in nothing:--Years are coming fast upon us all. We are here marked as an inferior, little race of men, and are considered the same as sticks and straws that are wafted on the face of the river, heeded by few, and neglected by all, while themselves are like the lofty ships that are seen afar from the hills. But they should remember that both the weed and the big ship afloat on the same stream, and that straws and bulrushes may be lodged in the same quiet creek, while the ship may be left to be dashed to pieces on the wild shallows of the ocean.

Sketches on Different Subjects[64]

1. On the difference between Ancient and Modern Kings

The generality of the monarchs of antiquity, tho' perhaps as bitter enemies to the quiet and happiness of mankind as any modern princes or kings that met at the convention of Pillnitz in 1788[65] for the purpose of leaguing against the spread of a Republican system in the world, yet in their warfare they maintained consistency enough with their principles, and generosity enough of spirit to march out in person and run some risque of being cut to pieces with their miserable subjects, or rather slaves. Of modern times, Charles the 12th of Sweden and the late Frederick of Prussia were the only two monarchs that have thought proper to fight in person, and these were both enthusiasts, and the former not far removed from madness. As to the other European kings of modern days, contrast their characters with those of the ancient crown men, bad as they were, and the modern will be found to sink into insignificance itself. What is a king of these days! a creature shut up in a palace and kept almost as much in the dark as the grand Lama, the pope of the East-Indies. If a modern king goes beyond the environs of his palace, it is sure to be in a carriage fortified with iron and surrounded by guards. The grounds round his palace or country residence, besides being defended with artillery, must be thickly planted with man-traps, concealed just below the surface of the earth. All this betrays a consciousness that a people are robbed of their rights, and assassination is dreaded as the just reward of perfidy and theft. --Besides all this, at their very meals, royal families have had their tasters for ages innumerable. They dare not swallow a mouthful until a number of their attendants or guards, who are responsible for their safety, have eaten several mouthfuls. This alone shews something wrong;-- none knew 'till guilt created fear, what poison'd or rats-bane were. --Such is the picture of a king--a being that lives (if he may be said to live) in the midst of splendour, pomp, affluence, satiety, and delicacy, who knows nothing of mankind, nor is known by them except as a star to be gazed at at an immense distance, who hears, or reads in his court gazette, of wars and warfare, but is as ignorant as a horse of the whole system in practice, and is in fact no other than the leech of a nation, but at the same time the mere tool of nobility, pensioners, royal families, and royal progenies that are one great cause of involving a nation in wars and making them poor indeed.

2. The origin of navies

Royalty originated in the usurpation of the rights of a people, and nobility was the excrescence of royalty. Others, however, have arranged these matters differently, and say that nobility first usurped the rights of the people by making some popular character of their own body, who has in some instances been little better than a highwayman, the centre or polar star of usurpation, and had the cunning to attract the adoration of the people to a being who was evermore kept at a distance from them, and who enslaved a nation while they were taught to worship him as something supernatural. Nobilities have in all ages made it their study to keep the individuals of a nation poor, and thus made themselves rich. The superfluous wealth of the nobility was the natural cause of riot and good living. Hence your demi-gods among the old Greeks. High living and spontaneous plenty have always been the parents of idleness and an abundant increase of mankind. The fruits of their amours were of course lofty in spirit, and as they advanced to maturity became fit for treasons, stratagems and spoils, or any thing but honest industry. In insular governments, where a landed territory is not very extensive, and of consequence there was not room for a superabundance of military chieftains or independent men of titles, employment for the offspring of nobility was to be sought for on the ocean. The sea, at first view, presents nothing to man but two objects worthy of attention; it is a field of fishery or commerce. Neither of these prosecutions were thought to be attended with much honour, and certainly some toil, risque and difficulty. Something more honourable, and consequently more idle, was to be contrived. Hence began navies, and artificial quarrels between governments to give those navies something to do. The maintenance of armies and navies would not be supported by any people without some colour for national antipathy and animosity. Hence too, what is called the natural enmity of

318

nations (all men of the same species being natural enemies to each other.)

Previously to the attempts for an American navy, a race of well borns was to be found in our Republic, and we now see them popping up their heads like the frogs in April from the fresh ponds, singing and rejoicing at the sight of three frigates.--War, war, war! my sentiment is for war! when the people of America are wise enough to see that war is hatching only for the benefit of comparatively a few individuals, they will be cautious of listening to men who are artfully endeavouring to draw them into a snare that has produced the misery of all nations, and made the world a slaughter house, or, almost literally, a den of thieves and robbers.

Detached Observations[66]

1. Endless are the revolutions of opinion among men. They are fond of being thought a steady, settled animal, and yet are in reality the most unstable of any of nature's mundane creation. They call themselves firm and fixed, and yet are everlastingly in motion. Thus unexperienced passengers sitting in the cabbin of a ship under sail imagine the land and trees passing by them, and suppose themselves and the vessel in a state of quiescence. Instances of sudden revolution in popular opinion are daily taking place, and which would lead a reflecting man to put little confidence in the common sense or understanding of mankind.

2. In New-York, twenty or thirty years ago, the whole magistracy believed, and with them the whole town, that the dray carts of the city, with wheels of immense bulk, weighing several tons and without a tire, were the fittest on all accounts for the business of the streets, for

the ease of the horse, and to prevent injury to the pavement.

3. To have argued against popular and magisterial opinion, at that day, would have been speaking to the winds, and would have almost condemned the arguer to a madhouse.--And yet, in the slow progress of events, it began to be perceived that a snug, light cart-wheel bound with a strip of iron was the best calculated, both for the ease of the poor animal that draws the cart and for the preservation of the pavement.

4. About the year 1650, and indeed from the first settlement of this island (called by the ancient Indians Manhattan) dwelling houses with the gable end to the street were all the fashion in New-York. For a man, at the present time, to build a dwelling house in that position would entitle him to the character of "a fellow of no taste--a Dutchman, and the Lord knows what. "

5. Thirty years ago or less, Play-houses and Players were so detested in Philadelphia (the Athens of America) that it was with the greatest difficulty license could be obtained from the provincial government to build a Theatre in Southwark; and in erecting it, the proprietors were careful to go 12 or 14 feet high with a brick wall before they attempted to begin the wooden work, for fear of incendiaries.

6. Such was the popular prejudice in those days against the Drama--at the same era to have talked of erecting a Theatre in any one of the eastern provincial governments would have been little less than committing high treason against established authority--A performer on the stage would have been considered as a sort of excommunicated being, an animal to be hunted down and slaughtered by the common consent of mankind. For any one to have reasoned

in behalf of the drama, at that day, would have subjected
him, if not to prosecution and persecution, at least to contempt, slight, and the character of a wrong-head. --But
TIME has done great things. In those very towns and capitals, (such as Boston, Hartford, &c.) where dramatists
would have been persecuted with bitterness twenty years ago,
they are now invited, courted, caressed; and costly buildings
are erected for their exhibitions.

7th. The popular phrenzy in America, as far as regards sentimental pleasure, is in favour of theatres. Buildings of immense price are erected to gratify the public
taste. But how is this pleasurable phrenzy to be turned to
the interests of republicanism, and the good of mankind?

8th. They are much mistaken who suppose that buf-
foonery, double-entendre, and mere amusement are the real
purposes of a theatre. Fancy and imagination among mankind are every thing. Aristocracy and Royalty, by taking
hold of these leading faculties in human nature, have rendered the theatre subservient to their own purposes. In a
Republic like America, in whose exalted system the voice of
all former Republics is "like the singing of frogs," the theatre (especially when countenanced by the public will, as expressed by legislative permission) should be a school of virtue and public good. On an American stage, nothing appears more ineffably ridiculous than the idle distresses of
kings and queens, a sort of beings who for the weight of a
straw are in hysterics, hipt or suicides. All plays, therefore, commiserating the distresses of royalty, ought to be
discarded. The divine Shakespeare, indeed, will lose part
of his popularity by a strict adherence to this rule: but his
morality & poetical excellence will remain on a basis that
cannot be shaken.

9th. To render a theatre useful, and not to suffer it to be degraded into a mere vehicle of aristocracy and royalty, the primary virtues of man are to be recurred to. A play (a mean word for those lectures which ought to be exhibited on a republican stage) has endless topics to dilate and en-large upon. On a reformed republican theatre, patriotism will soon be a popular subject; and writers, no doubt, will be found who will erect their fabrics on this basis; but even this fine sentiment wants a check. Mankind have never been more deceived than in what is called patriotism. A German author (Zimmerman) says, "Patriotism is a hog fighting for his pen." The idea of love of country is, no doubt, both nat-ural and flattering to man, and highly commendable in prac-tice; but it is a principle fatal to their peace if confined to islands, continents, or any thing less than the globe on which he exists. Man should be "the citizen of the world," not of Africa, Europe, England, France, or the United States:[67] when his ideas dwindle into insignificance and partiality, he becomes the tool of tyranny; and the artful and unprincipled of his species trample upon his liberties.

The Sorrowful Petition of U, G, H
to the American Printers [68]

SHEWETH,

That your petitioners, as well as other letters in the English Alphabet, have had their respective sounds and uses long since determined by the first scholars and the best grammarians; that in their several capacities your petitioners have always been ready with their service and assistance, and have even (as is frequently the fortune of other letters in your worthy employ) been pressed into such situations as were contrary to established rules--to which they have always submitted without a murmur; that your petitioners have, besides, by a certain use allotted to them collectively, become like brothers, or friends so intimately connected that they may be said to form a kind of partnership which cannot be dissolved without altering or corrupting the English language; and your petitioners humbly conceive that you gentlemen have no proper authority to deface and mutilate a language which is already full established by custom, and reduced to a standard of grammar.

Your petitioners beg leave to represent, That they have always been found together in the words 'thought, brought, sought, taught, wrought, fraught, naught, taught, laugh, cough, dough, &c.' and they are alarmed to find that from the two first they are excluded entirely by the greater part of the printers in America, who, no doubt, think the new fangled spelling very neat and fashionable, and besides lay their account in finding at the year's end a considerable diminution of expense in the article of types.

Your petitioners have long since, by a sign of contradiction, been arbitrarily lopped off from the words "through and though," to their great injury and vexation; but their mutilators, in this case, had the modesty to substitute an apostrophe in their place; and your petitioners beg leave to suggest that when they are cut out of the middle of a word, there ought to be an ellipsis, thus, "tho-t," &c. and you, gentlemen, will thereby prove that it is with diffidence you make those innovations, and may save your types as before.

Your petitioners are aware of an objection which may be urged against their claim; namely, that the words "thought, brought," &c. may retain their original sound, though they be written without our assistance, by recollecting that the O is sounded as in the word 'soft,' and by just as good a rule might the words, "sought, thought, naught, fraught," be written "sot, tot, not, frat," to the utter confusion of analogy and etymology; for wherever your petitioners are used, the O, which precedes them, resembles that in "soft;" and when an a, it is like that in "hall;" but though your petitioners do not really sound in any of these words, they are clearly of opinion that such orthography can never be defended; and they further think that your ingenious "tho't" and "brot" are equally ridiculous.

Your petitioners, therefore, earnestly request that they may be restored to their original uses, as well for the reasons already given as because by printing every word at length, you may more easily fill your papers without retailing stale news from day to day, and raising reports in one paper to contradict them in the next; and lastly, if you persist in curtailing us of our rights, it will turn out that you are very ill "taught"--your dough will never do, and the laugh will be entirely against you.

The Lack of Principle in the Rich[69]

Many of those who held elevated situations in the American revolutionary war have been more than once reproached with at least a partial abandonment of those principles for which they then contended, and having rather cooled in their affection for the people and a republican interest. The truth is, these persons have generally become rich, and as was said in another case by divine authority, it is easier for a camel to pass through the eye of a needle than for a rich man to pass into the kingdom of heaven; the same may be almost said in respect to an overgrown rich man being a republican. --The answer on the part of the rich has generally been, "When I was a child, I spoke as a child, but now that

I am a man I do the things of a man"--that is to say, while I wanted the assistance of the people, I courted their favour and interest, but the moment I found I could do without them, I turned my back upon and despised them. It is remarkable that men of great wealth have generally in no age possessed for any length of time any uniform principle in favour of human rights; the people, and what is called the middle and lower classes, have always been the guardians of this deposit, and with them it appears it will eventually remain. The great are continually fluctuating, while what is placed low possesses stability.

> Thus, on yond' steeple towering high,
> Where clouds and storms at random fly,
>   The weathercock is plac'd,
> Which only while the gale does blow
> Is to one point of compass true,
>   Then veers with every blast.
>
> But things are so appointed here
> That weathercocks on high appear,
>   On pinnacle display'd,
> While sense and worth and preaching wights
> And clerk, that tunes grave Music's flights,
>   Sit humble in the shade.

A Sketch of Biography,
By Hezekiah Salem, Late of New England[70]

It was my purpose to have said something more on the subject of pumpkins. In verity it may be said, this is a subject that cannot easily be exhausted. One of the philosophers of the old world, we are told, spent his whole life in contemplating a butterfly's wings and penning down such meditations and reflections as therefrom occurred.

I once raised a pumpkin in my garden (whose history deserveth to be recorded for the information of posterity) that beggared all description. The vine grew and flourished, and expanded its goodly leaves. At last three pumpkins appeared from one single small shoot of the vine, partly connected and yet separated. At gathering time I took them in safe and sound, each five feet in length, and although veritably conjoined, they were yet not one pumpkin, but really and truly three pumpkins.

I might disgust my readers by dwelling too long on this subject, so shall proceed to other matters.

In commencing a course of papers that shall induce men to the perusal thereof (not I hope without some small degree of edification) I will previously give some brief hints of my own life and conduct.

I am a native of the state of Connecticutt. My father was a weaver of no mean degree, and from the annals of the family it appears that during one year of his life he kept three looms a going, almost without intermission. Sister Dorothy managed one of them, one David Dismal had the charge of the second, and the third appertained to my father, as his own particular charge. Thereto he would suffer no man to approach; and being of stern countenance and unpleasurable manners, he did keep at strict distance such as wished to intermeddle with his threads, to throw the shuttle, or sit upon the weaver's beam.

My father, at times, used many serious arguments with me, while young, to embrace the calling and occupation of a weaver; but I resisted him thoroughly, well knowing that as there are many stars in the firmament of different degree, order and occupation, so in a family as one son might be destined to preaching, to farming, or to be engaged in the delightful art of psalmody.

In these opinions I grew up to man's estate; but at length, taking a serious turn of mind, I at first became a deacon, and at length, finding increase of knowledge beyond that of my teachers, I procured myself to be made a preacher; and no less than twenty five years did I pass in that benevolent occupation, honouring and honoured, doing good and, honourably be it said, receiving good.

I had ever an unlucky propensity to be fond of playing at bowls: this practice I had carefully concealed from my parishioners. At length, however, being one day engaged divertising at this game, both wholesome and manly, with some confidential neighbours in a place where we imagined ourselves secure from all vulgar observation, a deacon popped in who cast an angry eye at me and immediately reported the affair all abroad, that he had caught "Hezekiah Salem, the grave preacher, playing at nine-pins on the bowling green!"

An assemblage of my brethren soon pronounced me unworthy of the pastoral calling. I was accordingly dismissed and left to find out some other profession wherein to exercise my abilities.

This disappointment, I own, was great: It at once threw me from the more elevated part of mankind to a situation among the low and simple. But disappointments are necessary to man. I was even prepared for this change. I remember in the days of my early youth my father took me in his cart with him, along with a parcel of pumpkins (a present) some twenty miles distant, to pay a visit to an old kinsman, a farmer that lived like a hermit by the side of a lofty, solitary hill, covered with tall woods, from which flowed a right pleasant stream. It turned[71] prettily, and I was so delighted with my handy-work that I wished never to be absent from that stream or my water mill. Our tarry, however, was confined to one week, and we then departed.

Three years afterwards we re-visited the same place. On arriving at the old farmer's house, our kinsman, I sprang out of the cart, and immediately ran down to the brook to look for my water wheel.

It was gone! The torrent from the hills had, I suppose, swept it away, and I could not discover a single vestige of my favourite work. I have felt angry ever since at the disappointment; but what avails it? This disastrous event served to reconcile me to all the succeeding misfortunes of my life, has impressed me with a lively idea of the transient nature of things, and inclined me to bear with patience and fortitude the real losses occurring in the process of human things and times.

Soon after my dismission from the pulpit on account of the nine-pin affair, I sailed over to the east-end of Long Island in a canoe with all my worldly appurtenances, consisting of a dog, a cat, a chest of old sermons and other writings, &c. seven pumpkins of the best and largest kind, a hoe, a spade, a straw bed, and some apparel of coarse sort and quality. I soon fixed on a spot of about half an acre in extent, of such poor soil that I was sure no man, in his senses, would ever contest with me the right of pre-occupance or property. There I built a cabbin or hut, near the sea-shore, and at my first settling, made frequent excursions in New England vessels on whaling voyages, in quality of steward, and, on occasion, harpoon-man. Weary, however, of the fatigues of the main great sea, I have re-occupied my hut last year, and by way of eschewing idleness, have, with some little exertion of ingenuity, adopted the trade of basket-making. I find this will maintain me comfortably (being an old batchelor) during my declining years. As I now and then send down a parcel of baskets to

New York city for sale, I shall at times inclose in some
one of them certain extracts from my old trunk of papers--
Sometimes my lucubrations will appear in a portion of some
one of my old sermons: at others as a sketch of my travels. Let not my readers, however, expect too constant a
supply. The vessel may now and then be retarded during
her passage down the Sound by head winds--in which case,
they must be patient.

On Imprisonment for Debt[72]

"Hast thou, which art but air, a touch, a feeling
Of their affliction; and shall not myself
One of their kind, that relish all as sharply
Passion as they, be kindlier mov'd than thou art?
Tho' with their high wrongs I am struck to the quick,
Yet with my nobler <u>reason</u> 'gainst my <u>fury</u>
Do I take part--the rarer action is
In virtue than in vengeance--they being penitent,
The sole drift of my purpose doth extend
Not a frown farther! Go, release them, Ariel:
My charms I'll break; their senses I'll restore,
And they shall be themselves."
<u>Shakespeare.</u>

Man, it has often been said, is the creature of habit;
he imbibes prejudices in the dawn of his existence which,
taking his species in the bulk, are not easily eradicated. He
is born, lives, and dies the slave of custom, and rarely has
strength of mind or leisure to consider well on what has
preceded him, or whether those forms of policy, adopted in
the infancy of society, when man first emerged from his
savage state, should be continued to an era and in an age
when, from an impulse of Providence, Reason, or Nature,
or from some cause unknown, he has thought proper to cast
an eye of reflection upon himself, to look within himself,
and to consider his rights, what is due to the dignity of his

nature, and to scan the means of preventing the great family of mankind from being preyed upon, vitiated, and harassed through life by those hereditary tyrants whom a perverted and mistaken system of things has placed at the head of human affairs.

Men of sentiment and those who deal in moral and philosophical theory, which is a kind of dawn to practical policy, have long seen that there is something wrong in restraining the persons of men for what is called debt. Few, if any, however, have assigned a reason why, in the common cause of things, society should not punish those who wilfully forfeit obligations, or by loose habits of life, and without industry, embezzle, purloin, or destroy the property of others. It is not every one that reflects sufficiently on the nature of society. Metaphysical arguments might be brought in abundance to shew that in the social state, as well as in every other which man has thought proper to adopt, an individual has a clear right to the products of his labour, however they may in part, by abuse, be filched from him by kings, courts, and those destructive systems which originate in the opinion that by making man a poor base reptile, he is more easily governed, and more to his own advantage, than if enlightened, instructed, humanized and taught to consider himself, in the aggregate, a rational, subordinate governor of the globe on which he exists.

In the career of things, so diversified are the natural abilities, understandings and energies of mankind that there will evermore be an inequality in point of individual property. The matter is clearly so ordained by nature. Let us not consider man alone as a constant exemplar of the instability of things. Look at yonder hive of bees; the faculties of those ingenious winged insects are endlessly diversified.   One comes home laden with honey; he baffles all the efforts of the king birds, who are in perpetual pursuit of him--evades their dexterity, and deposits his treasure.   Another, with equal industry, comes back to his hive with a poor return--he has lost one of his limbs--a leg--or he has had his eye pecked out by some warrior wasp.   The whole hive are instantly in arms against him: he is put in coventry--he is killed or ruined.

Jails and the whole system of civil debitorial co-ercion have probably had origin in a wrong system of legislation. Equivocal laws are the worst of all nuisances; and designing men are continually taking the advantage of such, to favour themselves and wrong others.   What a monstrous system must that be--how absurd--how unjust--how cruel--which allows a man to carry his ill-gotten millions with him into a prison, to defraud the industrious, ruin the orphan, and desolate all that had been within his reach or connexion!--

The voice of the world is against all creditors--altho' frequently unreasonable, it is still the voice of nature, and is one of those reliques of the original benevolent movements of the human heart before it became hampered with absurd laws, rules, regulations, society.   On a view of this subject, the question naturally arises, how, where, and when the idea of coercion in these cases originated.

In the investigation of truth, it is the business of the philosopher to revert to simple principles.   Look at man in savage state: there the outlines of his general conduct are the same as under civilization.   The Missisago Indian wanders through the forest with his bow and arrow--he kills a deer and returns to his wigwam.   He happens to have a humane heart: The deer is more than he wants for his present occasion.   A poor adjacent Indian, perhaps unfrugal or

331

unthrifty, comes to him, and purchases a quarter, promises the same in return from the deer he is going out to hunt to morrow. He goes out but has no luck, and comes home empty. What is the conduct of the creditor Indian?--Bring me positively to-morrow (says he) a quarter of venison as large as that you had from me, and all will be well--otherwise you shall, by the general consent of our village, be put to labour until you make restitution.

Last Will and Testament of a Democrat on a Sick Bed in the Last Stages of an Aristocratic Consumption[73]

In the name of ----- A-----, to whom C----- have given all power amen, being of sound mind and memory, and considering the mortality of the body politic, and the uncertainty of my political existence, do publish this, my last will and testament; I commit my political soul to ----- A-----, believing in the Federal -----, which lately died by the hands of T. L. H. &c. for the political sins of the Republic and its resurrection at the last day, the dead laws, and the life of the republic to come.

My body I commit to the care of the surviving '76 Democratic Republicans, to be interred in a decent manner, at a respectable distance from all aristocrats; having never associated with them while living, I do not wish them near me when dead, first enjoining them to have my body dissected for the purpose of ascertaining the cause of a Republican being all at once seized with the disease of Aristocracy.

My real and personal estate I do dispose of in the following manner:

Item 1. The 600 acre lot I drew for my services as a soldier in establishing the independence of my country, I give to the Democratic Society for a burying place, upon this express condition, that not but Democrats be interred therein, who, as a proof of their being such, shall confirm it by the following oath--I swear by the Republic, I have lived and die opposed to monarchy, Aristocracy, and every other species of Tyranny.

Item 2. I give and bequeath my French musket, sword, bayonet, catouch box, knapsack, &c. furnished Congress by the French to establish the Independence of America, to Mr. Tracey, member of Congress from Connecticut, who proposes arming every woman and child in America against every woman and child in France, to carry on his war of Extinguishment.

Item 3. I give and bequeath to Mr. Lloyd and Sewall, from Massachusetts, authors of the Sedition and Alien Bills, my share in the patriotic presses in the United States, being of no use to my Democratic heirs, and all my claims to the pride of being an American, if the people suffer them to--

Item 4. I give and bequeath to my old friend Mr. Brooks, from New-York, whose circumstances are needy, forty quire of old Continental Money, which, like an old coat laid aside, may shortly come in fashion.

Item 5. I give and bequeath to the P----- [74] all my share in the superlative excellencies of the British Constitution and government.

Item 6. I give and bequeath to the good People of the United States the example of the late glorious revolution.

And do hereby appoint as my Constitutional Executors our trusty and well friends to the equal rights of men, George Washington and Alexander Buonaparte.

Your correspondents, in their examinations of several measures which have of late very much engaged the attention of the public, have, in my opinion, reasoned from a very erroneous principle, namely, that princes or presidents ought always to act fairly, openly and ingenuously: that they ought not only to see that the laws should be obeyed by others, but should, in all their actions, strictly act in conformity to both the letter and spirit of the law themselves. If this indeed were so, that princes were bound by laws, and could never cause right to bend to convenience, I, for my part, would as soon be a dray-man as a secretary of state, as soon tug at the oar, as fill the presidential chair--But I am bold to affirm that I can prove the contrary, first, by the authority of the most learned and wise ancient sages, and, secondly, by the practices of princes in all ages.

No man, says Pliny, ever presumes to prescribe to princes, or include them within the verge of any laws but their own inclination. In the highest post, justice is always on the strongest side. That which is most profitable can never be unlawful. Holiness and piety, faith, truth, and common honesty are the virtues of private men--princes are above these vulgar dispensations.

It is allowed by all that it is lawful for governors to use dissimulation. Says one of high authority, "The same dissimulation, which in persons of private condition would be vicious and abominable, is in princes highly commendable: there is no discharging their weighty affairs without it; yea, the very thing which ruins private conversation is the best support of government. A prince or governor must appear open, honest, sincere; but in his mind deceit, deep design, and cunning must hold their seat. If he wishes to govern wisely, he must know, like Cromwell, the art of employing SPIES and the almighty power of BRIBERY--of compassing his designs by deep devised and unseen methods; by equivocating and ambiguous terms; by refined subtilties and deep intrigue; by good words, fair promises, compliments and congratulations, formalities of EMBASSIES and letters; and by these outwardly fair pretences and amusing stratagems, bring the matters about on which his whole soul is steadily fixed. " And to accomplish this, says Plato, "governors ought to make no scruple of having frequent recourse to lies and tricks;" and Pliny asserts that it is a part of prudence to deceive as occasion and the present posture of affairs shall require. Suppose, for instance, that in any state or country whatever, there should be a citizen or subject turbulent, over-ruling and rebellious, head of a strong and determined party, would it not be just to employ the assassin secretly to stab him, or bribe one of his intimates to hand him the poisoned draught? Or suppose some great man, who was every day increasing in popularity and strengthening his interest, who undoubtedly had it in his power to do mischief, if he were so inclined, I say, would it not be prudent for the governor to clip his wings--check his popularity by well devised and plausible stories, forged letters, and secret correspondence, that so he might not be able to annoy, if he would? To me it appears evident that in both these cases the ruler would be perfectly justifiable. One thing is certain; princes ever have acted thus, and in so acting have found advocates. "In order preserve justice in greater and more important matters, there is sometimes a necessity, says Plutarch, of deviating from it in those of less moment; and in order to do right to the gener-

335

ality, it is allowable to put some hardships and to do some wrong to particular persons." Commonly speaking, says Tacitus, the noblest exploits carry somewhat of injustice in them. A prudent prince, says Plutarch, must not only know how to govern according to law, but know how to govern the laws themselves: that is, if the laws are not willing that he should do what is necessary at that time, he must make them willing. And, not to tire you with quotations from the ancients, Aristotle's rule is, if a prince cannot be good in all, it is sufficient that he be so in the greater part of his administration.

I now think I have fully established my position by authorities, that princes are not bound to be, like other men, virtuous. Were I to enter on the proof of it from the practice of princes, it would be giving a history of their lives, which abounded, according to their abilities, in every species of dissimulation, deceit, and cunning; and if the most diligent historian can select one eminent for virtue, he will stand rara avis in terra, nigroque similima cygno.[76] From this disquisition, of governors or princes being in certain cases supreme above all law, I would deduce the following particulars:

1st. An irrefragable argument for the justice of the Alien Bill. Those people who are most affected by it, and against whom it was made, are inimical to all good government. Witness the troubles they raised in Ireland, where at present, and for many hundred years past, the government hath been temperate, humane, and just.

2nd. It was necessary, by the Sedition Law, to clip the wings of some men, and to shew the heinous nature of speaking against persons high in trust. What would have been the consequence if a stop had not been put to such abuse?--Colonel Lyon's imprisonment and fine[77] did more good to America, by inculcating a proper submission to our rulers, than any thing that could be devised, short of cutting off his head: which indeed might have been wrong in itself, but would have been right nevertheless, for great advantages would have sprung from it.

I was in great spirits a few days ago, expecting that the tale of a tub with a double bottom would have proved our governors well skilled in developing the secrets of foreign courts; but I am now quite chapfaln, for the tub appears to have lost both its bottoms. But I hope they will be more fortunate in their next attempt. I trust also that the people will soon open their eyes, to see that the paltry sums of money which are granted by their representatives in Congress, for the use of government, will never serve to answer any valuable purpose: if ever they wish to see their government respectable, they must give freely, and not stand trifling for a few thousands, like women on a market-day higgling for halfpence; for when all is done, no sword can cut so deep as that with a silver edge; it serves with zeal, obeys without grudging, and draws the world after it. Let us never judge governors by those rules by which we ourselves are to abide and be governed, but rest satisfied under whatever laws, decrees, or ordinances the rulers frame, still remembering this grand advice, (which is my last authority) whosoever resisteth the power, resisteth the ordinance of God, and they that resisteth shall receive to themselves DAMNATION.

Changeable Orthodoxy[78]

Some time ago, I thought that I had gained such an entire mastery over my fears that the whole troop, so remarkable for printer-flogging here or elsewhere, could not make me tremble--and so I walked about in open day, ventured even to talk in favour of the Aurora in the little beerhouse at the corner, and indeed was so fool-hardy as to assert that the clergy were now behaving in the most inconsistent manner by praying for the success of Suwarrow, the pope, and the re-establishment of the Romish religion, for the downfall of which they, and their fathers before them in the church, have prayed heartily for at least these two hundred years--But this conduct raised such a buz about my ears that I have been forced to run away in good earnest. What chiefly led to this was the following--One day, having gained a little time, I took my stick in my hand, adjusted my wig, and walked out to see an acquaintance. Who happened to be there, as ill luck would have had it, but his reverence--So after some chit chat about dry weather, water works, sickness, and some thoughts on death, which I thought made the parson's face longer than ordinary, though it is not short at any time, he thus addressed me--So Robert, I am informed that the reason why you no longer attend to hear God's word preached on the Sabbath is because you neither like our prayers nor our preaching. I confess, Mr. Editor, I knew not what to say--I looked on the one side, and then on the other, rose from my chair, spit in the sand box, and threw a segar I had but just lighted into the fire. --I had never contradicted the clergy because my good father had often said to me, "Robert, never meddle with the clergy--they are edge-tools;" but father's advice had slipped out of my memory at that time--so, giving three pretty loud hems, by way of practice, I answered--And pray your reverence, said I, can I have a better reason? If, Robert, answered he, our preaching or praying were not orthodox,

338

then you would have a right to quit us and go elsewhere; but what fault have you?--Why sir, said I, as to what is orthodox, and what do you call it, the other dox--Heterodox, replied he--Aye, aye, says I, that's it; I never clearly knew what they meant--I have but a poor head at best, and these are hard words--I would be much obliged to your reverence to tell me what they mean, and then I will try to answer your question. The parson, putting on one of his airs, went on thus: I am astonished, Robert, to hear you talk thus-- You have appeared in public, censured men and measures in that democratical sheet called the Aurora, and your name is familiar in every company. Some say you're a man of sense; others, that you are a fool; yet both laugh at your productions; and you ask what is the meaning of two plain English words.--They may be English or Spanish for me, said I, much ashamed of my own ignorance; but if you please to tell me, I'll thank you kindly sir, and if I can I won't forget what you say.--Why, said he, with a smile of superior wisdom, orthodoxy is the whole body of principles taught in our church--and every opinion contrary thereto is heterodox--So, said I, this is indeed to me very strange--but I'll remember it--But, added I, can a principle be heterodox one year and orthodox another year?--No sir, answered his reverence, with much authority; orthodoxy is ever the same; the principles I have the honour to preach were taught by Christ, his apostles, and so on to the present day, without the smallest alteration.--It may be so, answered I; I have but a poor brain--but I confess I think otherwise. And pray, sir, said the parson, what is this great fault that we have been guilty of, and of which your wise head is so full?-- Sir, says I, before you came to preach at our church, the reverend Dr. **** never went into the pulpit but he prayed

for the fall of Antichrist, that man of sin, and this I think
was orthodox praying--He preached very often against the
errors of the church of Rome, and from the prophecies
proved that the Pope was Antichrist; and this, because you
know it was taught in our church, was orthodox preaching--
Now sir, you pray for the re-establishment of the Romish
religion, and preach that the French have committed a
damning sin in pulling Antichrist from his chair, converting
images into money, consecrated bells into democratic cannon,
shutting up the nunneries, and sending the poor girls into the
world to answer the end of their creation--Now sir, is this
also orthodoxy? Undoubtedly sir, answered he, for you
know it is taught in our church. But, says I, how sir can
this be? You told me but just now that orthodoxy did not
change, but was always the same--I acknowledge, said his
reverence, that you have, Robert, stumbled on something
like a contradiction, and it deserves a reply. We prayed
for the downfall of the Pope because we thought religion
would be benefitted by it--we now see that religion is much
hurt by it, and therefore we wish it restored--If indeed God
had brought down Antichrist in some other way, and established the true Calvinistic Presbyterian religion in its room,
then we would not have desired its restoration--and this is
orthodox. It may be orthodox, said I, for ought I know to
the contrary, but one thing I'll venture to say, that it is
neither agreeable to Judaism or Christianity--I hope, Robert,
said his reverence, you don't pretend to argue religion with
me!--God forbid sir, says I; excuse me for speaking rash-
ly; but if you please sir, I'll tell you a story--Let's hear it,
says he; but I tell you aforehand, there must be nothing a-
bout the French in it, for I hate them heartily--Indeed, said
I, there is not one word about the French in it, for I be-

lieve it is somewhere in the Bible or Testament--Once upon a time, there was a very great man, but he was not a
Jew, who had the bad fortune to be afflicted with the lepro-
sy--all the doctors in his own country were consulted in
vain, and he was pronounced incurable. At length he was
informed that in the land of Jewry there lived a very good
man who could cure him in an instant. The great man set
forward immediately on his journey. His equipage was
splendid--his retinue numerous. He arrived--the man of
God paid no respect to him, although he was very great--
but sent him word to go and wash himself a number of
times in the river Jordan. The great man was enraged.
Are not, said he, the rivers of my own country much better than the rivers of Israel? I thought he would have come
out to me--put his hand on the place, called on God, and so
healed me. However, being a man of some sense, and having some wise men about him, he was induced to obey the
prophet. He did so, and was cured. You have my story.
I can make nothing of it, said the parson. Well, said I,
I'll apply it. God had his way (like the prophet) of bringing
down Antichrist; but you, like the great man, say his way
was not a good way, and if he had taken counsel with the
very wise Christians of the day, they would have taught him
that it would have been much better to have left him standing than to have made use of such instruments; and now you
would instruct him to govern his providential dispensations
by your advice, and once more erect spiritual Babylon,
bring back the images, catch the poor nuns, and shut them
once more in their cells. As I said this, his reverence
leaped to his feet. I declare, Robert, said he, you are unfit to live in society; 'tis such men as you who are bringing
the curse of God on our city. I pronounce you an infidel, a
341

despiser of the clergy, constituted authorities, holy customs, and a dangerous man in society, and I hope we shall shortly have it in our power to lay such fault-finding, ignorant fellows by the heels, that so they may learn to reverence the most useful and honourable of all men, the clergy. Having said this, he stalked out of the house with great consequence. Shortly after I took my leave. The story ran like lightning--Robert Slender is an infidel, said one--Why, he argued with the Reverend-----, and the parson told him he ought to be imprisoned for the good of society. Mrs. Slender went to visit her neighbour--I am very sorry, says Goody Rattle, that it is so bad. What's the matter, said she? Why, I need not hide it--Mr. Slender is an infidel-- a speaker against the clergy--a puller down of religion-- and his reverence says so!--In short, I had once more to shut myself up in the house; and I have moved into the country among my friends till the story blows over.

P. S. Your papers have come safe to hand. Lord bless me! what a story about horse-thieves, and busy-bodies, and proclamation-mistakes, and Kingston-cargo! But I cannot say I understand it all--but I'll read it over along with my friend the Latinist, (for he came out along with me) and perhaps I'll steal time to send you our remarks. [79]

Freneau, Jefferson, and the National Gazette [80]

A pamphlet has been published some weeks since in this city by William P. Young, addressed to the citizens of South Carolina, in the 13th page of which occur the following words; in speaking of the conduct of Mr. Jefferson while secretary of state, the writer says,

"He endeavoured to influence the public mind to adopt

342

his opinions by calling to his aid instruments to vilify the measures of the administration. He invited a printer, thus employed in another state, as a clerk for the translation of the French language in his office, where he had already a fit person. This man came into his office in the summer of 1791; and in the autumn of that year he set up a National Gazette, which continued its existence till about the time of Mr. Jefferson's retreat. Mr. Jefferson manifestly established, supported, and was the patron of this Gazette. The editor was his pensioned and confidential agent; the paper was as clay in the potter's hands. This Gazette, so patronized and so edited, commenced the system of abuse against Washington and the measures of his government which was afterwards carried on by the Aurora. His proclamation of neutrality, issued most timely and maintained most firmly for the peace of our country, was the subject of long continued denunciation and slander; and the President was openly charged with having transcended his power and violated the constitution. "National Gazette," under the influence of Mr. Jefferson, openly encouraged the insolence of Genet, and justified him in insulting the people in the person of their beloved chief magistrate, &c. &c."

The above mentioned pamphlet came to my knowledge only a few days ago; and as far as the passage quoted regards myself, I should not have thought it worthy my while to pay any attention to what I consider an impotent effort of malice and slander to prejudice the citizens of this state against Mr. Jefferson, and, so far as such assertions would serve, to prevent his election to the chief magistracy of the United States.

Justice, however, to Mr. Jefferson seems to require that I should state a few facts to exculpate him, as far as in my power, from the charge of influence in the establishment, publication, or editing of the National Gazette.

Early in the spring of the year 1791, being then resident at my usual home in Monmouth, (New Jersey) I was invited by Mr. Jefferson, by letter, to come to Philadelphia, with information that the place of translator of foreign languages, being in his appointment as secretary of state, was then vacant, and if it would suit me to accept it, it might possibly be in his power to introduce me to some other employment of more importance, on a proper opportunity offering.

Upon receiving this letter, I consulted several of my friends, who advised me to accept Mr. Jefferson's overture; but as the salary for this business was no considerable object, it being only two hundred and fifty dollars a year, at the same time they gave it as their opinion, if I established a twice a week newspaper in Philadelphia for the purpose of supporting the genuine principles of the American revolution, which were becoming unfashionable with some from whom a different conduct was expected, it might in time prove an establishment of value.

In this view of things, in the month of June, 1791, I engaged Messieurs Childs and Swain, printers in New York, to embark with me in the business, and to undertake the printing work of a paper, stipulating at the same time that pecuniary advances were made by them, and the loss, if any, to be their own, after the debts of the paper should be collected, myself in the mean time to be considered as concerned as a third partner in that paper.

Being engaged in my agricultural concerns in New Jersey, I did not, however, proceed to Philadelphia until early in October, 1791, uncertain and not very much concerned whether the office of translator to the department of state was occupied or not, as I had in the interim given myself no trouble about the matter.

On my arrival in Philadelphia, having been introduced to Mr. Jefferson several months before in New York, I called on him at his house, when, after some conversation on different matters, he informed me that the translator's place in his office was still vacant, and if I would accept it until something of more consequence should be in his power, the appointment should be made out on the following day.

In all this not a single word passed on either side on the subject of the National Gazette, in the establishment of which I was influenced by no one, but undertook it from the powerful necessity of such a paper at the seat of government, to expose in some degree, as far as my abilities were adequate, the approaches of royalty, and to hold up to America the baseness and duplicity of certain influenced characters in their desertion of almost every principle of the revolution of 1776.

I was accordingly sworn in as interpreter of languages to the department of state, some time in October, 1791, which place I held two years under every species of the most illiberal newspaper abuse, and with very trifling advantage to myself, as there were sent from the several departments of government so many foreign papers and letters, directed to official characters in this country from Russia, Holland, Prussia, Germany, and elsewhere, the translations of which I was obliged to procure at an exorbitant rate of charge; the place was beginning to be rather a loss than a matter of emolument, particularly during the last year I occupied it.

Apprehending therefore that official dispatches might

345

soon arrive from, perhaps, his very sublime majesty, Kien-Long, the emperor of China, written in Chinese characters, of which not a soul in Philadelphia had the least knowledge, from the brother of the sun and moon at Constantinople, in Turkish--or from the dey of Algiers, in Arabic, with which sort of people or their writings I wished to have no concern, I resigned the translator's office into the hands of Mr. Jefferson, in October, 1793, as well for the aforementioned reasons, as to an end to the clamor that was raised against me in several New-England papers of a particular cast, in which I was basely aspersed by men of illiberal and malignant minds, and whom I wish never to think of again.

Before the conclusion of the first year's publication of the National Gazette, I had acquired nearly, if not quite, seventeen hundred subscribers to that paper, in different parts of the United States; but such, I do aver, were the strong obstacles generally thrown in the way of its circulation, that a great part of the time I received little more from the great body of subscribers than letters of complaint at the irregular or non-reception of the Gazette. This circumstance, of course, prevented in a great degree the expected remittance of money at the proper periods; and I must have abandoned the publication short of its continuance for a year, had it not been for the complaisance and good will of Messrs. Childs and Swain, who furnished me with the necessary sums for carrying it on.

In September, 1793, Mr. Childs, having recently returned from England, wrote to me that he could no longer consent to be connected in a paper which was to him a perpetual loss, and directing me at all events to discontinue its publication immediately if its continuance was to depend upon his advances.

I, however, found resources of my own, and from some little money that was collected in, continued the gazette until two years were completed, when I notified the subscribers of its temporary suspension, and at the same time of the probability of its speedy renewal when I could make the necessary arrangements for the purpose.

Upon this event, which was extremely mortifying to me, I returned to my accustomed residence in New Jersey; but circumstances of a various nature and my own immediate concerns prevented a revival of the National Gazette.

I should have mentioned that no sooner had this famous National Gazette become an object of terror to the enemies of liberty and equality, who were continually abusing the secretary of state in papers devoted to their cause, but who never did or could, or can at this moment, (in this instance at least) support a charge of corruption, than I considered it my duty, as far as in my power, to clear Mr. Jefferson of the imputation of any agency whatsoever or any concern in the National Gazette, or of any influence upon it more than if he had not been in existence. I imagined that the most ready means of effecting this purpose would be to make oath before the mayor of Philadelphia that no such connection as was asserted by Mr. Jefferson's enemies, influence, or agency, existed. This was accordingly done, and the affidavit published in several of the Philadelphia papers, which proved another fertile source of abuse and misinterpretation from those who thought it their interest to ruin the political character and consequence of Mr. Jefferson.

In order to prejudice the citizens of this state against Mr. Jefferson, and if possible to prevent his probable election to the presidency of the United States, the old unfounded

347

charges above alluded to have been again brought forward in a pamphlet printed by William P. Young, and addressed to the citizens of South Carolina.

I therefore, in justification of Mr. Jefferson, do declare in this public manner, and in the face of South Carolina, or of the United States, that Mr. Jefferson did not, any time, establish, support or patronize the National Gazette, and that I was neither his pensioner nor confidential agent.

Secondly, that I acted from my own motives and with my own views in the publication of that paper.

Thirdly, and lastly, that the author of these charges, whoever he may be, has, to say the least, been guilty of a shameful misrepresentation of facts, and, whether from being misinformed or not I will not pretend to say, has perverted the truth and imposed upon the public a statement of the affair as remote from the truth as it is destitute of candor and liberality. [81]

PHILIP FRENEAU.

Coxe and Jefferson [82]

Mr. Duane:

You see that I am fond of what the great writers call "trimming the midnight lamp," which I have construed like the leader of the other party "sitting up all night for the benefit of mankind:" indeed if I could cease to think, after putting out my lamp, I should be well off; but you and your politics follow me to my very bed, to the great distress of my loving spouse, Polly Bunker--I think of you all day, and I dream of you afterwards.--My uncle has so ingratiated you in my favour that my wish to advise increases with the evidence of the folly of doing so: poor man, how uncle Joe grieves for you; ho! you're a mortal enemy of the Bunkers!

To make it clear as the sun that you are wrong, I have told you what France has become by giving way to the majority, that is, the rabble: if you would use your brains, you would discover that the ruin of all nations has proceeded from three causes, first, too extensive a territory, second, the admission of foreigners, and thirdly, from the want of energy in the government proportioned to the democracy of the governed.

Our country, Mr. Duane, was once governed by federalists, who would have done very well had they placed such men as Mr. Coxe in their front rank; if they had made him secretary of the treasury certain things would not have happened; so they were turned out for their neglect of talents and incapacity; and the present administration appear to be forming the same system of neglect of great men. Mr. Jefferson is in my mind responsible for keeping Mr. Coxe in the back ground, and he may rue it when too late, as Timothy Pickering said. So, sir, since the federalists did wrong and Mr. Jefferson has done wrong, we have a party, neither federalists nor democrats, who want offices out of pure love of the people and to keep them from ruin. Our purpose is to oblige every body, to be like St. Paul, all things to all men--for the good of our country, and let me tell you this party must have offices--or it will send all parties to the devil in the end.

Already, sir, we have discovered three great objections to Mr. Jefferson which will have their weight. I told you all nations were ruined from these three causes; now Mr. Jefferson has encreased the first cause by procuring Louisiana. The Roman empire fell because it was too unwieldy; it had your wildernesses and salt mountains in abundance, but it went to pieces when those great men, the Clodiuses, and the Caius Caesars, and the Mark Antonies were refused places; and so shall our country, unless you let such men as Mr. Coxe and others of similar virtues govern us.

In the next place, Mr. Jefferson is a friend to emigrants, and we third party men are not, for you would know if you had read books that the introduction of foreigners was another cause of Rome's downfall--the Romans had their Goths and Vandals, and we have the Irish and Germans, and their descendants, I believe--so that we third party men are no friends of Mr. Jefferson for introducing them--and a friend of mine, a grocer at the corner of Market street who is one of the most moral men of our party, as his father in law can tell, says nothing can be more absurd than to allow an Irishman, from the bog of Alan for instance, to think as freely as one of us aborigines; I believe he had this sentiment from a great officer who writes these witty things called "quids and quiddities"--the world is given to change--the Irish, it appears to me, are imported like our coloured population, for no other purpose than to keep up the stock, take care of our plantations, and trim our cabbages: a very great man, as he assures me himself he is, once told me that he would oppose the importation of any more Irish if we did not want them to counterbalance the blacks--and I voted to make him a senator for the soundness of his principles.--In their own country these Irish would be glad enough of potatoes and herrings, but here nothing will serve 'em but eating as we do: every body knows Ireland is a country inhabited by uncivilized people, and I have a great repugnance to associate with such. But what is worse than all, these Irish "have too much influence;"

350

and this we may thank Mr. Jefferson and your friend Leib for--Then there are the Germans; they have monopolized the best farms of this state particularly, to the great injury of us aborigines; to be sure, there are many Irishmen and Germans who were born here, but as they had not native parents like us, they are Irishmen and Germans still, for even the Irish themselves allow there are Irish of all countries, and the Germans must admit the same or we'll make them --you have now our two first objections to Mr. Jefferson, and also Leib; our only hope of keeping these Germans and Irish in their proper places is to make 'em fight with one another.

The third objection to Mr. Jefferson, as well as to your Michael Leib, is that they are opposed to energetic government; they give in to democracy--and democracy produces anarchy and bloodshed. For my own part I believe that all the wars of the world for a thousand years past have been owing to democracy, even the thirty years war, tho' the historian pretended it was all about religion--order --and law. That our case is the same is obvious; for instance, Mr. Coxe wanted a higher salary than his predecessors, which he was justly entitled to, and it was not granted, forsooth because the money belonged to the people! this was a reason indeed--and did not his services belong to the public also? Why did not the government agree at once to give him, along with his present office, that of Mr. Harrison and general Irvine--were not his talents adequate to the discharge of all the three!--I tell you, sir, no wise man but knows great services deserve great recompense, an able statesman will give any thing for rare talents, but you democrats can't be brought to believe Mr. Coxe has great talents, tho' he has been telling you of it in a thousand

351

shapes for years past--I tell you what, sir, Mr. Jefferson should have called every man of "virtue and talents" to Washington; he ought to have made Mr. Coxe secretary of the treasury or some other secretary, (with a high salary) and he would have taken care to write enough in quantity to supersede all dread of the frowns of a mere populace--I had great expectations, myself, of promotion, and once set a-bout learning decimal arithmetic and geography to qualify me for some genteel office--but I see a democracy is un-friendly to talents, and I have given up those studies and keep at my old trade of pump boring--If the people had not acted like the cock on a dunghill, who passed a jewel by to get at a corn cob, they'd have encouraged my studies--but then I see them so foolish as not to have chose Mr. Coxe governor instead of McKean, another of your democrats, and an Irishman into the bargain. I see no hopes for myself or my friends getting into places of profit or trust but by thrusting you all out. If Mr. Coxe were governor, we'd have no trouble from the Connecticut intruders; his interest in that quarter is amazing--and only equalled by his indus-try in quieting the people, and if he were president we'd have a navy equal to that of England; and who knows but we might make a naval superintendent of our friend Penrose--who, we all know, differs from Mr. Jefferson on a navy.

You have now all my objections to your democratic president, and to Leib, who always acts with him, and who is foolish enough to think that we cannot have a large navy.

All history is against you--when two dogs have been fighting for a bone 'till they are exhausted, a third comes in and carries it off very quietly; you see, I am a third-party man and think no motives can govern any one but those of which I tell you--I therefore repeat to you, we are

352

the third and are resolved to bear off the bone.

If you stay where you are with your cursed Aurora, you may expect ever to remain a sorry printer, a most disgusting business--or if you are fond of the name, you may retain it and live on the people! if you join us, now you will catch the tide leading to fortune--the summum bonum in this world. Being a minority, of course there will be two offices to each man, and you may get on if you behave yourself and obey orders--if you don't join us, but continue to make your remarks, you'll find interest enough making with our party in congress to make you quit there--and here will hamper you in the banks--and at length like old Jacob Bright you'll be put into prison till you rot; you had better follow the example and come round the corner--you'll find me at Shinkle's every day about eleven or twelve.

Yours to serve,
JONATHAN BUNKER.

The Old Indian School Must be Abandoned[83]

In times past, when Indians have barbarously murdered our women and innocent children, we have generally solicited a treaty. After some time these savages have assembled and feasted for weeks at our expense; in the end a treaty was made with great professions of friendship; the hatchet is finally buried, and large presents are given as evidences of our sincerity and friendship. These are deemed by the Indians as evidence that we fear them... when the presents were consumed, they pretended to have some cause of war; but the real design is to get more presents; for they are a lazy, idle set of wretches, and consequently always poor and needy. The British know this...

We have tried treaties long enough, according to the

old school, to convince us of the inutility of that method...
Some years ago we had a treaty at the mouth of the Mus-
kingum, where these savages received liberal presents; but
the perfidious British soon bribed them...to invade and murder us again...

Mr. Johnston[84] in congress has lately made a speech
with a view to form a winter campaign against the Indians,
in which he has exactly expressed my sentiments...I fear a
winter campaign will be attended with more difficulties than
appear at first sight. The forage will be scarce and the
horses will soon become weak; if this can be provided for,
the plan is excellent, and will have a happy effect; for if all
their towns and provisions are destroyed, their distress will
be extreme; and this will still be aggravated if we can succeed in making their squaws prisoners.

The Need of a Larger Navy[85]

Public motives need no apology, and therefore I offer
the result of my reflections and observations on the proposed encrease of the navy.

The policy of a naval establishment having long been
the subject of political discussion...let us now approach the
subject without prejudice and discuss it with candor...The
foe we have to contend with is of a character inflexible, energetic, proud and desperate. Her hostile councils have recently acquired new strength, and it behoves us to prepare
for the utmost vigor of her arms by sea and land. A just
estimate of these objects and a proper disposition to meet
the crisis will fill us with confidence...I shall indeed be
mistaken if the war on her part does not assume a character of malignancy and desperation proportionate to her disappointment, chagrin, and injustice. It is therefore vain to

354

look for honorable peace, but through the blood and perils of honorable war.

The important question then presents itself; shall we employ all the means which nature, habits, and circumstances have placed within our power...or shall we rely alone upon the military ardor and patriotism of the nation ...? There can be but one rational answer--employ the whole force of the country, naval and military...

As an efficient means of annoying the enemy...I am for an extensive encrease of the naval force.

Our naval operations, to be effectual, must necessarily be predatory, and the capture or destruction of the enemy's frigates and smaller cruisers, and of her commercial fleets will...be the most effectual means of protecting our commerce...Hence it is evident that large frigates and sloops of war are the most effective vessels we can employ.

The frigates President, United States, and Constitution are of a class perfectly original, and decidedly superior in force, strength and velocity to any frigates in Europe. Experience has demonstrated these transcendent qualities--let us adhere to them. Fleetness of sailing close-hauled is of all other qualities the most essential to an inferior force. It enables the commander to avoid or attack... Sloops of war of the description of the Wasp and Hornet are a most useful class of vessels for predatory warfare. They are inferior only to a frigate, and superior to any number of merchantmen combined...

HAWSER TRUNNION.

On the Spots in the Sun[86]

"There are more things in heaven and earth, Horatio,
Than is dreamt of in your philosophy." [87]

The dark spots in the Sun, and what are called spots
in the Moon, seem to be of an entirely different nature.
The latter appear to be oceans, lakes, and extensive bodies
of water, or some liquid substance, that in a great measure
absorb the sun's rays, and only partially reflect light. The
same may be said of the spots in Venus and Mars; but in
Jupiter, besides his spots, there are several remarkable
dark zones or belts that seem to be vast bodies of clouds
floating in his atmosphere, and perhaps somewhat similar to
what are called spots in the sun, or owing to a similar origin, being exhalations from the body of the planet, or vapours mounting into its atmosphere and suspended at different altitudes, according to their different degrees of density.

It was not discovered that there were any spots in the
sun until, I think, the year 1610, when they were seen by
Galileo. History mentions, indeed, that in the time of Julius Caesar the sun suffered great obscurations, probably
from these spots, so that the seasons were considerably affected thereby, and that they continued, more or less, above
a year, to the astonishment of all who then lived. To this
circumstance Shakespear alludes in one of his tragedies:[88]

"Some time before the mighty Julius fell
Disasters veil'd the sun, and his bright orb
Was sick almost to doomsday with eclipse."

The great circular spots plainly visible to the naked
eye during part of the late spring and summer were not un-
precedented in modern times. One appeared in the year
1612, whose diameter was equal to one twentieth part of the

sun, or about forty thousand miles. The spot seen this summer, 1816, was two minutes of a degree in diameter, or very nearly, and therefore the diameter of the spot could not have been less than fifty thousand miles, and its circumference one hundred and fifty thousand, a very considerable blot on the disk of that glorious orb, whose circumference is twenty four hundred thousand miles!--Some have asserted, from their observations, this spot was a solid globular body. But many reasons would lead one to suppose their assertions and opinions to be erroneous. All planetary bodies that we know of, that transit the sun's disk, do remain in that position but a short time, as they are constantly in motion with immense rapidity, say sixty, seventy, or eighty thousand miles an hour. As far as I could observe, the spot in question either adhered to the surface of the sun, or was suspended immoveable in his atmosphere, or above it. The apparent motion was from east to west, produced by the real rotation of the sun in his axis from west to east, in 25 days, 15 hours, and 16 minutes.

This, and similar spots on or near the sun, it is not irrational to think, are nothing more than exhalations from the globular surface of the sun, and condensed in his atmosphere, where they remain stationary until dissipated by some cause or causes unknown to us.

It has been observed frequently that many small spots have, after some time, formed themselves into one large one, and at other times one would be separated or subdivided into many small ones. Such fluctuations could not take place in solid globular bodies. It is well known that the telescope discovers spots on the face of the sun at all times, but it is a rare thing that we see them with the naked eye, even when looked for through the stained glass of a quadrant.

It is a fact well known that in different ages of the world several fixed stars (or suns) have disappeared entirely from human view, and never appeared more. Others have disappeared, and after a certain lapse of time re-appeared. Perhaps nature employs this interval in new moulding, modelling or re-creating some old globe, or solar orb, that has been exhausted by length of time. But such changes are probably owing to the solar spots, which may obtain such a power, gain such an ascendancy as to obscure, or incrust, a whole solar orb; and, of course, a whole system of primary and secondary planets perishes and all that exist thereon!--Thus these brilliant solar orbs, the blazing suns of the firmament, like the systems of government contrived by man, seem to contain the seeds of their own dissolution. Nature will take her time, I should rather have said the God of nature, either to renovate or to leave their place a blank in the creation, as best suits the will of supreme wisdom.--Intellect alone, that emanation from the Deity, is secure from the effects of these changes in the material world; and MIND, we have powerful reasons to conclude, will survive when matter is no more:[89]

"The sun himself may waste away with age,
And all the Starry system sink in years,
But MIND will flourish in immortal youth,
Unchanged amidst the war of elements,
The wreck of matter and the crash of worlds."

Doing Without Tea[90]

Sometime in the month of June, 1773, there were thrown overboard in Boston Harbour from the British Tea-ships, by a combination of the Townsmen, upwards of three hundred and fifty chests of choice India Teas, to prevent their being landed and paying the new three penny parliamentary duty to the Royal custom House. Soon after, in consequence of speculations in this article, and from other causes, Tea became a real scarcity, not only in Massachusetts Province, but generally throughout the then thirteen colonies. --Resolves were every where entered into and brought forward, to dispense with the use of tea and to admit none to be landed or imported into the country until the very odious tax was abolished. The female part of the community were instantly thunderstruck at the prospect of being deprived of their common and favorite beverage. Lamentations, groanings, and howlings were heard in every quarter --Rachel mourning for her children!--and never was loss more deplored or regretted than the three hundred and fifty chests submerged into Boston Bay, and which, sad to tell! could now do nobody any good! There were, however, thousands of patriotic females, and many of the first condition, who concurred in the determination to abandon the use of Tea altogether rather than acquiesce in the accursed Tax, as it was called, and entered into combinations and adopted Resolves accordingly. --Immediately every thing was mentioned as a substitute for real Tea. Ginseng, Catnip, Sage, Balm, Carolina Yoppon, and what not? All these failing and being of ephemeral date, a reverend and pious Clergyman, then settled at Lewes Town, near Cape Henlopen, about this time published in Philadelphia a great and important discovery he had made, that the leaves of the Peach-Tree-Oak were the genuine green Tea of China, or at least so nearly resembling it as not to be easily distinguishable therefrom. He also published ample and minute directions how to cure and preserve the leaves for general use.

Now every countenance brightened up, and poor John

Bull and his thousand ships of war, with all his menaces, was laughed at. The Peach-Tree-Oak was universally sought after, and the good man's directions carefully and punctually attended to. But alas! after long and patient trial it answered not expectation! The good parson was left to drink his Tea with his own family, who soon became tired of it also, and no wonder, as it was really insipid and void of the true flavor as well as the qualities of India Teas. It was also highly sudorific, and no more like the Tea from Canton than a decoration of dog wood bark. So it fell into disuse.

To add to the evil, about this time a captain Isaac Sears, an influential and overbearing character in New-York, had issued, upon his own authority, a sort of Proclamation denouncing all Tea Drinkers as political heretics, and menacing Tar and Feathers to such Tea consigners as should receive any foreign teas on shore. Such was the quixotism of the Times--Sadness, tribulation, and mourning now returned upon the land when it was discovered that no effectual substitute for Tea could be found, and that the days of Butter milk would probably return. At last it was concluded to make a virtue of necessity and to abandon the usage of it altogether until times should take another turn, which they effectually did after the Fourth of July, 1776, when tea again became plenty. On occasion of the before mentioned event in Boston in 1773, the following colloquial conference was printed in a New-York Half sheet weekly Paper of those times called The American Whig, now long since forgotten, and perhaps shot away in cartridges during the Revolutionary War. The lines were lately recovered in a bundle of old manuscripts.

Liberty Poles 91

The origin of Liberty Poles is very ancient; Polybius and Xenophon, historians of the first credibility, both mention them as distinct from Columns of brick, stone, or marble. It is not probable, however, the idea they attached to them was the same as has been so prevalent in America. Perhaps they were only signals of public resort, and erected on spots where orators and demagogues harangued the populace. It is certain from history that the Greeks, as well as the old Romans, had such Poles set up on festivals of national rejoicing for gaining a victory, and other occasions of minor importance. In no country, however, as far as we know, were they so generally adopted as in this in the Revolutionary war of America. In 1774 and 1775, and even anterior to those dates, they were to be seen at almost every tavern, beer house, and other places of public assemblage, in the front of Court houses and other provincial public buildings, and hardly any place was excused from their august presence and commanding attitude except churches. --Early in the month of April, 1775, one of these Liberty Signals, upwards of eighty feet in length, including its topmast, was set up in the city of New York, nearly in the centre of the spot where the superb and elegant City Hall now stands. About this period the City was infested with considerable numbers of people who continued their attachment to Great Britain, and had even imported from London and erected in the Bowling Green, as it was called, a large Equestrian Statue of George the third in his old Roman Drapery and habiliments, notwithstanding the insults, outrages, provocations, and degradations the country was almost daily experiencing from the mother Island, its

King, Ministers, Governors, and naval officers. --These
People, not a few of whom were of the first rank and families in the city, had their agents every where, as well as
spies on the public conduct of the whigs, which spies and
emissaries had at this time private orders to destroy, when
a convenient opportunity offered, every Liberty Pole that
was accessible. Accordingly, one stormy dark night towards
the latter part of May, 1775, a little before Generals Washington and Lee arrived in New York from Virginia on their way
to Boston, a gang of the disaffected to the American cause approached the unguarded Pole at midnight, hacked it down,
and separated it with their axes into thirteen different por-
tions or lengths, probably with a view of gaining a triumph
over the predominant party by burning them--An alarm,
however, was given, and they thought proper to decamp before any of them could be detected and seized, and they
scattered and ran off without effecting their purpose of con-
flagration.

This outrage produced a spirit among the whig populace and their leaders almost bordering on frenzy; and,
could the perpetrators of this deed have been discovered, it
would have fared badly with them. Tar and feathers would
have been the mildest punishment.

All that could now be done was to procure and erect a
new Pole to supply the place of the one demolished, and
show the disaffected that the Liberty, or Whig Party were
the majority, and were determined to carry their point at
all events.

Instantaneously a party of axe men were despatched up
the North River, beyond Haverstraw Bay, to cut a new Pole,
which was speedily brought down, a beautiful stick of Red
hickory about 75 feet in length. No sooner had the maker

362

done with it than a Mr. Boyd, a first rate democratic master Blacksmith, was engaged to arm the Pole against future insults. Iron bars, case hardened, were prepared, about sixteen feet in length. These were perforated with many spike holes, and then spiked on to the Pole so as completely to inclose its whole circumference and present an adamantine face on every side to the edge of any tool or force whatever. The Bars extended about four feet down into the earth, and twelve above the surface. These provisions rendered it, with the addition of a nocturnal Guard, and two three pounders (called bull-dogs) perfectly secure and iron proof against all invaders and assailants. When all was completed and the Pole erected, a number of respectable people, and of the whig persuasion, were appointed Guardians in rotation of said Pole, one of whom always, when the Evening Guard was set, required from each individual of them the following solemn acknowledgment, with the hand laid on General Simes's Military Guide, a book at that time much read and in fashion:

You do swear, promise, and engage, as a man of honor and a good whig, truly and faithfully to guard, preserve, and watch this Liberty Pole while on duty?

"I do, to the best of my knowledge, abilities, strength, and capacity. "

You do also obligate yourself, and promise to suffer no disaffected person, or of suspicious character, to come within twenty-five yards of the pole, by night or by day?

"I do promise this also, as far as I shall be able to know them. "

They will be pointed out to you by some of the Committee men. -- You will permit no person whatever to approach the Pole during the hours of your standing Centry, by night or by day, unless he presents a Ticket signed by a Committee man, or the Liberty Pole Chairman of the day, or his Secretary, or Deputy?

"Yes, please Your Honor"--Go on duty.

This Pole stood the brunt of the enthusiastic ferocity and severity of the times until Lord Howe arrived with his fleet at New York in August, 1776, when on the retreat of Washington, it was left to his mercy. It is almost superfluous to mention that on the English troops taking possession of the City, it was one of the first offensive objects destroyed by them.

At the inauguration of the Pole (for mankind will have something to worship, whether a pole or a broomstick) the following stanzas, composed for the occasion, were read by a Committee man to the surrounding multitude. They were also printed in a hand-bill and circulated in all directions, carried thro' every street, and thrown into every floor in the City.

LETTERS

Letter to James Madison[92]

Somerset County in Maryland--
November 22d: 1772.

Sir--

If I am not wrongly informed by my memory, I have not seen you since last April, you may recollect I was then undertaking a School at Flatbush on Long Island; I did enter upon the business it is certain and continued in it thirteen days--but--"Long Island I have bid adieu, with all its bruitish brainless crew, The youth of that detested place, are void of reason and of grace, From Flushing hills to Flatbush plains, Deep ignorance unrivall'd reigns," I am very poetical but excuse it--"Si fama non venit ad aures" if you

364

have not heard the rumor of this story (which by the by is
told in various Taverns and eating houses) you must allow
me to be a little prolix with it--Those who employed me
were some gentlemen of New York, some of them were bul-
lies, some merchants, and others scoundrels: They sent me
Eight children the eldest of whom was 10 years--Some could
read, others spell and a few stammer over a chapter of the
Bible--these were my pupils and over these was I to pre-
side--My Salary moreover was £ 40,--there is something
else relating to that I shall not at present mention--after I
forsook them they proscribed me for four days and swore
that if I was caught in New York they would either Trounce
or maim me: but I luckily escaped with my goods to Prince-
town--where I remained till commencement--so much for this
affair--I have printed a poem in New York called the American Village, containing about 450 lines, also a few short
pieces added; I would send you one if I had a proper oppor-
tunity--the additional poems are, --1. a Poem to the Nymph
I never saw--The miserable Life of a Pedagogue--and Stanzas on an ancient Dutch house on Long Island--As to the
main poem it is damned by all good and judicious judges &
my name is in the title page, this is called Vanity by some
--but "who so fond as youthful bards of fame?"--I arrived
at this Somerset Academy the 18th: of October and intend
to remain here till next October--I am assistant to Mr.
Brackenridge. This is the last time I shall enter into such
a business, it worries me to death and by no means suits
my "giddy 'wandring brain"--I would go over for the gown
this Time two years--but old hag Necessity has got such a
prodigious gripe of me that I fear I shall never be able to
accomplish it--I believe if I cannot make this out I must
turn quack--and indeed I am now reading Physic at my lei-

sure hours, that is, when I am neither sleeping, hearing classes, or writing Poetry--for these three take up all my time--

It is now late at night, not an hour ago I finished a little poem of about 400 lines, entitled a Journey to Maryland--being the Sum of my adventures--it begins--"From that fam'd town where Hudson flood--unites with Streams, perhaps as good; Muse has your bard begun to roam"--&c. I intend to write a terrible Satire upon certain vicious persons of quality in N. Y. --who have also used me ill--and print it next fall--it shall contain 5 or 600 lines--Sometimes I write pastorals to shew my Wit--

"Deep to the woods, I sing a Shepherds care, Deep to the woods, Cyllenius calls me there, The last retreat of Love and Verse I go--Verse made me mad at first and--will keep me so"--I should have been glad to have heard from you before now; while I was at College I had but a short participation of your agreeable friendship, and the few persons I converse with and yet fewer, whose conversations I delight in, make me regret the Loss of it--I have met with a variety of rebuffs this year, which I forbear to mention, I look like an unmeaning Teague just turned out of the hold of an irish Ship--coming down hither I met with a rare adventure at Annapolis--I was destitute even of a brass farthing--I got clear very handsomely--could I/one Expect ever to be free again, if I travel through Virginia I shall stop and talk with you a day or two--I should be very glad to receive a Letter from you if it can be conveniently forwarded --In short "Non sum qualis eram" as Partridge says in Tom Jones--My hair is grown like a mop, and I have a huge tuft of Beard directly upon my chin--I Want but five weeks of twenty one years of age and already feel stiff with age--We

366

have about 30 Students in this academy, who prey upon me like Leaches--"When shall I quit this whimpering pack, and hide my head in Acomack!"--Shall I leave them and go "Where Pokomoke's long stream meandring flows--Excuse this prodigious Scrawl--without stile or sense--I send this by Mr. Martin who will forward it to Col. Lee--and he to you I hope--Mr. Martin lives in Acomack in Virginia, this side the bay--Farewell and be persuaded I remain your

truly humble Servt and friend

Ph. F-r-e-n-e-a-u--

A Sailor's Philosophy[93]

Sir,

Amongst a number of my good natured acquaintance, who have lately sympathized with me on account of what they term my misfortunes during a great part of the last year, I know of no one more entitled to my acknowledgments on the occasion than yourself. When an old woman talks of witches, ghosts, or blue devils, we naturally make an allowance for bad education, or the embecillity of intellect occasioned by age. When one man seriously supposes another unfortunate for the sake of two or three successive disasters, which no prudence or foresight could have avoided, the same allowance ought to be made, provided the same excuses could be assigned.

Can you be serious then in advising me to quit all future intercourse with an element that has for some years, with all its dangers and losses, afforded to your humble servant attractions far more powerful than those of Apollo! --Formerly, when I wrote poetry, most of those that attended to it would not allow my verses to be good. I gave credit to what I deemed the popular opinion, and made a safe retreat in due time to the solitary wastes of Neptune. I am not, however, inclined to believe people so readily now, when they alledge my vessel is not sound, and when several gentlemen, for reasons best known to themselves, and perhaps not over willing to risque the uncertainties of the world to come, affect to doubt of her ability to waft their carcases in safety.

But my ambition is greatly concerned in this matter: a schooner is confided to my care, humble indeed, when compared to those lofty piles which I have seen you so much admire, but which is, nevertheless, really capable of an European, nay of an India voyage. Read all history, ransack libraries, call tradition to your aid, search all records, examine a million of manuscripts on vellum, on parchment, on paper, on marble, on what you please, and I defy you to find the most distant hint of any poet, in any age or country, from Hesiod down to Peter Pindar, having been trusted with the controul or possession of any thing fit to be mentioned or compared with this same barque, which, you say, I have the misfortune to command.

To be serious: misfortune ought to be only the topic of such men as do not think or reason with propriety upon the nature of things. Some writer says it is but another name for carelessness or inattention: Though that may not at all times be the case, it is in the power of every man to place himself beyond the supposed baneful influence of this inexorable deity, by assuming a dignity of mind, (if it be not the gift of nature) that will in the end get the better of the untoward events that may frequently cross our best purposes. --Indeed, the sea is the best school for philosophy (I mean of the moral kind); in thirteen or fourteen years acquaintance with this element, I am convinced a man ought

368

to imbibe more of your right genuine <u>stoical</u> stuff than could be gained in half a century on shore. --I must add that, be our occupations what they may, or our fortunes what they will, there is a certain delectable, inexpressible satisfaction in now and then encountering the rubs and disasters of life, and I am entirely of the opinion which (says Dr. Langhorne)

> --"Weakness wrote in Petrarch's gentle strain,
> When once he own'd at love's unfavouring shrine
> <u>A thousand pleasures are not worth one pain!</u>"

I must now conclude this scrawl with telling you that I am receiving on board my vessel a small cargo of lumber at a place called Yamacraw, a little above Savanna. The weather is extremely warm, I am tired of my letter, and must, of course, conclude. I do not know whether you ever mean to make a voyage to sea--if you should, thrice welcome shall you be to such accommodations as my little embarkation affords. Poets and philosophers shall ever travel with me at a cheap rate indeed?--not only because they are not generally men of this world, but because, even supposing the barque that bears them should make an eternal exit to the bottom of the ocean, the busy world, as things go, will regret the loss of most of them very little, perhaps not at all.

Letter to James Madison[94]

Monmouth, May 20th--1795. --

My respected friend,

By some accident your kind letter of April 6th was a long time in finding its way hither, having not come to hand 'till the 17th inst. I sincerely thank for the interest you have taken in favour of Mr. Bailey. He is a good republican and a worthy honest man, which qualifications, I have thought, entitled him to some notice from the Government, in his line of business--I was heartily laughed at, however, a few weeks ago in N. York, by some aristocrats, for having in my letter to you or Mr. Beckley, I forget which, extolled his military services in the late war.--I am sensible he never cut off the heads of giants or drove hosts before him, as some have done; at the same time it ought to be remembered that he was an officer in the Pennsylvania Militia in the season that tried Men's Souls (as Paine says) and I believe never acted otherwise than became the character in which he acted.--

I meet you at least half way in your congratulations on the public intelligence received from Holland. It is but another step toward the advancement and completion of that great and philanthropic system which I have been anticipating for many years, and which you as well as myself, I hope, will live to see realized.--When I first went to reside in Philada. in 1791 I wished to be one of those who would have the honour and happiness of announcing those great events to the public through the medium of a newspaper: a variety of circumstances, however, needless to trouble you with, urged my departure from that city after completing a two years publication.--As I mean to pass the remainder of my days on a couple of hundred of acres of an old sandy patrimony, I have, by way of filling up the necessities of time, set on foot a small weekly newspaper calculated for the part of the country in which I am--Should you have any curiosity to see it I will forward it to you free of all expence except that of postage. I will not make high promises in regard to what it may contain. It will scarcely be expected that in a rude barbarous part of the country I should calculate it for the polite taste of Philadelphia.--Should your fixed residence be in Philada. I can transmit the papers to you once a week by the Public Post, who stops every Wednesday at my door. A letter put into the Post office at Philadelphia on Saturday Morning, will be sure to reach me on Wednesday. --The public papers sometime ago announced your marriage. I wish you all possible happiness with the lady whom you have chosen for your companion through life --Mrs. freneau [sic] joins me in the same, and desires me to present her best respects to your lady and yourself--and should you ever take an excursion to these parts of Jersey, we will endeavour to give Mrs. Madison and yourself--"if not a costly welcome, yet a kind. "--

I am, Sir,

with Great Esteem

Your friend and humble Servt.

Philip Freneau

Letter to Peter Freneau[95]

New York, March <u>1st.</u> 180 <u>/1/</u>

Dear Brother,

Having been here a day or two, and finding the Brig Echo, Capt. Webb, to sail for Charleston, I take the opportunity of dropping you a line by him. I left all well at home last Thursday, and the place &c. as well as could be expected after my four months absence. I have been and shall be for some time busy in repairing old fences, and making new ones, a new garden, and some other small improvements as far as I prudently can with the money you let me have.

Helen goes to school here, the other two girls are at home, but agnes will come here next Month for the same purpose, for a while. Nelly I find is forward with another

371

one, which is expected in a few weeks. Thus are new cares and vexations coming on, but still they must be got through with at some date. Probably I shall have to embark on some new expedition or plan before long, wherever or to whatever the devil shall see fit to drive me: But I shall attempt nothing, if I can avoid it before I see you here, in April or May, as you promised. --Mr. Napier accepted the 300 dollar Bill of Exchange, which I left at the Bank--The statement of that and the 233 doll. are from the Manhattan Bank, with the expences due [illegible] as follows--

> 233 dols. paid for advertising in your Paper
> 300 Bill of Exchange
> 533 --

Paid out to Stewart, my debt, which was --	100 dols.
To Bush do. --	118 --
Your balance due to Hunn[96] --	39
To Greenleaf --	98
To myself --	157
	512
To myself	20
	532

So that what I have now left is 157 dollars after all these payments have been made, which I will turn to the best uses I can: Part of it I leave in Mr. Hunns hands, out of which Mamma[97] and Polly can have occasional supplies, as they have already of some small stores to make them easy. --

We all hope You will not fail of coming in the spring; and Nelly will be glad of Miss Eliza's company as long as she pleases, should she come with You, and the Same here at Mr. Hunns. --

I return this morning to Jersey. Mr. Hunn, Peggy,

Mamma and Polly all desire their love to You--My best respects to Mrs Freneau and Miss Eliza with her Mother and family--remember me also to Mr. Parine and Judge Burke, who I hope continues on his recovery.

May I expect to have a line from you by Capt. Pelôn. C. C. Linchelson from the Gazette has spent two or three days with me at Mt. Pleasant. Tho', not acquainted with you he desired me to have his services sent to You / He married you know Helen Ledyard, and is therefore a sort of connexion--

Yours affectionately

Philip Freneau

Letter to James Madison[98]

Philadelphia, May 12th. 1809--

Sir,

After a month's ramble through the States of New Jersey and New York, I returned to this place on Saturday last, and found your friendly Letter on Mr. Bailey's table, with the contents. There was no occasion of inclosing any money, as your Name was all I wanted to have placed at the head of the Subscription list. --I hope you will credit me when I say that the republication of these Poems, such as they are, was not a business of my own seeking or forwarding. I found that last winter an Edition would soon be going on at all events and in contradiction to my wishes, as I had left these old scribblings to float quietly down the stream of oblivion to their destined element the ocean of forgetfulness. However, I have concluded to remain here this summer, and have them published in a respectable manner, and free as possible of the blemishes imputable to the two former Editions, over which I had no controul, having given my manuscripts away, and left them to the mercy of chance.--I am endeavouring to make the whole work as worthy of the public eye as circumstances will allow. 1500 copies are to be printed, only; but I have a certainty, from the present popular frenzy, that three times that number might soon be disposed of.--I will attend to what you direct on the subject, and will forward the ten you mention by the middle of July or sooner.--I will consider of what you say relative to the insertion of a piece or two in prose, but suspect that any thing I have written in that way is so inferior to the Poetry, that the contrast will be injurious to the credit of the Publication--I feel much in the humour of remaining here about two years to amuse myself, as well as the Public, with such matters as that of the fat man you refer to, and if the public are in the same humour they shall be gratified. [99]-- But I am intruding on your time and will add no more at present.--I had almost said

> Cum tot sustineas et tanta negotia solus
> Res Italas armis tuteris, moribus ornes
> Legibus emendes, in publica commoda peccem
> Si longo sermone mores tua tempora, Caesar--

My best wishes Sir, will ever await you, and in particular that your Presidential Career may be equally honourable though less stormy than that of your predecessor.--

> My best compliments and respects to Mrs. Madison,
> And remain with esteem and respect
> Your sincere friend
> Philip Freneau

Letter to James Madison[100]

New York, March 3d. 1815

Sir,

When I mentioned in my few lines to you, dated from my residence in New Jersey on the 22d. of January last, the two Volumes of Poems publishing in this city by Mr. Longworth, I did really think to have had a small box of Poems at Washington by the middle of february [sic] at farthest, with a particular direction of a couple of copies to Yourself bound in an elegant manner. Finding, however, that the business went on slowly here, and a little vexed to be under the necessity of leaving my solitude and the wild scenes of Nature in New Jersey for the ever execrated streets and company of this Capital, I embarked near Sandy Hook in a snowstorm, about the last of January, and shortly after arrived here, fortunately unnoticed and almost unknown--At my time of life, 63!!!, abounding however in all the powers of health and vigour, though I consider my poetry and poems as mere trifles, I am seriously out of humour on my arrival here to see my work delayed, as well from the cold, which has been unremitting for more than a month past, and perhaps to some other causes It would not be prudent <u>here</u> to explain. By my incessant exertions in spurring on the indolence of typography, the work, such as it is, is now finished, in two small Volumes of about 180 pages each.--The moment they are out of the bookbinders' hands, Mr. Longworth will forward you a Copy, and by the first Vessel to Alexandria, Georgetown, or Washington a Box of them to his Correspondents in those places--a copy or two of the Revolutionary poems will be forwarded to your direction--I am sorry the copies You had were doomed to the flames, but the author had nearly suffered the same fate in the Year 1780.--Yesterday I received from New Jersey a copy of Your friendly letter of the 1st february: a copy, I say, for my wife, or some one of my four girls, daughters, would not forward me on the original, but keep it until my return for fear of accidents.--

Tomorrow morning I embark again for Monmouth, and among other cares, when I arrive at my magical grove, I shall hasten to exert all the poetical energy I may possess, on the grand subject of the Repulse of the British Army from New Orleans. There is a subject indeed! far above my powers, I fear. If there be any thing in inspiration, it will be needful on such a theme. Eight hundred lines in heroic measure I mean to devote to this animating subject. --In due time you shall hear more from me on this business, if I am not anticipated by some one more muse beloved than myself--Hoping that all health and happiness may attend you, and that your libraries in future escape the ravages and flames of Goths and Barbarians--

> I remain, dear sir,
> Your obedt. humble servt.
> Philip Freneau

Letter to John Francis[101]

1815--

Mount Pleasant, near Middletown Point, May 15

Sir,

Doctor Hosack's and Your own attention and civility to me when in New York was of such a candid and sincere character, that I cannot avoid addressing to You a few lines, now I am returned to my old Shades and gloomy Solitudes, and am withdrawn from the noise and observation of the

Streets of Your City.--I remained there much longer than I had intended, not a little out of humour that my two little Volumes Seemed to have fallen Nearly dead-born from the Press, owing to the enmity of Some, the politics of others, and the general inattention of all--I suppose, however, the truth is, that almost every person in Your City has other and More serious matters to think of than mine, or at least Such poetry as mine, happens to be. Had I written a Volume of psalms, hymns and Spiritual Songs, I believe the Success would have been infinitely greater. Some of the democratic party, I was told, positively refused to purchase the Books because they were published by a High Federalist, or, according to others, a Tory. Now, I never had enquired into Mr. Longworths politics and should have Supposed it a Matter of indifference who published the books, or who printed them, provided the typographical part was well executed, and the poetry worth reading.--Others Smelt out deism in the Book because it contains a few Stanzas, insignificant enough, to the memory of poor Tom Paine, first printed in Philada. Near Six Years ago. Others again, execrated the address to Thomas Jefferson, first published at Trenton, and afterwards in Philada. in 1809. In short, I have reason to believe that there is Scarcely a Solitary trifle through the two Volumes but has its personal enemy, all combining in damning the work and Sending Author, publisher, printer, bookseller and even the binder to the devil.

I almost wonder at there not being people who have enquired what were the politics of the Paper-Maker, a Mr. Pitt, of Bloomfield near Newark. Certainly, he must be either Neutral, federalist, Monarchist, or democrat: Not one of these grounds but would afford Sufficient argument for condemning my poor Poetry.--These party men have done the work much harm, God reward them according to their works!--I should scarcely have noticed this strange manoeuvring had it not deprived me of about two hundred dollars which I had calculated upon from the Booksellers, but they are either very poor, or will risque nothing at present even to the Value of 10 Copies at 33 1/3 d. discount.--All this, as I have said, has rather disgusted me with authorship. However, I am transcribing a poem of about 1400 lines on the Repulse of the British Army from New Orleans in January last.--To this will be appended Some shorter poems generally on light Subjects. This will make about an half dollar Volume. Mr. Longworth, or rather Nicholas Van Riper, will Set about printing it in about three weeks.--Heaven prosper the poor Bantling; it has a dramatic air; as I thought the Subject demanded Something like progressive Action, and not the Monotony of Addison's celebrated Campaign and Glover's Leonidas--

After all, as I take it, the genius of the City of New York is So entirely Commercial, that I suspect it swallows up all ideas of poetry, or refuses any attention to poetical production, further than what is calculated for the fly market Stalls, or to be sung at Some Tammany convivial meeting or the Bachanalian Sons of the Hotels. A drop of water might exist, merely as Such, in a furnace as poetry, where all the ideas of people Seem to be devoted to Commerce, Speculations, Bank Shares, &c. &c. What use would there be for physic or physicians were there no diseases, what use for poetry where men have no idea of its efficacy and influence over the human mind.--

When I visited with Yourself and Mr. Stephenson Your academy of fine arts I felt a strange propensity to be Searching and Scrutinizing into Your collections of manuscripts and printed papers, the labours of past ages as well as the present--but I am not So entirely out of the Literary World, that I can only muse upon such things, without the opportunity of taking an active part in the Business--

The Two Volumes of the Historical Collections you were So kind as to present to me, I had not leisure, or rather was Not in a humour to read through with attention, while in New York. Doctor Hosack's papers, also, with the Engravings of Elgin Garden, I left for a short time with John Kearney Esqr. at No. 94 Pearl Street, for his perusal. He is a worthy good man, a friend of mine, and with whom You and Doctor Hosack may possibly be acquainted. -- Please tell the Doctor that I feel a strong inclination to write 4 or 500 flowing Lines in the poetical Style of <u>Darwin,</u> on the Elgin Garden, as Soon as I can get materials into my hands sufficient for the ground works of the Poem, and that I may not go to work merely on imagination, without any Semblance of reality. --

Our packets leave New York, Coenties Slip, every friday morning for Middletown Point, about two miles from which place I reside: Should You have any Communications to make, I shall receive them in that way without any expense of Postage--My best respects to Doctor Hosack and family--

And am, Sir, with respect and esteem, Your's

Philip Freneau--

Dr. Francis--No. 6 Vesey Street, N. Y.

Be so good as to mention to Doctor D. Hosack that I look forward to be in Your city, for a day or two, on or about the 10th of June ensuing--Doctor William Reynolds, of Middletown Point tells me he will be there at the same time, and will be glad to make a visit to the Elgin Botanic Garden:

He is a man, as I take it, of real science, not only in his particular profession, but the relative arts of Chemistry, &c. Since he returned from Italy and the coast of Barbary in the Year 1800, I think, the fancy took him to Settle at the above mentioned place. He is not only a Single but a Singular man, and has a tolerable knowledge of Natural History &c-- Neither Doctor Hosack nor Yourself will I hope be displeased with his acquaintance. I will also introduce him to Mr. Clinton (the late Mayor) with Some Specimens of the Spermaceti I mentioned to You---[102]

P. F.--

Letter to John Francis[103]

Mount Pleasant, Near Middletown Point,
Monmouth, New Jersey, May 14, 1822.

Sir:

As I promised, I now inclose to you a sort of Prospectus for the republication of my Poems. In my own Judgment, I have said all that is necessary. But perhaps you may think otherwise. Should you disapprove of it in general, you can correct, change or modify it as you see proper. In fact, I have ever found that, after all is said and done, a Judicious Bookseller, well hackneyed in business, such for instance as Mathew Carey, and some others I might mention, brothers of the craft, can always draw up a Paper of this kind to better advantage than any mere Author of a Book. Generally speaking, they have a better knack at so wording and managing a thing of this kind as to produce a respectable subscription from a publication, when it is within the bounds of possibility to do it at all, when every man seems to set his face against the whole Subscription System.

Should the matter go on as you seem to think it would, Be so good as to let me know, when convenient. If Messieurs Bliss and White should be induced to undertake it, I shall be ready with the copy when I have information. Very sure I am that from 500 to a thousand copies could be sold at the City of Washington toward the conclusion of the next session of Congress--and I think New York and South Carolina would not be backward in forwarding the Publication. I can expect nothing from the Bible Societies--and so much the worse. I believe I must write no more against the Witch of Endor. I have made several Enemies by rather making too free with her. [104] I must try and compromise with her as well as I can. My best respects to Your Brother. Our Packets sail away Friday and Saturday from the Old Fly Market Slip.

Yours respectfully

P. Freneau

Notes

1. "United States Magazine," Feb., 1779. Rest of title: "Containing an original Poem on the Beauties of that Island." After title: "In a letter to A. P. Esq. (Extract.)" Introduces poem, "The Beauties of Santa Cruz," in USM with 52 stanzas.

2. This gives an impression that there were three towns. There were and are only two--Christianstadt and Frederickstadt. Bassend or Bassin was the old French name for the former.

3. The essay closes with "I believe the best thing I can do with the rest of this paper is to transcribe a few dull heavy lines which I composed near two years ago on the spot." The poem follows, dated as writ in 1777.

4. From the manuscript at Rutgers University. Published in 1899, edited by Jay Milles, with numerous small errors. Milles assumes, without giving evidence, that Freneau "built and fitted out the ship Aurora"--but this seems to have been only a rumor. Leary assumes (p. 378) that he was an active member of the crew, a third mate; but Freneau in the ms. (with no apparent motive for falsifying) describes himself as a passenger who had paid for his passage, but had been mistakenly enrolled as part of the crew. In the battle he relates that he was merely an onlooker. From the last paragraph, it is evident that he was intending to visit someone in Santa Cruz, probably Captain Hanson, with whom he had resided from 1776 to 1778. The account is dated July 14, 1780. As Freneau was captured on May 26 and freed on July 12, it is clear that his actual imprisonment was a bit over six weeks. This experience embittered Freneau towards the British, for whom he found hardly a good word for the rest of his life.

5. It is not clear for what purpose Freneau wrote this account of his experience. It does not appear to be a letter to anyone, or part of any journal. Probably he intended to publish it, but was diverted by converting it into a poem, "The British Prison Ship," which was published as a broadside early in 1781.

6. There is no connection between the account and this note, which was evidently written to Freneau's Santa Cruz friend, Captain John Hanson.

7. "Freeman's Journal," Nov. 21, 1781. Addressed "To the Printer of the Freeman's Journal. Sir," and signed "Your and their humble servant, The Pilgrim." First of the 'Pilgrim series' of nineteen numbers, ending Aug. 14, 1782, the basis for the 'Philosopher of the Forest" series in Freneau's "Miscellaneous Works" (1788). Example of Freneau's primitivism. Evidently intended as an American "Spectator."

8. "Freeman's Journal," Jan. 9, 1782. Eighth "Pilgrim" essay. Untitled--title supplied. Freneau rarely wrote prose in this epic strain--here, a fairy-tale story of America. Same as "Philosopher of the Forest, X," in "Miscellaneous Works."

9. The fantasy with which Freneau began has become, first, an essay championing the Indian and condemning the colo-

nizers--then an attack on Britain. America's future and greatness occupy the rest of the article.

10. "Freeman's Journal," May 8, 1782. "No. 14" of "The Pilgrim"--title supplied. A favored subject with Freneau, here treated in the Addisonian manner. Note that now the Pilgrim, a "primitivist," resides "in the northern suburbs of this city."

11. "Freeman's Journal," Sept. 4, 1782. Marked by Freneau as his in his personal file, and signed "W. H.," the initials of Shakespeare's friend, to whom he dedicated the sonnets. This oratorical essay is very similar to Goldsmith's "A City Night-Piece," and in tone to the "graveyard" poems.

12. "Freeman's Journal," Nov. 20, 1782. Signed "G." Untitled here, but in "Miscellaneous Works" titled as above. Typical of Freneau, who hated pomposity.

13. Preface to the poem, "Journey from Philadelphia to New-York, By way of Burlington and South-Amboy," By Robert Slender, Stocking Weaver. Extracted from the Author's Journals. Philadelphia, 1787. Interesting as the first formal introduction of "Robert Slender," a favorite pseudonym of Freneau, and as using the Addisonian device of "finding" a manuscript of a departed writer. Here, as in MW, Slender is a stocking weaver. "Slender II" emerged in the "Aurora" of 1799 as a much-wed cobbler, with a different personality. "Slender I" strongly resembles Freneau's college pal, Hugh Brackenridge.

14. Shakespeare's "Hamlet," Act II, Scene 2, line 413: "They say an old man is twice a child."

15. This is the only known use by Freneau of the pseudonym "Adam Buckskin," though he often used the initials "A. B."

16. "Miscellaneous Works" (1788), offered as "By the late Mr. ROBERT SLENDER.*" The asterisk leads to a long footnote describing this character, who closely resembles Freneau's friend, Hugh Brackenridge. "Slender" supposedly wrote many of the essays in MW. The device of the "discovered" manuscript had been used by numerous authors, including Addison (in "Spectator 50"), to whom Freneau was devoted. The footnote follows:

* Many people, no doubt, will be anxious to know something of the history and character of the above named "Robert Slender;" and the Editor is really sorry it is not in his
power to afford them the most ample information. Of two
things, however, the reader may be assured, that he was a
Pennsylvanian by birth, and a stocking and tape weaver by
trade, and has now been dead something more than a year
and an half, having been buried with very little ceremony by
a few of his most intimate friends and neighbours.--Notwith-
standing he was an author as well as a weaver of stockings
and tape (both of which articles he manufactured on a curious loom of his own invention) we cannot say he ever possessed the least faculty or turn of mind for amassing the
treasures of this world, so that when his executors came to
examine his strong-box, little or nothing was discovered
therein more than a bundle of manuscripts penned in a very
antiquated, obscure and perplexing hand, from which, however, we shall now and then present such extracts to the
public in the course of this work as shall appear to be best
deserving of their notice: Indeed, had our old friend stuck
closer to his loom for any length of time than he was wont
to do, it is highly probable his box would have been stored
with riches of a very different nature; but such as they are,
gentle reader, they are wholly and sincerely at thy service.
--ROBERT SLENDER was, in his person, a tall spare man
with a meagre aspect, of a sociable disposition, fond of
travelling from place to place, and was known to have made
frequent visits to the several capitals of the American continent and islands, while his brother weavers were more
profitably employed at home at their looms. Writing and
weaving seem to have been rather his amusements than his
serious occupations; and one proof of his having been a man
of sense is his not having depended upon authorship alone
for a subsistence. In his temper he was extremely iras-
cible; but I have often remarked that when he saw his writings treated with malevolence, contempt or neglect, he never became angry or outrageous, whereas, when his stockings or tape were calumniated, he was instantly changed into a monster of passion and revenge, breathing out nothing
but menaces and curses against the enemies of his loom.

He was extremely fond of sunning himself in clear winter mornings, and has been known to sit three hours together on the south side of a hill in December or January,
enjoying the salutary beams of the great and splendid luminary.--Reader, if these few particulars will at all gratify
thee, our purpose is answered. In this miscellaneous col-

lection of original papers we shall now and then present thee with an essay, a paragraph, a sentiment, or a poem of the late facetious "Robert Slender," all of which, it is hoped, will be treated by the critics with more indulgence than the rest, since these effusions are to be considered as the works of a deceased author who, it does not appear, ever intended his lucubrations, at least the greater part of them, for the eye of the public. The first piece of his with which we shall present thee is the above, containing his "Advice to Authors," which, from several circumstances, we conclude was written in the latter part of his life. [Freneau's note.]

17. In the controversies between the "Freeman's Journal" and "Independent Gazetteer" in 1782, he was called "poet-aster" and "imitator." See Leary, "That Rascal Freneau," page 116.

18. "Miscellaneous Works." Originally in "Freeman's Journal," Feb. 16, 1785, by "A. B." Good example of sailor's dialect and philosophy, which Freneau had learned in several voyages. Beneath the humor is a serious recognition of the sailor's plight ashore. Another "manuscript discovery."

19. In this paragraph Freneau reveals his lifelong bias against Catholicism and his sympathy for the veteran soldier. Government bonds were selling far below the face value in 1785.

20. "Miscellaneous Works." Subtitled "A Fragment." Supposedly by "Robert Slender." An Addisonian dream essay, similar to "Visions of Mirzah" ("Spectator," No. 159). The idea that traditions may not be true is reminiscent of Swift's "Gulliver's Travels," in the visit to Glubdubrib, where history's concept of famous men is exposed as untrue.

21. Used in the old meaning of "wonder."

22. Note the odd "system" of quotation marks, often for every other speaker only, with introductions included within the marks.

23. "Miscellaneous Works," eighth essay in the "Philosopher of the Forest" series, with title supplied. Resembles Addison's "Visions of Mirzah" ("Spectator" essay 159) and no. 5 of Goldsmith's series, "The Bee." Fame was a fav-

orite subject with Chaucer, Fielding, and Johnson.

24. Having begun by satirizing the folly of fame, Freneau has ended by picturing a deist's heaven as the essence of virtue, reason, and benevolence--discouraging curiosity about man's destiny and encouraging a Popean content with life.

25. "Daily Advertiser," June 29, 1790. Also in "Tomo Cheeki" series, "Jersey Chronicle," Aug. 15, 1795. Reflects Freneau's personal interest and observation of the seafaring men of his time. Other specimens of the character essay appear in the "Miscellaneous Works," but on the whole Freneau did little with the type.

26. "Daily Advertiser," Sept. 17, 1790. Also in "Jersey Chronicle," Aug. 1, 1795, as No. IX in the "Tomo Cheeki" series. Here by "Opay Mico," supposedly a Creek Indian chief who had recently visited New York, translated "from the Talassee Language." Satire on the whites' superstitions.

27. "The Creek Indians have no word for a ship: " Thlagachle, "which I here translate as Canoe, strictly means one of their canoes of the largest kind, and which are commonly hollowed out of the solid body of the Cypress, a tree that, in the most southern states and Florida, grows to an enormous size. [Freneau's note.]

28. "Daily Advertiser," Nov. 16, 1790. Evidently an editorial. Satire aimed at the Connecticut wits who wrote epics, particularly Timothy Dwight ("The Conquest of Canaan," mostly about Joshua's battles) and probably Joel Barlow ("The Vision of Columbus"). Both epics are clumsy, pompous attempts at grandeur, full of grandiose, artificial expressions.

29. "National Gazette," Jan. 12, 1792. In "Tomo Cheeki" series, "Jersey Chronicle," July 25, 1795. Title supplied. Typical of Freneau's early romantic attitude toward the Indian; in later years he assumed a more realistic view. Published coincident with our wars against the Pennsylvania and Ohio Indians. Perhaps in reply, Hugh Brackenridge presented a more prevailing, practical view in "Thoughts on the Present Indian War" (NG, Feb. 2, 6, 1792.)

30. Certain doubts about the justice of war on the Indians

were in the air. On Jan. 9, 1792, Freneau reprinted some
of these from the "American Daily Advertiser:" "Is the war
with the Indians a 'just' one? Have we purchased the territory from them on which we have lately erected several new
forts? Have they not the same right to their hunting grounds
...that we have to our houses and farms?"

31. "National Gazette," April 26, 1792. Evidently an editorial. Freneau now felt sure enough of his ground, surrounded by many strong Whigs, to attack the "Tory" or
Federalist element of the government. Many Whigs, including Jefferson, were sure there was a plot afoot to make
Washington king, led by Secretary of the Treasury Hamilton. No such plot existed, though there were many luke-
warm supporters of the republic who admired the British
form of government.

32. "National Gazette," July 4, 7, 1792. Evidently by the
editor. Like Franklin's satire of England, "Rules by Which
a Great Empire may be Reduced to a Small One." A sum-
mary of Whig criticisms of the Federalists, aimed particularly at Hamilton and his chief newspaper supporter, "Gazette of the United States."

33. In XI "general welfare" is a phrase Hamilton used to
justify his proposals. He also championed a program of
manufactures and controlled the excise collections; and he
had sponsored the funded debt, the national bank, the assumption of war debts, and the excise system. In XII the
"military defeat" is St. Clair's, by the Ohio Indians in late
1791. In XIV the "particular monarchy" is England, whose
government Hamilton greatly admired. XV continues the
"National Gazette's" contention that criticism of government
was a patriotic duty, in reply to the protests of the "Gazette of the United States."

34. "National Gazette" editorial (title supplied), Dec. 26,
1792. Part of Freneau's championship of the new France,
but also a statement of the faith that distinguished Whigs,
Republicans, and Democrats from Tories, Federalists, and
conservatives.

35. "National Gazette" editorial, title supplied, Dec. 29,
1792. Satire of Hamilton's practice of managing financial
legislation through his friends in Congress--good contrast to
the editorial of December 26, which is fervent rather than
satirical.

36. "National Gazette," Jan. 2, 1793. Title supplied. Evidently an editorial. Here bitterness against Hamilton, Fenno's "Gazette of the United States," the Federalist Connecticut wits, and monarchy lovers generally is expressed. GUS originally paid much attention to titles of the official families, even referring to wives as "Lady Washington," "Lady Adams," etc. Freneau hated the celebration of the President's birthday, as if he were a king--but it nevertheless went ahead, much publicized by Fenno, with banquets, balls, and elaborate (but amateurish) birthday odes to Washington.

37. Sir Richard Blackmore, 1655-1729, voluminous English epic writer of little distinction.

38. The Connecticut wits, Timothy Dwight, John Trumbull, and Joel Barlow all had written epic poems.

39. "National Gazette," March 6, 1793. Title supplied. Prefaced by "(From a Correspondent)" --a common device with Freneau, Fenno and others to introduce editorials, often obliquely, via a reference to a correspondent, but often without any. Similar in ideas and style to other editorials on the subject by Freneau, who strongly resented the dominance of the royal tradition in plays.

40. "National Gazette," April 20, 1793. Title supplied. Evidently an editorial--on Freneau's humanitarian views of men and war, that "man is naturally good," and debased by evil forms of government, yet reformable (he hoped) through democracy. The essays seem to reflect ideas of Rousseau and Paine.

41. Charles Fox, English Whig Parliamentary orator and foreign minister.

42. "National Gazette," May 22, 1793. By "An Old Soldier" --evidently Freneau in a thin disguise; the pseudonym followed him to the "Jersey Chronicle," the "Time Piece," and the "Aurora." Philadelphia merchants had presented to Washington a document approving his proclamation of neutrality in the French-English war; and he had received Genet, the new French ambassador, very coolly, despite the popular enthusiasm for France. Very likely this impudent article--with sarcasms about himself, the proclamation, and the ungrateful "big men," besides a suggestion of joining France in the war--impelled him the next day to explode a-

gainst the "National Gazette" to Jefferson, who recorded in his Anas (May 23):

> He adverted to a piece in Freneau's paper of yester-day; he said he despised all their attacks on him personally, but that there never had been an act of the Government... which that paper had not abused... He was evidently sore and warm, and I took his intention to be, that I should interpose in some way with Freneau, perhaps withdraw his appointment of translating clerk to my office. But I will not do it. His paper has saved our Constitution, which was galloping fast into monarchy.

43.   From Pope's "Essay on Man."

44.   "National Gazette," Aug. 21, 1793. By "An Old Almanac-Maker." Title supplied. By style and ideas evidently by Freneau, who wrote a poem, "To Mr. Blanchard, the Celebrated Balloonist," and apparently a letter to another balloonist, Decker (NG, July 17, 1793), in a similar spirit of imaginative banter about the heavens. "Mr. R-----e" is probably David Rittenhouse, the Philadelphia mathematician and astronomer. The "Brunswickean Quixote" is doubtless Duke Charles of Brunswick. Jean Blanchard, 1753-1809, the French balloonist, made the first air crossing of the English Channel.

45.   Psalm XVIII: "He did fly upon the wings of the wind."

46.   These gay references to solemn Bible names--St. Peter, Jacob, and Abraham--must have again shocked the orthodox, who long since had attacked Freneau as a flippant skeptic, if not an unbeliever.

47.   "National Gazette," Sept. 28, 1793. Editorial filler, evidently by Freneau. Yellow fever had evacuated a third of the city, and other communities were wary of refugees.

48.   Freneau used the dramatic form frequently, in both poems and prose. Note the nautical terms--"poop-lanthorns," "avast"--which he used habitually, often apparently unaware of their inappropriateness, as here in the talk of a farmer.

49.   "National Gazette," Oct. 19, 1793. Editorial. Title supplied. Evidently Freneau's valedictory as his newspaper was dying--the end came a week later. He was sure he had participated importantly in a "great political reformation"--

from an aristocratic-monarchistic trend in government and society to a republican-democratic one.

50. "Monmouth Almanac," 1795--Freneau's only almanac, which he wrote, edited, printed, and distributed. Freneau was always prejudiced against lawyers after his father became entangled with them, and lost most of his property, just before his death. This despite the fact that two of his best friends--William Bradford, Jr., and Hugh Brackenridge--were lawyers.

51. "Jersey Chronicle," Jan. 30, 1796--from (but not acknowledged) the "Aurora" of Dec. 15, 1795, where it was signed "An Old Soldier." Very strong evidence, if not proof, that the "Soldier" was Freneau--as here the last line is altered, and the signature and source omitted. Editor Freneau would not have altered any line or omitted the source, had he not been the author. The last line in the "Aurora:" "are partizans of war and confusion, it is false as respects me. AN OLD SOLDIER."

Title supplied. The essay assumes a prejudice to France that is not evident--revealing Freneau's strong bias for France.

52. Thomas Pinckney, American minister to Great Britain. He negotiated the Treaty of San Lorenzo, signed Oct. 27, 1795.

53. "Jersey Chronicle," May 2, 1795. Editorial. Thus Freneau, beginning his rural weekly, initiated the instruction of his farmer readers in the ways of international politics. The Jay Treaty was to become the biggest American political issue for the year, but the French-English war was still big news.

54. Evidently used in the old meaning of "make certain" or "make sure."

55. This is a typical Freneau editorial in its rambling, discursive quality. Beginning with the Jay Treaty, it moves to France, English ways, America, British naval depredations, and finally the advantage of France in the capture of Holland.

56. "Jersey Chronicle," May 2, 1795. Editorial expressing a typical Whig reaction to the British-favoring treaty Jay

negotiated.   Jay had been outmanoeuvred by Grenville, the
foreign secretary.   Nevertheless, Washington eventually
signed it as, apparently, the best available.   But this act
aroused a furor of disapproval and made the President, for
a few months, unpopular.   It must be noted, by the way,
that few Americans were as biased against Britain as Freneau.

57.   "Jersey Chronicle," May 30, 1795.   First number of
the "Tomo Cheeki" series, by "Tomo Cheeki, the Creek Indian in Philadelphia," supposedly translated from a manuscript left in Tomo's hotel room.

58.   The Creek Indians reckon the distance of places not by
miles or leagues, but by a day's journey, which they estimate at about twenty English statute miles. [Freneau's note.]

59.   The word here used in the original is "Kitchi Manitou,"
God, or the Great Spirit: "manitou" is the word for spirit
in general.--They denominate the devil or Evil Spirit "Mat-
cho Manitou." [Freneau's note.]

60.   This criticism of white ways reminds us of the primitivism of the "Pilgrim."   But not only is the "Tomo Cheeki"
series primitivistic; it is also romantic; the ways of the Indian are idealized.   Freneau, as far as is known, never had
any contact with Indians, but doubtless read many books a-
bout them.   Very likely he was influenced by William Bartram's "Travels" of 1799, in which the southern Indians' customs are romanticized.   See also Bartram's "Observations
on the Creek and Cherokee Indians, 1789," "Am. Eth. Soc.
Transactions," III (1853), 1-81.

61.   "Jersey Chronicle," July 18, 1795.   No. 7 in the
"Tomo Cheeki" series--title supplied.   Under the series
number is "(WRITTEN ABOUT MIDNIGHT.)"   This is about
the best essay in the series, and vividly presents the contrast between unhealthful city life and the vigorous natural
life of the red men.   Freneau, of course, says nothing of
the dangers, insecurities, lack of sanitation, and the ever-
present lice in the way of the wigwam.   These essays,
somewhat enlarged, reappeared in "The Time Piece," which
Freneau edited, in 1797.

62.   Used in the sense of "craftsman" or "mechanic."

63.   "Time Piece," June 16, 1797.   A new essay, added to

the "Tomo Cheeki" series for TP. The mystery of the tides and the problems of Indians in the city are here discussed, often in poetic terms. One chief has fallen in love with a white woman and has, in an effort to be like her, cast off his blanket. Another is homesick--and Tomo longs for his homeland and the "simple people of the forest, " to escape from the hypocritical whites, who look on the redmen as inferior. This is the last "Tomo Cheeki" essay. Full title: "To OPAY-MEEKO-- (the old man of the Lake) in the Creek country. "

64. "Time Piece, " June 21, 1797. Editorial in two parts -- a typical form for Freneau, who often wrote under "Reflections" a series of comments on several subjects, unsigned. Here he discusses kings and navies, with a weird idea of the origin of the latter--to provide easy employment for the nobles. This is part of his opposition to the rising American sentiment for war against France.

65. Freneau had the date wrong. In August, 1791, King Frederick of Prussia and Emperor Leopold of Bohemia and Hungary met at Pillnitz, near Dresden, Germany, and called on Europe to restore Louis XVI--aggravating the French revolutionists to destroy their monarchy.

66. "Time Piece, " Sept. 6, 1797. Editorial--here on changes of opinion or fashion, emphasizing the new favor toward actors and plays. Again Freneau recommends a republican stage and condemns the use of aristocratic or royal characters and ideas.

67. Here is evidence of Freneau's genuine liberalism--his criticism of narrow patriotism and his advocacy of internationalism.

68. "Time Piece, " Sept. 15, 1797--Freneau's by every evidence but a signature. Good example of the whimsy in which he often wrote, and a satire on American-English spelling and pronunciation.

69. "Time Piece, " Oct. 2, 1797. Editorial with original verse. Good example of the loose practice of the day--inserted under "Communication" (as if by an outsider), yet in a news column (where short editorials usually appeared), and closed by a Freneau poem--in the 1809 "Poems" as "The Political Weathercock, " with two more stanzas--but unsigned! Title supplied.

70. "Time Piece," Oct. 25, 1797. One of a series of seven satires on the Yankee--rather clumsy, but evidence of a lasting bias brought on by Freneau's hatred for John Fenno, his editorial enemy, and the Connecticut wits, who had raucously ridiculed him. Freneau used the pseudonym for some items in the 1809 "Poems."

71. Either Freneau forgot to mention Salem's building a mill (unlikely), or a line was omitted here by the printer.

72. "Time Piece," Dec. 13, 1797. By "A. B."--a Freneau pseudonym--and the first of three essays on the subject. It is practically certain that Freneau wrote it, from style and ideas, and the fact that at the time he was being threatened with prison for his own debts. The Shakespeare quote is from "The Tempest," Act V, Scene I, lines 21-31. Of all the many authors he read, Freneau admired Shakespeare most of all.

73. "Time Piece," July 4, 1798. Another "Old Soldier" essay. Satire on the Feds and the Alien and Sedition Bills, passed in June and July, 1798, by the Federalist Congress --aimed at troublesome immigrants and editors who criticized the Adams administration. The acts expired in two or three years, and were not renewed by the Jefferson administration. "A----" means Adams; "C----," Congress; and "T. L. H." probably means Hamilton, who had used "T. L." as a pseudonym in attacking Freneau and Jefferson.

74. Obviously this means "President." In Item 3 the blank probably means "pass." In the first paragraph, the last blank probably means "Constitution."

75. "Letter I" in Freneau's "Letters"...by Robert Slender, Philadelphia, 1799. This first appeared in the "Aurora," March 25, 1799, signed "A Monarchist." Title supplied. Freneau had evidently been in Philadelphia most of the time since the death of B. F. Bache, editor of the "Aurora," in September, 1798, probably helping the widow edit and print the paper. This letter, like most of those to follow, is a satire on the Alien and Sedition Acts and Federalism, but also on Adams, whom both Freneau and Jefferson regarded as a monarchist. He was also a Yankee and a friend of John Fenno, rival editor--another reason for ridicule. Adams, in later years, apparently thought of Freneau as the prime reason for his defeat in 1800. The letters are addressed to the editor, now William Duane, a Democrat far

more radical than Freneau or Bache. Here the facsimile edition of the "Letters," New York, 1943, H. H. Clark, ed., is used.

76. A rare bird on the earth, very like a black swan. [Freneau's note.]

77. Matthew Lyon, congressman from Vermont, the first to be prosecuted under the Sedition Law, was sentenced to four months in prison and a fine of $1,000, in October, 1798. In 1840 Congress remitted to his heirs the sum with interest.

78. "Letter XIII" in the "Letters," first published in the "Aurora," Aug. 8, 1799. Title supplied. Good illustration of Freneau's free-wheeling unorthodoxy and critical attitude toward preachers. Also a good example of the familiar style typical of most of the letters. This "Slender II" is a much-married cobbler who pretends an ignorance and humility he does not feel.

79. "Slender" wrote on religion several times. He wrote again on the inconsistency of orthodoxy in the "Aurora," Nov. 9, 1799; and his letter for Oct. 9, 1800, was entitled "Robert Slender Argueth with the Parson," the result again the parson's discomfiture; obviously Freneau was skeptical of the ministry.

80. "Aurora," Aug. 14, 1802--originally in the Charleston (S. C.) "City Gazette," Jan. 5, 1801, published then in reply to an attack, and republished now, when Jefferson was again attacked. Freneau's elaborate explanation of the founding and conduct of the "National Gazette" has historical importance, as Hamilton had accused Jefferson of founding and controlling it for political purposes. There is no good evidence to support Hamilton's charges.

81. In the main, Freneau's account of the "National Gazette" and his translatorship is apparently true. He was, however, a little "off" on certain facts. The agreement with Childs and Swaine was completed--according to his letters--in late July, not June, 1791. And he was appointed translator in August, not October, 1791--and went to Philadelphia at that time. But these are unimportant details; Freneau's mind was not a factual, but a dreamy, unrealistic one. And the major point of the letter is evidently true --that he founded and edited the "National Gazette" without any real help or influence from Jefferson.

82. "Aurora," Sept. 3, 1804. One of twenty "Bunker" essays by Joe, Joe, Jr., Jonathan, and Polly Bunker--part of a local political campaign between factions in the Democratic Party. These essays or letters are in almost every way the same sort as the letters of "Robert Slender," and may be considered as, in all probability, the work of Freneau. He was free from sea duties at the time, and was used to gravitating to Philadelphia. Of all the Bunkers "Jonathan" sounds most like Slender--apparently meek, but satirical of his enemies. Tench Coxe had been made purveyor of public supplies by Jefferson. He was a good man, hardly deserving the ridicule that Editor Duane and others turned on him. Penrose was favored for Congress by Coxe, and Leib by Duane. Pickering had been Secretary of State under Adams, and was now Senator from Massachusetts. Title supplied.

83. "Aurora," Nov. 24, 1812. "No. II" of a series of four by "The Old Soldier," a favorite pseudonym of Freneau, apparently. Here the romantic concept of the Indian, featured in the "Tomo Cheeki" essays, is abandoned for a realistic, "hard-boiled" one. A year before, Governor Harrison of Indiana Territory, faced by the treacherous Tecumseh and his brother the "Prophet," had been attacked and forced to disperse the savages and destroy their town, Tippecanoe. Tecumseh then joined the British, and was killed in a battle in Ontario, October 5, 1813.

84. Probably Congressman Richard M. Johnson of Kentucky.

85. "Aurora," Dec. 22, 1812. By "Hawser Trunnion," a Freneau pseudonym in "Freeman's Journal," Aug. 28, 1782. Another essay on the same subject, by the same author, was in the "Aurora" for Dec. 24, 1812. Freneau knew much about ships, and his advice appears sound. Note that his early pacificism has disappeared; he is for the "blood and perils of honorable war." Title supplied.

86. "New-York Weekly Museum," Sept. 7, 1816. Signed "P. F." Freneau wrote many poems and essays for this magazine. In the "Aurora" for June 21, 1816, a paragraph by "Z." (a Freneau pseudonym) discussed the same subject. A good example here of Freneau's interest in astronomy, which he mixes with literature. Note his naive theory of the "spots" in the moon.

87. Hamlet in Shakespeare's "Hamlet," Act I, Scene 5.

88. Horatio in "Hamlet," Act I, Scene 1.

89. Cato in Addison's "Cato," Act V, Scene 1.

90. "True American," July 27, 1822. Second of "Recollections of Past Times and Events." Signed "U.," a Freneau signature, and used as introduction to a poem on the same subject, "Margery and Patty. A Boston Dialogue"--see Leary, page 53. Title supplied. Interesting comment on the effect of the Boston Tea Party, not usually described in histories--the patriotic struggle to refrain from tea and to find a satisfactory substitute for it.

91. "True American," Aug. 17, 1822. Fourth in the series, "Recollections of Past Times and Events." Introduces poem, "The New Liberty Pole.--Take Care!" Signed "R.," a Freneau signature. The events here described amount to a choice bit of local history. The liberty pole may possibly be related to the Maypole and May Day in origin and tradition--even to the flag pole and the human urge to set up a symbol on a high point--by monument, pole, balloon, or satellite--representing some kind of supremacy or ideal.

92. Ms. "Madison Papers," Library of Congress. Note in Madison's hand beneath date: "Rec. Feby. 19. 1773," which indicates a very slow "mail." Here is a youthful, gay, collegiate Freneau still seeking a profession and making first attempts at literary fame. He was teaching under his friend, Hugh Brackenridge, the master of the school--Somerset Academy, near Princess Anne. The letter may be found in Mary Austin's "Philip Freneau" (pages 80-82), along with others by him (pages 183-4, 187-8, 196-9, 204-7).

93. "Freeman's Journal," July 8, 1789--letter to "A.B.," who may have been Andrew Brown, editor of the "Federal Gazette." Writ at Savannah, March 14, 1789. Here may be the reason why Freneau loved the sea, which helped him be a Stoic by giving the satisfaction of meeting the "rubs and disasters" of life. Title supplied.

94. "Madison Papers," Library of Congress. Freneau had recently started the "Jersey Chronicle," which he printed on his own press at his farm. Madison was married to a charming widow, Dorothea (Dolly) Todd, in the fall of 1794. He was now a congressman, and was to be Secretary of State under Jefferson and President, 1809-1817. "Mr.

Bailey" was Francis Bailey, publisher of "The Freeman's Journal" and several of Freneau's books and pamphlets. "Mr. Beckley" was John Beckley, Virginia lawyer and clerk of Congress.

95. At Rutgers University Library. Year date is incomplete, but from internal evidence is evidently 1801. The letter is interesting for its details. Helena and Agnes were his first two children; the third was Catherine, and the fourth, born in June, 1801, was Margaret. There is a rare reference to Peter's wife, "Mrs Freneau." "Miss Eliza" is not identified, but may have been a relative of Peter's wife. Judge Burke was Aedanus Burke, a warm friend of Freneau. The Ledyards were related by marriage into the Forman family.

96. Margaret Freneau, the poet's sister, had married John S. Hunn, and lived in New York City.

97. Freneau's mother now lived with the Hunns. "Polly" was probably Freneau's spinster sister Mary, who also lived with the Hunns.

98. "Madison Papers, " Library of Congress. Freneau had now retired from the sea, and apparently was spending most of his time in Philadelphia, helping print and edit the "Aurora" and contributing to it. This letter tells the story behind the 1809 two-volume edition of his poems, his most elaborate and largest in size and numbers. Note that Freneau had a low opinion of his prose; he considered himself primarily a poet, though he wrote more prose than poetry. He felt in the mood to stay in the city "about two years"-- so it seems his duties on the Jersey farm were very small. It appears he was in and out of Philadelphia much of the time till after 1820. The "two former Editions" were evidently those of 1786 and 1788, published by Francis Bailey while Freneau was at sea.

99. There were many essays in the "Aurora, " in 1809 and the years after, that seem, from style and ideas, to have been written by Freneau.

100. "Madison Papers, " Library of Congress. This letter concerns Freneau's last edition, a tiny two-volume affair containing new poems not in the previous editions, and many not previously published. They include naval poems celebrating events of the War of 1812, others about islands he

had visited, and a group of philosophical and deistic poems. These last may have damned the sales, for American readers were in no mood for any deviations from orthodoxy. The set sold poorly, and was a sharp disappointment to the author, who was in real need now. The letter reveals his genuine dislike of New York, his birthplace. Madison had lost his books in the burning of the White House by the British in August, 1814. The planned poem of Jackson's victory in New Orleans was apparently never written.

101. Monmouth County (N.J.) Historical Association. Wrongly dated 1819 in "Unpublished Freneauana," C. F. Heartman, ed. Freneau, disappointed at the sales failure of his 1815 "Poems," is at pains to find reasons. But by 1815, the active political bias against him was nearly dead. Democrats were dominant, and Unitarianism (like deism) was tolerated. Paine was largely forgotten, and Jefferson was still popular. New York was not a literary city--but Irving's writings were popular there, and Bryant's poems and Cooper's novels were about to be. Freneau's poems were regarded as oldfashioned; the new literary fashion was smart, sophisticated. Paulding, Neal, Willis, Irving, and others were to set the pattern. In Freneau's petulant protest is the frustration of an old man out of step with his time. The poem on Jackson's victory apparently never appeared; nor did that on the Elgin Garden; but the "shorter poems" were probably published in the "Weekly Museum" in 1816 (Leary, pp. 475-476). Freneau's acquaintance with Dr. John Francis was a happy event, leading to many congenial associations in New York.

102. The letter reveals some of Freneau's interests in his old age besides poetry--history, engravings, botany, even spermaceti, and science generally--which kept him an interesting conversationalist throughout his last years.

103. "Unpublished Freneauana," C. F. Heartman, ed., New York, 1918. Here we see part of Freneau's last attempt to collect his writings, this time a "miscellaneous works" with prose as well as poetry. Evidently Dr. Francis had encouraged him to plan the edition. The prospectus (at Monmouth County Historical Association) mentions "Poems and Miscellanies...written previously to, during the American Revolutionary War, and at different periods since that Event, down to the Year 1822." The volume never appeared, probably for want of demand. But many of the intended contents did appear, it seems, in "The True American" (Trenton),

1821 to 1823. See Leary, pp. 349-361. Carey was a successful Philadelphia book publisher-seller whom Freneau had known when he edited the "National Gazette."

104. In the 1815 "Poems" Freneau included "Pythona: or the Prophetess of En-dor," a dialog in which, at Saul's request, the prophetess raises Samuel from the dead. Saul asks his advice, whereupon Samuel predicts his early death and defeat by the Philistines. Saul is consoled by the witch.

Date Due